HEIDEGGER AND THE PROJECT OF FUNDAMENTAL ONTOLOGY

It is in any case a dubious thing to rely on what an author himself has brought to the forefront. The important thing is rather to give attention to those things he left shrouded in silence.

—Heidegger,
lecture course on the *Sophist*, 1924

SUNY Series in Contemporary Continental Philosophy

Dennis J. Schmidt, Editor

HEIDEGGER AND THE PROJECT OF FUNDAMENTAL ONTOLOGY

Jacques Taminiaux

Translated and Edited by
Michael Gendre

State University of New York Press

First published in French by Editions Jérôme Millon
entitled *Lectures de l'ontologie fondamentale.*

Published by
State University of New York Press, Albany

For information, address State University of New York
Press, State University Plaza, Albany, N.Y., 12246

Production by Dana Foote
Marketing by Bernadette LaManna

Library of Congress Cataloging in Publication Data

Taminiaux, Jacques, 1928–
    [Lectures de l'ontologie fondamentale. English]
    Heidegger and the project of fundamental ontology / Jacques
Taminiaux : translated and edited by Michael Gendre.
        p.   cm.—(SUNY series in contemporary continental
philosophy)
    Translation of: Lectures de l'ontologie fondamentale.
    Includes bibliographical references and index.
    ISBN 0-7914-0685-7 (alk. paper).—ISBN 0-7914-0686-5 (pbk. :
alk. paper)
    1. Heidegger, Martin, 1889–1976—Contributions in ontology.
2. Ontology. I. Gendre, Michael. II. Title. III. Series.
B3279.H49T3513   1991
111'.092—dc20   90–43592
                                                           CIP

10 9 8 7 6 5 4 3 2 1

Contents

Translator's Preface

The English title of this book does not communicate a nuance that is *expressed* in the French title:[1] that these essays approach Heidegger's works from the perspective of his *readings* in the tradition of metaphysics. In this collection, Jacques Taminiaux investigates the manifold topics addressed by Heidegger in his diverse readings (in French, the plural word: *"lectures"*) of this tradition. On the other hand, the English title reveals something not immediately apparent in the French one, namely that the essays of this collection deal essentially with Heidegger's initial philosophical project, "fundamental ontology." This term refers to a project involving the complex set of problems which emerged in the wake of *Being and Time* (1927), the Marburg lecture-courses (1923–28) and the Freiburg lectures (1928–35), which have been published in the *Gesamtausgabe*. According to Taminiaux, this set of problems reveals that in a debate between Heidegger and previous thinkers in our tradition there is more at stake than a question of influence. Heidegger's thought converts the past of metaphysics into food or fuel for his thought: "His thought turns everything from the past into timber for its own fire."[2] Hence the question of how Heidegger read and reappropriated the past of metaphysics is crucial, since he claims that fundamental ontology is the completion of metaphysics, i.e., of the tradition of *prote philosophia*, or *prima philosophia*.

Heidegger's own way of approaching classical texts was guided by the following maxim which we find in his lecture course on the *Sophist* (1924): *It is in any case a dubious thing to rely on what an author himself has brought to the forefront. The important thing is rather to give attention to those things he left shrouded in silence.*

In this book Taminiaux adopts the same maxim as a guide to his readings of Heidegger. Heidegger's silence concerning some of his foundational sources is a fact recognized by those who have carefully read his work. The objective of this book is to explore and assess these sources *systematically and critically*, and thus to shed light on the discretion and reticence of the

---

1. *Lectures de l'ontologie fondamentale*, essais sur Heidegger.
2. "Cette pensée fait feu de tout bois" (a remark made by Taminiaux in private conversations).

author of fundamental ontology in their regard. The principle sources discussed by Taminiaux are Husserl's *The Idea of Phenomenology,* Aristotle's *Nicomachean Ethics* (Book VI), Hegel's *Phenomenology,* and various works of Nietzsche and Descartes.

What emerges is a profoundly original reinterpretation and reassessment of *fundamental ontology.* Heidegger's project is an essay in finitude because it focuses on the temporality and self-understanding of human *Dasein* as the key to the various meanings of Being. Yet, because at the same time this project aims at the deconstruction of the history of ontology and attempts to reappropriate the spiritual energies of both German idealism (Fichte, Schelling, and Hegel) and of its criticism (Nietzsche) which had equated Being and Willing, it eventually culminates in the pretensions of a new absolutism. At the time of the second part of his lecture course on *Nietzsche,* Heidegger himself realized that fundamental ontology contained an internal paradox. Far from overcoming the metaphysics of subjectivity, it "had run the risk of reinforcing subjectivity."[3] Taminiaux traces the evolution of fundamental ontology from its inception in a double reappropriation of Husserl and Aristotle to its fulfillment of the pretensions of the modern metaphysics of subjectivity, as evidenced in *An Introduction to Metaphysics* (1935).

Taminiaux's essays bring a *systematic* approach to the problems inherent in the project of fundamental ontology. They focus on Heidegger's brilliant reappropriations of various tenets from the tradition, which never simply repeat the past, but rather seek to uncover the ground upon which the original question of philosophy emerged. One of these tenets is Kant's thesis: "Being is not a real predicate." This thesis comes to the forefront in the essays on Husserl and Kant. The first essay of this collection shows that Husserl sought to disengage philosophy from the abysmal difficulties entailed by psychologism, biologism, anthropologism, and historical relativism. Thanks to the phenomenological reduction, Husserl reinterpreted the notions of transcendence and immanence in such a way as to free philosophy from the unbridgeable dichotomy between objective and subjective realms. In order to reach toward a universal ground, the Husserlian project considers an eidetic realm. But instead of focusing upon facts and their relationships with other facts, phenomenological seeing reveals the eidetic structures of intentionality, without which perception, imagination, and judgment could not reach their intentional objects. This chapter also shows

---

3. *Nietzsche IV,* trans. Franz Capuzzi (New York: Harper and Row, 1982), p. 141, modified.

why Heidegger found in Husserl's theory of categorial intuition conceived against the backdrop of intentionality the ground from which his own inquiry would emerge. Heidegger says that "categorial intuition is possible only on the basis of the phenomenon of intentionality having been seen before it."[4] In spite of his thesis on the surplus character of Being (given to an eidetic seeing as *a priori*), Husserl accepts the dichotomy between two modes of being: material and spiritual. For Heidegger who rejects such a dichotomy as foreclosing our access to the meaning of Being, the positive impulse received from Husserlian phenomeneology calls for concretion and radicalization.

This concretion and radicalization of the Husserlian analyses will be sought on the ground of Dasein's comportment. Only thus is the question of Being radically formulated so as to reveal the ontological difference between Being and beings: this formulation of the problem will show that our understanding of Being is always presupposed when we understand any being and that the clarification can only be made by projecting such beings against the Being—that is, existence—of Dasein, or finite temporality. Two topics emerge as foundational: Truth and Time.

Taminiaux shows that Heidegger finds in Aristotle an intimation of the notion of truth as primordial unveiling, whose disclosing character does not take place exclusively in judgment. Any perceiving, producing, or acting comportment is grounded upon the moments of *synthesis* and *diaresis,* without which *logos,* and Being, come to no fruition. Heidegger thus reformulates the Husserlian discovery of intentionality and its associated thesis on Being in such a way as to retrieve Aristotle's position on Truth. For Heidegger this task can only be performed radically if we formulate the question of Being, the *Seinsfrage,* in terms of the comportment of Dasein.

This project discards the notion of immanence and gives a new meaning to the term transcendence, welding together world, Dasein's comportment towards other beings, its understanding of their Being, and most importantly its self-understanding. The essay on Husserl shows that in spite of the attention that Heidegger brings to bear on Aristotle, whom he claims to be the real master of phenomenology, he retains Husserl's notion of phenomenological seeing while criticizing its implicit commitment to an interpretation of Being as *Vorhandenheit.*

Concerning time, we witness a similarly complex connection between Aristotle and Husserl. Taminiaux shows how Heidegger's overcoming of the Aristotelian concept of world-time (the time of the *Physics*) was made possible by his reading of Husserl and how his radicalization of the Husserlian

---

4. *History of the Concept of Time,* trans. Theodore Kisiel (Bloomington: Indiana University Press), English trans., p. 72; German, p. 98.

consciousness of time was facilitated by his reading of Aristotle (who suggested that *praxis* is not ruled by the physical category of physical movement, *kinesis*). We know that in fundamental ontology the authentic comportment of Dasein calls for a radically finite conception of temporality. Taminiaux's analyses demonstrate that this authentic concept of temporality (connected to the self-referential comportment of care) owes much to the ec-static dimension inherent in Husserlian intentionality and also to the notion of truth found in the Aristotelian analyses of the comportments of man as *zoon logon echon.*

The essay on Kant—and the Kantian equation between Being = Position = Perception—indicates to Heidegger who reads it that the *perceivedness of the perceived* must be construed and radicalized as the Being of *Vorhandenheit.* Thanks to this reinterpretation, Heidegger evokes the ontological difference in the case of a theory of perception. Heidegger comments at length on the dual aspects—positive and negative—of Kant's ontological thesis ("Being is not a real predicate"). Because of this unresolved duality, Kant's thesis is indeterminate. Only by posing the problem in terms of the comportment of Dasein with respect to the beings it encounters in the world, can fundamental ontology remove the indeterminacy of Kant's thesis and reappropriate it in the framework of its project.

I previously indicated that the rigor of Taminiaux's deconstruction of Heidegger's project of fundamental ontology derives from the fact that he *systematically* explores Heidegger's areas of interest in the tradition. These areas could also be called tenets and directions within which the tradition of metaphysics constantly approached—but continuously failed to reach—the status of fundamental ontology, i.e., of the analytic of Dasein itself. One of the most important tenets and directions should be mentioned: it is the reappropriation of the distinction between *poiesis* and *praxis* in Aristotle. The chapter on Aristotle shows that this distinction, whose importance Heidegger did not acknowledge as such, is at the core of his enterprise. Taking his clues from the seminal retrieval of these notions by Hannah Arendt and her phenomenology of action,[5] Taminiaux shows that Heidegger follows Aristotle in the phenomenological account of the comportment of fabrication (*poiesis*); it is made possible by the specific light in which the Being of the beings produced (or dealt with in this comportment) is understood, and is contrasted to a higher comportment: that comportment is action, or *praxis,* which involves the essential characteristic of self-reference

---

5. See *The Human Condition* (Chicago: The University of Chicago Press, 1958).

because it aims at the life of the individual agent. For Aristotle and Arendt, this comportment must be essentially seen in the light of the ground that makes it possible. The ground upon which this phenomenology of action is conditioned is the basis in which the agent's operations originate and to which they return: the *polis*. For the Greeks of the classical age, the *polis* allows the possibility of a mode of living concerned with a specifically individual type of excellence and virtue in the midst of a plurality of agents. Yet Heidegger essentially dismissed this vital reference to plurality in his notion of Dasein's existence for the sake and in the care of itself (*Dasein existiert umwillen seiner*) while at the same time integrating the notion of action as self-referential activity, critically necessary to establish Dasein's Being in its superiority over the involvement or preoccupation in the world of extant beings, or *Vorhandenheit*. Since this comportment of self-referential care leads Heidegger to the reappropriation of Nietzsche's injunction not to "become too old for [one's] victories"[6] and to the meaning of finite temporality, the openness of the ec-static threefold (in which each ec-stasis temporalizes in conjunction with the other two), finite temporality is the *theoretical focus* which permits the *Seinsfrage* to be answered in the most authentic manner. Thus the *moment of vision* (*Augenblick*) contains within itself the characteristics of action (a term whose equivalent in Aristotle's Greek is *praxis*) and structurally reveals the stakes of Heidegger's theoretical enterprise. Heidegger rejects the traditional contemplation of eternal beings, but rather seeks what the moment of vision reveals about Dasein: that as a thrown being, it exceeds every other being and can think their Being, and its own Being, only by projecting its finite time upon them. In this projection, the treatise of fundamental ontology reaches its center and brings ontology to a mature science.

It is a fact however that one tenet of the tradition of metaphysics (namely the absoluteness of willing, as linked to the modern metaphysics of subjectivity) is exacerbated, rather than held at a distance in the unfolding of fundamental ontology. I already mentioned *An Introduction to Metaphysics* as the text in which Taminiaux shows that the pretensions to absoluteness conflict with its objective of authentically grasping the requirements of finite existence. At that time, Heidegger applied Dasein to the people-State of Germany and, in the first lecture course on Hölderlin which continues and prolongs the *Introduction,* compared the Führer to a demigod (one of the few mortals capable, with the thinker and the poet, of authentically temporalizing the time of history) and dismissed as idle talk the "realities of racism, of national characteristics (*Volkstum*), the slogan *Blut und*

---

6. See *Being and Time,* trans. Macquarrie and Robinson, (New York: Harper and Row), 1962, p. 308 English; p. 264 German.

Boden, mass organization and normalization''[7]—themes which, surely, are neither idle nor mundane.

In the wake of the media stir around the "Heidegger affair," the most relevant question is the *philosophical* significance of Heidegger's association with Nazism. This collection of essays—some of which were conceived well before the recent debate—discusses both the ambiguity and coherence of Heidegger's involvement, and for the first time exposes the work of the young Heidegger to a rigorous and wholesome *internal criticism.* By delineating the origins of fundamental ontology in phenomenology, and by presenting its subsequent shifts and final outcome, these essays allow us to reflect on this difficult question at its depths and origin.

---

7. See Chapter 8.

Acknowledgments

I owe a very special debt of gratitude to Professor Cobb-Stevens of Boston College. He graciously agreed to review carefully and critically more than half of this manuscript, and in doing so resolved many difficulties and ambiguities and gently corrected my less than perfect English. Each time he suggested looking at the French original, his reason was well-grounded and resulted in a clearer, more accurate and concise translation. His expertise in Husserl turned out to be decisive with respect to the terminology used in that chapter. His assistance went beyond mere suggestions as his knowledge of French was also the key to unlocking several recalcitrant expressions. Without Professor Cobb-Stevens' expertise, patience, and encouragement, this book could not have been edited.

Joanne Avallon reviewed with me the drafts of various chapters (Foreword, Aristotle, Hegel) with an eye towards copyediting. I requested her help on many other points of expression. She looked critically and painstakingly at every word of text put in front of her and raised the most simple and pertinent questions of sentence construction and word usage. Without the countless hours of her probing into the syntax and lexicon of those drafts, the final text of the chapters would not have the polish it seems to have acquired. Her unrelenting help and persistent encouragement were most needed and crucial in the last months, weeks, and days of the editing process.

Dr. Vincent Avery of Philips Academy, Andover, made helpful suggestions in the editing of the chapter on Hölderlin and of the Epilogue after reading the French original. On several occasions, he presented me with alternative translations which clarified for me how the author's intent could best be expressed in English.

Dr. Peg Birmingham provided assistance in the editing and copyediting of the manuscript at its early stage.

Professor Dennis Schmidt identified quotes from Hölderlin and made helpful recommendations especially on the appendix to the first chapter. He went beyond the requirements of duty to help and encourage me in the completion of this project.

Finally, from the outset Professor Taminiaux encouraged and challenged my understanding of the various sources mentioned in these essays and of the important issues he raises. The scope of his scholarship, the breadth of his remarks on Heidegger, and the perseverance of his encouragement made my task of translation worth the trouble for which he had kindly warned me to be prepared.

Foreword

"Fundamental ontology" is the title of the project that guided *Sein und Zeit*. The publication of this work had an impact comparable to the fall of an asteroid: "Calm block here fallen from a dark disaster" (Stéphane Mallarmé, *The Tomb of Edgar Poe*, trans. Mary Ann Caws). Because the book opens with a dedication to Husserl and because its very first page begins with a quotation from the Sophist, its readers had every reason to suppose that it should bear some relationship to the entire tradition of philosophy from Plato to phenomenology. Yet, no one was able to assess fully the nature of that relationship. Furthermore it was difficult to determine its relationship to the master of phenomenology to whom the dedication paid homage. Key notions of Husserlian phenomenology (natural attitude, reduction, intentionality, noetic-noematic correlation, constitution) seemed to have been entirely abandoned. At the same time however, Heidegger stressed that it was thanks to Husserl that the path toward the "things themselves," i.e., toward the meaning of Being, had been made possible, even crediting Husserl with securing the "ground" upon which further research in that direction could be conducted.[1] Yet, the work remained silent regarding the specific question of Husserl's exact contribution to the question of the meaning of Being (*Seinsfrage*) and also to the conquering of that ground. The obscurity which surrounded Heidegger's relationship to the thinker nearest to him also shrouded those most remote, particularly Aristotle. On the one hand, by linking the concept of time articulated in the *Physics* to the level of fallen everydayness, Heidegger clearly distanced himself from Aristotle, while on the other hand, by crediting Aristotle with understanding truth as unconcealing and with having assigned to truth a site other than judgment, he seemed at a crucial point to claim allegiance to the Greek thinker. Yet on the question of what this different site for truth was for Aristotle, once more the book was remarkably reticent. Heidegger, without any further commentary, simply limited himself to referring the reader to the *Nicomachean Ethics*, Zeta, and to the *Metaphysics*, Theta. In

---

1. *Being and Time*, trans. John Macquarrie and Edward Robinson (New York: Harper and Row, 1962), p. 62; (German text, p. 38).

both cases, Heidegger at the same time said too much and too little. More generally it was immediately evident that a prodigious amount of reading in the texts of the tradition had accompanied the work's preparation and, thus, it was clear that the references appearing in the notes and in the body of the text were more than standard practices of academic scholarship. One could therefore have suspected that Heidegger's readings concerned the very core of the enterprise called fundamental ontology. But the principle which guided these readings remained mysterious. On the one hand, when *Sein und Zeit* thematically treated the great texts of the tradition—such as Descartes on world or Hegel on Spirit and time—it was always with a view toward stressing that the project of the book was leading somewhere else. On the other hand, many signs could be found to indicate that the intended demarcation was not the final word on how to deal with the tradition. We indicated this shift concerning Aristotle. Similar reflections could be made about Descartes and Hegel. A theme such as solipsism ("existential" though it becomes in Heidegger) obscurely evokes some indebtedness to Descartes; likewise the central role played by anxiety in the opening of Dasein to its ownmost possibility, its Being-toward-death, echoes the analysis of the emergence of *Selbstbewusstsein* in the *Phenomenology of Spirit*. Furthermore, recall that the book promised a second part that would provide the phenomenological *Destruktion* of the history of ontology. Heidegger warned that such a deconstruction would not attempt to destroy the ontological concepts inherited from the tradition; rather he claimed that it would have the positive status of a genealogy. It would produce a justification of those concepts along with the "originary experiences" which founded them, but which were immediately covered up when the concepts were applied beyond their boundaries. But with regard to this promised genealogy, the published part of the book, the only one we have, said so little that what would be involved in this deconstruction remains enigmatic.

The goal of this collection of essays is to contribute to the clarification of these obscurities. The first generation of Heidegger's readers had to rely exclusively on *Sein und Zeit* to understand the inroads of fundamental ontology, and *Kant and the Problem of Metaphysics* provided only a glimpse into the nature of the deconstruction of the history of ontology. Since then, our approach to fundamental ontology has been facilitated by a number of retrospective reassessments made by Heidegger himself in the closing years of his life, in private seminars or in pieces written for special occasions (letters, prefaces, dedications in praise), but mostly by the publication of his lecture courses in the *Gesamtausgabe*.

In the account of his life in Germany before and after 1933, Karl Löwith devotes a few incisive and bitter pages to the man who had been his master at Marburg. The following statement may be found in these pages:

"His scientific training had been acquired firsthand. Far from being an assortment of books, his library contained only classical works which he had studied completely and thoroughly since the time of his youth. The fundamental books of ancient times, those of the Middle Ages, and of modern times, were all equally familiar to him."[2] This quotation concerns Heidegger at the time he conceived fundamental ontology. It seems to indicate to us the close connection that the philosophical project bears to the great texts of the tradition. It is through a close reading of such texts— ancient, medieval, and modern—that the project of this ontology was conceived. Heidegger's teaching at that period bears witness to the same preoccupation with texts rather than with themes. Even when he announced a thematic study (e.g., on the fundamental problems of phenomenology or on the bases of logic), it was through some texts (Suarez, Hobbes, Leibniz, Kant) that he sought to gain his approach to such themes. After considering this situation, it seemed more appropriate and prudent to follow Heidegger in his readings, and to attempt to read him, so to speak, as he was reading.

It seemed to me that such a task had to be conducted along three major lines, with the following requirements:

1. one would have to take into consideration what Heidegger said of his readings;

2. one would have to confront the readings with the relevant texts; and

3. one should try to take into account his later re-readings, whenever possible, since we know that Heidegger subsequently abandoned the project of fundamental ontology, yet never ceased to justify it in some respects, and kept returning to the very texts within which the project had been conceived.

However, for my research into the project of fundamental ontology (which incidentally became clear to me only gradually), none of these three lines could be taken separately and no simple guideline could be given once and for all.

Indeed, it very quickly appeared to me that while he made abundant references to his readings, Heidegger continued to maintain, or only partly discarded, the original reticence of *Sein und Zeit,* especially when discussing the most burning issues, such as the question of his methodology and the articulation of fundamental ontology. As for the reasons for this reticence [*sa discrétion*], I have no answer. Is it the pride of the pathfinder? Is it the fear of being misunderstood or lumped and leveled with all-too-common theses? Perhaps both.

I realized also—and this remark is in keeping with the above assess-

2. K. Löwith, *Mein Leben in Deutschland vor und nach 1933,* (J. B. Metzler, 1989), p. 44.

ment—that the thinkers he mentioned least often in his publications and in his lecture courses, Nietzsche in particular, may well have been those he had most in mind. And further, it occurred to me that when Heidegger talked about a thesis and its proponent, he was perhaps aiming his remarks at someone else. For example, while talking about Kant on Being, he was in fact also talking about Husserl, since the sixth *Logical Investigation,* read time and again by Heidegger, considers and endorses Kant's formula: Being is not a real predicate.

Concerning the confrontation of the texts with the reading that Heidegger made of them, it goes without saying that this objective could not be reached by means of those procedures by which one compares an original to a copy or a masterpiece to the work of a follower. This is because Heidegger happens to be the first one to have taught us how to read 'original' works anew and to seek their phenomenal pertinence beyond the traditional acceptance and the legacy of scholarship we have come to take for granted. Thus, between the 'original' text and the Heideggerian reading of it, I did not feel that I could adopt the position of an impartial, disinterested reader. It became therefore increasingly clear to me that analyzing the readings of fundamental ontology was not akin to a peaceful project of comparison between given 'originals' and Heidegger's specific readings of them. I discovered that neither the original nor the reading contained univocal properties. In both cases what had remained unsaid accompanied what had been said, and what had been already thought was still to be thought. However, I was convinced that some omissions made by Heidegger as a reader and by his way of selecting passages worthy of attention within the texts were meaningful and could cast new light on the major directions of the project of fundamental ontology and on some of its prejudices.

In no way did taking into account Heidegger's subsequent readings turn out to be an easier task. How can we accept without criticism later comments he made to justify *Sein und Zeit,* when, taken in their new context (i.e., in writings in which these comments appear or in other contemporary ones), such comments go hand in hand with a metamorphosis of the key notions of fundamental ontology, perhaps even with their own disappearance pure and simple? If we take this metamorphosis and disappearance into account, we may suspect that these comments, far from saying what they at first seem to ("I am saying now something that I have always said"), are in fact saying, "I am trying to think now something which I can only think by virtue of what I thought before;" or more simply yet, "The point that I am reaching in my thought is not separable from all of my past itinerary." This amounts to saying that Heidegger was the thinker of one question only, the *Seinsfrage,* but does not mean that he always maintained his first way of articulating the question or of answering it. Indeed, let us not forget that *Sein und Zeit* stops short of taking a decisive step, the one by which the treatise of fundamental ontology, then under the heading *Zeit und Sein,* was expected to demonstrate how the different meanings of Being point toward time as their single and converging center of intelligibility. This center was supposed to be the temporal movement by which the finite existence of Dasein takes it upon itself to claim its ownmost individuation and separates itself from anything that is not itself. Part Two of the treatise, the unpublished *Zeit und Sein,* was also expected to demonstrate—this is the goal of deconstruction—how the same center (finite temporality) was the unique key for reading the philosophical works of the tradition from Parmenides to Husserl. We might, I believe, be justified in anticipating that the very aim of the demonstration contains a sort of paroxysm of the modern metaphysics of subjectivity, a paroxysm to which, however, it is not entirely reducible. Indeed Heidegger argues that the key to the entire history of ontology is contained not only in the principle "that the 'I exist' must accompany all my representations," but also in the principle that "existence is in the care of oneself—for the Dasein that each and every time is mine." Thus a paradox appears to be at the very core of fundamental ontology and helps to explain its collapse: On the one hand the project offers the most sobering and unrelenting description of finitude, and on the other hand it turns out to be the last implementation of the absolute pretensions of metaphysics.

Indeed, the substitution of an onto-chrony for the various historical forms of onto-theo-logy preserves the claim made in onto-theo-logy that it can contemplate an ultimate source of intelligibility. Such a contemplation (*theoria*) was ascribed by the Greeks to that which within nature, or *phusis,* is spared from the process of being born and perishing, and is connected to the *aei,* which is divine. For mortals, this contemplation is the highest type of *praxis,* or existence, because in the exercise of *theoria, praxis* overcomes itself, draws closer to the eternal, and escapes the frailty that characterizes it as long as it remains inserted in the shifting world of human affairs. Aristotle says that no *sophia* could ever correspond to human affairs because they do not reveal first principles, hence only the provisional criteria of *phronesis* can apply to them. These Aristotelian views prompt a twofold approach [*double geste*] in the Heideggerian fundamental ontology: on an overt level, a critical thematization; on a covert level, a transformation and a reappropriation. When Heidegger thematizes Aristotle's views, he criticizes them as granting a privilege to the eternal and therefore underrating what is primordial in the finite time involved in our *praxis,* i.e., in the mortal mode of human existence. According to the Heideggerian deconstruction, this privilege originates in the fact that Greek *theoria* had originally aligned itself with the views of everyday preoccupation which, in order to manipulate tools and utensils, needs to trust in a stable presence-at-hand (*Vorhandenheit*) of *phusis*. But this critical thematization is accompanied by a transformed reappropriation of such themes. For it is from the Aristotelian confrontation between *poiesis* and *praxis* that fundamental ontology borrows its distinction between an everyday mode of being, which is alien or inauthentic, and a mode of being which is one's own and authentic. It is also Aristotle who inspires Heidegger with the notion that the highest form of *praxis* is *theoria*. Heidegger, however, radically diverges from Aristotle when he assigns to *theoria* the function not of dissociating itself from *phronesis,* but of reiterating it and of integrating it. In other words the only topic of *theoria* should be the finite period of human existence. Nevertheless, this transformation, by displacing the theme of *theoria*—no longer connected to the eternal, but to finite temporality—is still in line with the ambition of ancient onto-theo-logy since finite temporality is supposed to reveal the ultimate center of intelligibility for the Being of beings.

Similarly, when Heidegger thematizes the fundamental concepts of medieval metaphysics, he links their genealogy to the views of everyday preoccupation and to the productive behavior that supports those views. But it is from within this onto-theo-logy that he discreetly reappropriates the very central notion of *analogia entis*. Just as the Scholastics determined ontologically the hierarchy of beings, or the degrees of Being, by using the relationship of analogy between these beings and *summum ens* (the divine being whose activity is devoid of any potentiality and whose essence is identical with its existence), Heidegger determines analogically the hierarchy of the meanings of Being. He characterizes, for example, the being of the stone as "worldless" and the being of the animal as "poor in world," on the basis of a unique analogy with Dasein, whose essence, once it is, is to exist, or to be in the world.

And again, similar remarks can be made concerning the relationship of fundamental ontology to modern metaphysics which culminates in what the project of fundamental ontology calls onto-theo-ego-logy found in Hegel.[3] Yet here too, the Heideggerian approach [*geste*] is twofold including both a critical demarcation, or distancing (*Abhebung*), and a reappropriation. Furthermore, this reappropriation, unlike those concerning the ancients and the medievals, ends up extremely close to the views reappropriated, since fundamental ontology maintains, with Hegel, that the ultimate key to ontological intelligibility is not to be found in nature nor in a transcendent God, but in self-understanding.

Commentators sometimes present the Heideggerian meditation on the

---

3. *Hegel's Phenomenology of Spirit,* trans. Parvis Emad and Kenneth Maly (Bloomington: Indiana University Press, 1988), p. 126.

history of Being—which came in the wake of the dismissal of the project of fundamental ontology—as some sort of Hegelianism in reverse, in which the increasing density of the forgetfulness of Being replaces the progressive emergence into light of the Absolute. I believe rather that it is in the project of fundamental ontology that the strongest traces of Hegelianism are to be found in Heidegger. For at the core of his ontology, no matter how attentive it is to finitude, a quasi-speculative circle is operative: Authentic *praxis* culminates in *theoria* as the knowledge of Being, but, vice versa, *theoria* culminates in the speculative justification of resolute or authentic *praxis*.

Such a circle was foreshadowed—as we shall see—in the famous Heideggerian proposition that describes the mode of being of Dasein: *"Das Dasein existiert umwillen seiner"*[4] (Dasein exists for the sake of itself). The paradox that I am aiming at—namely, a combination of finitude and absoluteness—is condensed within that formula. In connection with this point, let me make an historical remark. I recall that during the first session of his last seminar, after indicating for the record in what way Husserl's *Logical Investigations* had provided him with the ground for the *Seinsfrage,* Heidegger stressed that in *Sein und Zeit* no mention is made of *Bewusstsein,* but only of Dasein. Upon which remark, he proceeded to ask of his embarrassed audience what they saw as the most essential characteristic of Dasein. The answer, of course, Heidegger duly provided: "It is simple. It is the 'ec-static' dimension of Dasein." And indeed, in *Sein und Zeit,* to exist means to stand in the open, in the open-ness of finite transcendence, in the in-between of Being and beings. Since the listeners in that audience knew Heidegger's late meditations on the clearing of Being, they might have had the temptation to add that Dasein is exposed to the secret of Being. However, in relationship to *Sein und Zeit,* Heidegger's answer in the seminar was actually nothing more than a half-answer, since it superbly neglected the last two words of the formula: *umwillen seiner.* These words signify that Dasein is always engaged in the care of itself, and of itself alone, and that Dasein wills itself exclusively. There is a paradox in the formula; the first two words indicate the ec-static dimension, but it is precisely this dimension that is cancelled by the last two words. The Dasein of *Sein und Zeit* is open only to make room for a circle leading back to itself. Dasein has an authentic understanding if and only if it wants to be itself.

One cannot fail to recognize here an echo of the Hegelian program, which had been prepared by Fichte, aiming at merging understanding and will, or theoretical reason and practical reason. Once we detect this connection, we cannot fail to notice that after stretching Dasein beyond the limits

---

4. See *Vom Wesen des Grundes* (Frankfurt am Main: Klostermann, Fünfte Auflage 1965), p. 38.

of the individuated *praxis* of a mortal to the *praxis* of a historical people, Heidegger confronts us with a new version of the speculative Hegelian circle: The history of the world—a world limited to the Germanic West, for Heidegger as well as for Hegel—is the judgment of the world. Therefore the thinker's task is to transcribe the historical judgment of the world—which is what was done in the Hegelian *Erinnerung*—or to contribute to the projection of future world-history—which is what Heidegger did between 1933 and 1936. But the project of fundamental ontology stumbled somewhere.

No simple answer can be given to the question as to when Heidegger realized the paradoxical nature—involving both finitude and absoluteness—of his project. I think that the *Rectoral Address* and the various Nazi proclamations of 1933–34 were for him still in accord with the project of fundamental ontology. I believe that, notwithstanding his resignation from the Rectorate, the first reading of Hölderlin (1934–35) in no way contradicts such proclamations. For his first reading bears witness to the same continuity that led him to maintain those two antithetical dimensions, perhaps even while reinforcing them. The same attempt to connect finitude and absoluteness was not disrupted by the lecture course on *An Introduction to Metaphysics*; the disruption occurred in the second part of the lecture course on Nietzsche (*Nietzsche IV*, "European Nihilism").

Whatever went awry in the project of fundamental ontology was never clarified by Heidegger who, once more, remained surprisingly reticent and discreet. Was this a reluctance to admit failure? Perhaps. More simply, I believe that this was due to the fact that a thinker moves forward and leaves it to others to describe and chart the vicissitudes of the work of the pathfinder. Furthermore some retrospective allusions made by Heidegger, publicly or privately, give us the impression of something other than self-justification. For example, in a statement from the *Nietzschebuch*, he said that the inquiry conducted in fundamental ontology had run "the risk of reinforcing subjectivity".[5] Also, in a letter to Kommerel, he said that the publication of *Sein und Zeit* was a disaster.[6] Finally, there is the acerbic assessment he made in front of Gadamer during their last meeting, "Nietzsche destroyed me." But beyond the reevaluations that Heidegger made of his own writings, the confrontation between the way he read some texts at the time of the project of fundamental ontology (notably those of Descartes, Hegel, Nietzsche and Hölderlin) and the way he began to read those texts

5. *Nietzsche IV*, trans. Franz Capuzzi (New York: Harper and Row, 1982), p. 141, modified.

6. See *Philosophie* (Paris: Minuit, 1987), Correspondence between M. Komerell and M. Heidegger, p. 16.

after the dismissal and rejection of that project warrants the hypothesis of a profound self-critique. Yet I cannot maintain that such a self-critique was even radical because it was conducted obliquely and in a cryptic manner. In addition, I am ready to acknowledge that some of the prejudices—and the blindness—involved in fundamental ontology are still maintained after the so-called *Turn,* in spite of the shift toward the meditation on the history of Being. But the first task is to identify and recognize what those prejudices were.

From One Idea of Phenomenology to the Other[1]

1. Husserl

The Idea of Phenomenology is the title of five lectures delivered by Husserl in Göttingen from April 26 to May 2, 1907, and edited by Walter Biemel in 1950. There is also a subtitle, given in parentheses following the title, which indicates that the title does not mean an *eidos* offered to contemplation, nor a general notion. The wording of the subtitle is deliberately programmatic: *Introduction to the Capital Points of Phenomenology and of the Critique of Reason.*

My objective here is to look to the text of these lectures in order to clarify the stakes of the debate that Heidegger initiated with Husserl, the master with whom he was in "direct contact" and to whom he owed the method later used in his fundamental ontology. And since the notions of immanence, of transcendence, also of Being, play a decisive role in the Husserlian lectures, their elucidation will permit us to clarify the debate.

In addition to the text of the lectures, the work edited by Biemel contains a summary of their progression. This summary was composed by Husserl for his own use. I shall refer to it as well as to the text of the lectures.

According to Husserl's summary, the train of thought pursued in the lectures proceeds through four stages. The first is a sort of preliminary stage corresponding to the recognition that a critical situation in the epistemological field requires a new form of philosophy. The next three stages correspond to successive stages within phenomenology itself. Husserl men-

---

1. A first version of Section One of this chapter was published in *Immanence, Transcendence, and Being in the Collegium Phaenomenologicum: the First Ten Years*, ed. John Sallis, (Dordrecht: Kluver-Nijhoff Phaenomenologica, 105) 1988, pp. 47–74.

tions either "immanence" or "transcendence" or both in his presentation of each of the four stages. Our task is to elucidate the meaning of these terms in each stage of the development.

1. Let us consider the preliminary stage, i.e., the description of the critical situation that motivated the new form of philosophical investigation called "phenomenology." This preliminary stage is the topic of the first lecture. The text of this lecture makes us realize very quickly that phenomenology has its origin in a perplexity regarding the very possibility of cognition, and that phenomenology was designed by Husserl as a method for overcoming once and for all the discomfort and perplexity that were prevailing at that time in the field of theory of knowledge.

Investigating that perplexity is tantamount (a) to asking what the theories of knowledge are by which it is brought about, and (b) to determining what it is in their methodological principles that inevitably entails perplexity.

Husserl gives only two examples of such theories of knowledge. In both cases the theories of knowledge ground their investigation of cognition on "a science of the natural sort" (13; 17)[2], i.e., a science originating in what Husserl calls the "natural attitude of mind."

Husserl insists that "the natural attitude of mind" *per se* does not experience any perplexity at all since it is "as yet unconcerned with the critique of cognition. Whether in the act of intuiting or in the act of thinking, in the natural attitude of mind we are turned to the matters (*den Sachen*) which are given to us each time and as a matter of course, even though they are given in different ways and in different modes of being, according to the source and level of our cognition" (13; 17). Within the natural attitude we have no doubt that our perceptions and judgments relate to the world. To be sure, the natural attitude often faces difficulties. This happens when our cognitions "clash and contradict one another" (14; 17). But this clash does not result in any real perplexity: it merely raises problems which can be solved either by restoring formal consistency if the clash turns out to be of a formal nature, or by refining our observation if it is a conflict between

---

2. In the case of a dual page number, the first number will always refer to the English edition, in this case *The Idea of Phenomenology* (The Hague: Martinus Nijhoff, 1964). The second number always will refer to the German original. When only one number is given, this indicates that the English translation of the German text was modified, and the single page number refers to the German pagination. (Trans.)

two empirical evidences. In other words, the natural attitude is basically unshaken.

Such is the case also for the sciences which originate in this attitude and which may therefore be called "sciences of the natural sort" (*natürliche Wissenschaften*). These sciences include those dealing with real actualities such as the sciences of nature (physics, chemistry, biology, *and* psychology), the sciences of culture (*Geisteswissenschaften*), and the sciences dealing with ideal possibilities, such as the mathematical sciences and the sciences which "investigate in their *formal* generality the *a priori* connections of meanings and postulated meanings and the *a priori* principles which belong to objectivity as such" (15; 19), such as pure grammar and pure logic.

All of these sciences progress with assurance. The difficulties which they encounter are always only provisional and are quickly resolved. There is never a doubt that their approaches will eventually reach its object.

> What is *taken for granted* in natural thinking is the possibility of cognition. Constantly busy producing results, advancing from discovery to discovery in newer and newer branches of science, natural thinking finds no occasion to raise the question of the possibility of cognition as such. (15; 19)

This question is raised not by the natural attitude, but by philosophical thinking and is the subject investigated in the philosophical theory of knowledge. Whereas the natural thinking is sure of its continued power and has no reason to turn the possibility of knowing into a problem, the philosophical theory of knowledge no longer takes for granted that possibility, but reflects upon it. It is "with the awakening of reflection about the relation of cognition to its object," that "abysmal difficulties arise" (14; 18).

As a matter of fact the theories of knowledge entailing these abysmal difficulties are based upon sciences of the natural sort; more precisely upon natural sciences in the usual sense of the word. Husserl's first example is the theory of knowledge that bases its investigation upon psychology. Psychology, in its leading version at the end of the 19th century (we might think of Wundt's work for example), was indeed a science of the natural sort inasmuch as it conceived cognition as a "fact of nature" (15; 19) occurring in a cognizing being, that can be treated as any other natural fact according to empirical procedures of observation, analysis, comparison, induction, hypotheses regarding the influence of other facts, and so on.

According to Husserl, it is by relying upon psychology thus understood that the philosophical theory of knowledge is led into an abysmal perplexity. Every philosophical theory of knowledge addresses the problem of the correspondence between the cognitive act and its object, which amounts to the problem of truth in the sense of the adequation between the two. But as soon as someone maintains, in agreement with empirical psychology, that knowledge is nothing but a mental occurrence, in the sense of a fact or mental process occurring like any other event in a sector of nature, within the organism with cognition, then the very possibility that "there exist not only my own *mental processes* . . . but also that which they apprehend" becomes enigmatic. Husserl argues that, logically, whoever maintains that cognition is merely a psychic fact has to become a solipsist: "He never does and never can break out of the circle of his own mental processes" (16; 20). Consequently, the psychological, or psychologistic, theory of knowledge is led to deny the very possibility of science in its double connotation: universality and objectivity.

The implications of a second type of theory are no less "abysmal." When a theory of knowledge is based upon biology, it treats knowledge as a biological fact, a characteristic specific to a biological species and determined in the course of a long process of natural selection and adaptation. The consequence is that the manner in which humans know, including the rules and the logical structures that regulate their judgments and their reasonings, is nothing but the outcome of some accidental peculiarities of a certain type of organism. In both cases therefore, it turns out that our cognition, understood as a natural fact, is not fit to gain access to the things as they really are.

The previous theories had been scrutinized thoroughly by Husserl in the *Prolegomena* to his *Logical Investigations*. He called the first "psychologism" and the second "biologism." Together with a third theory called "anthropologism," they were charged with many faults, including imprecision, inconsistency, self-contradiction, relativism, skepticism, all of which ultimately lead to absurdity.

These accusations are repeated in the five lectures, but the major criticism now levelled at psychologism and biologism concerns the *relation* between the cognitive act, its meaning, and its object. Introducing his own philosophical theory of knowledge, i.e., phenomenology, as a "critique of theoretical reason" (17; 22) that aims in 1907 at what Kant's *Critique* had done in its time, Husserl denounces as a "playground of unclear and inconsistent theories" (17; 21) the "natural" theory of knowledge—and the metaphysics which is "bound up with it, historically and in subject matter." And Husserl writes that the first task of his new theory is to "stigmatize the absurdities inside which natural reflection almost inevitably falls regarding the relation between knowledge, cognitive meaning and the object of knowledge" (22).

Since the philosophical theories of knowledge leading to those obscurities confine themselves to a reflection of the "natural" sort, the question arises as to what, in the methodological principles of such a reflection, inevitably leads to perplexity. This question is not raised explicitly by Husserl, but he says and repeats that a reflection of the "natural" sort on the possibility for the cognitive act to reach its intended objects ends up with a denial of that very possibility. This is why he insists so much, both at the beginning and at the end of the first lecture, that a sharp distinction must be made between science of the natural sort and philosophical science:

> In contradistinction to all natural cognition, philosophy lies . . . within a *new dimension*; and what corresponds to this new dimension . . . is a *new* and *radically new method* which is set over against the "natural" method . . . He who denies this has failed to understand entirely the whole level at which the characteristic problem of the critique of cognition lies, and with this he has failed to understand what philosophy really wants to do or should do, and what gives it its own character and authority vis-à-vis the whole of natural cognition and science of the natural sort. (21; 25–26)

In other words, Husserl's critique of the theories of knowledge already presupposes another theory of knowledge which no longer, in any way, is of the natural sort, but of a radically new sort, that is, of a truly philosophical one. Hence the preliminary stage presupposes stages that are internally contained in the phenomenological approach itself. To be sure, awareness about the perplexities generated by the natural philosophies of knowledge is what motivates phenomenology, but the very description of those perplexities is carried out in the light of "the new dimension" won by phenomenology. Husserl makes this clear when he states: "Only with epistemological (*Erkenntnistheoretische*) [i.e., with the phenomenological] reflection do we arrive at the distinction between the sciences of a natural sort and philosophy" (18; 22–23)

But one could perhaps object: Does all this have anything to do with the notions of immanence, of transcendence, and of Being? The answer is yes. And the text goes on to say:

> Only does phenomenological reflection bring to light that the sciences of a natural sort are not yet the ultimate sciences of Being. We need a science of Being in the absolute sense. This science, which we call *metaphysics,* grows out of a "critique" of natural cognition in the individual sciences. It is based on the insight (*Einsicht*) acquired in the general critique of cognition and what it is to be an object of cognition of one basic type or other, i.e., on an

insight into the meaning (*Sinn*) of the different fundamental correlations between cognizing and being an object of cognition. (18
modified; 23)

In its Idea[3] therefore, phenomenology implies, in a parallel with Kant's Critique, what Husserl calls a "metaphysical purpose" (*Abzweckungen*) (23).
In its properly critical phase, phenomenology proposes to elucidate the confusions "of the theory of knowledge, into which we are led by natural (pre-
phenomenological) reflection on the possibility of cognition." Husserl can
now propose in a second moment to deflect the metaphysical effects of
these flawed reflections: "They involve not just false views about the essence of cognition, but also self-contradictory, and therefore fundamentally
misleading *interpretations* of the being that is cognized in the sciences of
the natural sort" (18; 22). But because such a metaphysical purpose is
based upon a prior cognitive reflection finally liberated from illusions, only
in it will the correct interpretation of Being originate.

The notions of immanence and transcendence come into play when the
very conditions of this reflection are established by disengagement from the
"natural." When Husserl depicts the concept of knowledge engendered by
"natural" reflections, he writes:

Cognition in all its manifestations is a mental process (*psychisches
Erlebnis*); it is the cognition of a cognizing subject. The objects
cognized stand over against the cognition. But how can we be certain of the correspondence between cognition and the object cognized? How can knowledge *transcend* itself and reach its object
reliably? The unproblematic manner in which the object of cognition is given to natural thought to be cognized now becomes an
enigma. In perception the perceived thing is believed to be directly
given. Before my perceiving eyes stands the thing. I see it, and I
grasp it. Yet the perceiving is simply a mental process and act of
mine, of the perceiving subject. (15 modified; 20)

Logically according to Husserl, such a psychological conception of knowledge leads to Hume, who reduced "all transcendent objectivity" to the
level of "fictions" that can be explained psychologically, but cannot
be given a rational justification. This however does not prevent Hume—
at the cost of a contradiction—from "[transcending] the sphere of immanence," and so, instead of limiting himself to current impressions (the only
reality according to him), he treats "concepts such as habit, human nature,

---

3. The word is capitalized by the author to emphasize its Kantian connotation.

sense organ, vividness, etc. that are transcendent entities (and transcendent by his own admission)." (16 modified; 20)

We are now beginning to get an outline of the answer to the question of what in "natural" reflection leads to an abysmal perplexity. If, in principle, knowledge is nothing but the internal succession of mental events, it follows that knowledge, as a phenomenon of the mind in which it occurs factually, does not know any object. If there were a dividing line and a demarcation between knowledge (immanent by definition) and its objects (transcendent by definition), we would have no hope of ever crossing the line and reaching the objects. Certainly, in spite of his declarations of principle, Hume on many points, "as much as anybody else," according to Husserl, went beyond the line and acknowledged, in the very concepts with which he operated, that knowledge is much more than a stream of factual occurrences unfolding inside a singular mental agency. Yet it is one thing to acknowledge this state of affairs indirectly and in spite of oneself, and another thing to show how this is the case. This is part of the task of phenomenology. Let us therefore take our first phenomenological step.

2. The import of the preliminary step seems to be this: theories of knowledge of the natural sort are forced to deny the possibility of knowledge because they limit cognition to a succession of occurrences within an immanent sphere from which it is impossible to escape. Consequently, if we want to establish a theory of knowledge free from any form of perplexity, it seems clear that we should not establish it within the sphere of immanence. However the first stage of the phenomenological orientation situates itself explicitly on the ground of immanence.

How should we understand this decision? This is the way Husserl argues: Since the current theories of knowledge lead to unfathomable perplexities inasmuch as they are "natural" and rest on "natural" conceptions, whether these are scientific—e.g. psychological theories of cognition—or pre-scientific, then we must resolutely suspend all knowledge of a "natural" kind. "At the outset of the [phenomenological] critique of cognition the entire world of nature, physical and psychological, as well as one's own human self together with all the sciences that have to do with these objective matters, are put in question. Their being, their validity, are suspended" (22; 29). Such a universal suspension is the *epoche* and we should notice that it bears upon Being. That *there is* a world, a *phusis,* a *psuche,* this is what the *epoche* suspends in this context. "To be" means: to be pregiven (*vorgegeben*), as standing on its own (*an sich*), yet known. This suspension is a methodological decision which Husserl expressly compares to Cartesian doubt. In line with Descartes', Husserl's *epoche* aims at the indubitable: specifically at "making evident something which we have to acknowledge as absolutely given and indubitable." And, as in Descartes, this indubitable "Being" is the *cogito*: "While I am judging that everything is doubtful, it is indubitable that I am so judging" (23; 30). Similar remarks could be made concerning any other *cogitatio*: perception, representation, judgment, reasoning, etc.

The *cogitationes* that are given as a result of the *epoche* are nothing pregiven, they are given absolutely and indubitably: they form "a sphere of absolute givenness" (24–25; 32) that constitutes the ground from which the new theory of knowledge must begin.

But what is thus absolutely given in this first knowledge? Is it the fact that any specific *cogitatio* (perception of this or of that, judgment on this or on that, imagination of this or of that, etc.) is, *hic et nunc,* effectively experienced by myself? Husserl grants that in the wake of the *epoche* every *cogitatio* that is given is a lived experience, or *Erlebnis.* And in a way, the absolute givenness of the lived experience, or *Erlebnis,* which each *cogitatio* is, seems to concern primarily the fact that such *cogitatio* is being experienced by me, *hic et nunc.* As it is thus experienced, the *cogitatio* can, after the *epoche,* be given to a pure contemplation in which it is an absolute given: "It is given as something that is, that is here and now, and whose being cannot be sensibly doubted" (24; 31). But when Husserl stresses that "every intellectual *Erlebnis* and indeed every mental *Erlebnis* whatever, while being enacted, can be made the object of a pure 'seeing' and understanding, and is something absolutely given in this 'seeing' " (24 modified; 31), the point is not at all that I can see that this mental process *is* actually enacted by me *hic et nunc.* If the point were the existence of the *cogitatio,* Husserl would not stress concerning this pure seeing, that it is indifferent whether the *cogitatio,* which is to be seen, be real or simply imagined.

Whether we reflectively imagine a perception or reflectively consider a perception at the same time as we experience it in actuality, in either case, there is an absolute givenness of the *cogitatio* which is the perception. "All of these . . . can also be data in imagination; they can 'as it were' stand before our eyes and yet not stand before them as actualities" (24; 31). In other words, the absolute givenness of a *cogitatio* is not its factual occurrence, but the presentation of its essence.

In the entire sphere of *cogitationes,* what matters to the pure seeing directed at them is not to observe whether they really occur but to "intuitively consider their essence, their constitution, their intrinsic character" (31). Husserl adds: "The task of the critique of cognition is to clarify, to cast light upon, the essence of cognition and the legitimacy of its claims to validity that belongs to its essence; and what else can this mean but to make the essence of cognition directly self-given" (25; 32).

What happens to immanence and transcendence in this context? Precisely when he recapitulates the movement of this first intraphenomenological phase, Husserl writes that the absolute self-givenness of the *cogitatio* is a consequence of its immanence, and that it is "because of this immanence" that the point of departure of phenomenology is "free of the puzzlement which is the source of skeptical embarrassment" (26; 33). "Immanence," he says finally, "is the generally necessary characteristic of all epistemological cognition" (26; 33).

Now we are the ones who are puzzled. We thought that a bias for immanence was the flaw of the earlier theories of knowledge. Is Husserl contradicting himself? Or is he giving two different meanings to the same word? Indeed, he seems to have been aware of the difficulties caused by his terminology since, in a recapitulation of the first intraphenomenological phase, he devotes a long analysis to the controversial senses of both "immanence" and "transcendence." Let us follow his analysis.

> One thing one can mean by transcendence is that the object of cognition is not actually (*reell*) contained in the cognitive act so that one would be meaning by "being truly given" or "immanently given" that the object of the cognitive act is actually contained in that act. (27 modified; 35)

Then he adds:

> But there is still another transcendence whose opposite is an altogether different sort of immanence, namely absolute and clear givenness, which consists of a simply immediate "seeing" and apprehending of the intended object itself as it is. (28 modified; 35)

Let us try to elucidate this distinction. In the first sense, "*immanent*" means: actually contained in the *cogitatio* as a mental process, and consequently, "*transcendent,*" as the antonym of *immanent*, means: not actually contained in the mental process. In the second sense, "*immanent*" means: given in itself absolutely and clearly to an immediate seeing, and consequently, "*transcendent*" means: not given in itself with evidence, but rather only mediately.

To eliminate the apparent contradiction mentioned above amounts to understanding in what sense immanence generates perplexity in the case of the natural theories of knowledge, while immanence frees us from puzzlement and embarrassment in the case of phenomenological theory. Reaching such an understanding presupposes a closer inspection of the way in which natural theories pose the problem of cognition. Their question is that of a relation, of the relation between the cognitive *Erlebnis* and the object known. If the very manner in which they pose the problem contains the impossibility of ever solving it, the reason is that at the outset they base their inquiry on

> the unspoken supposition that the only actually understandable, un-questionable, absolutely evident givenness is the givenness of *the moment actually (reell) contained* within the cognitive act, and this is why anything in the way of a cognized objectivity that is not actually *(reell)* contained within the act is regarded as a puzzle and as problematic. (28 modified; 35–36)

Such a presupposition, is, according to Husserl, "a fatal mistake." Before understanding why, let us note immediately that the two senses of the words *"immanence"* and *"transcendence"* are implied in the unspoken presupposition of the natural theory of knowledge.

The natural theory of knowledge implicitly states at the outset that what is absolutely evident (second meaning of *"immanence"*) is what is actually contained within the mental process (first meaning of *"imma-nence"*). Therefore and inversely, what is not actually contained within the mental process (first meaning of *"transcendence"*) is not absolutely evident (second meaning of *"transcendence"*). Now it is clear that the object as a physical thing is not contained in the actual mental process. Consequently, the object is problematic.

The fatal mistake consists in believing that the cognitive act is not in-trinsically relational and open to the objectivities at which it aims, i.e., that "cognition and its object are actually separate" (30; 37) and that therefore their relation is not given either. Or, if we use the two terms of *"transcen-dence"* and *"immanence,"* the mistake consists in believing that the cog-nitive act is an absolute datum or seen entity (second meaning of *"immanence"*) if and only if it is limited to what is actually contained within the mind (first meaning of *"immanence"*). As a result the cognitive act turns out to be a non-relational process, radically separated from the object, which is neither seen nor integrated as a part of the mental process. As a result, it is impossible to understand how the cognitive act can be related to objects because the objects not only are not a part of the cogni-tive act, but are not visible within the cognitive act either. In other words, if the *relation* between cognition and object is not from the outset given to an immediate *seeing,* then every attempt to understand the possibility of a relation between cognition and object is, as Husserl says, "patent folly" (30; 37).

We are now able to understand in what sense immanence annihilates puzzlement and perplexity in the case of phenomenology, whereas it gener-ates them in the case of the "natural" attitudes of knowledge. What is at stake in Husserl's debate with the natural theory of knowledge is a question of "seeing." The "natural" theory of knowledge says: I only see cognition as an occurrence in the mind, I do not see objects, and therefore neither do I see the relation of cognition to the object. However, the "natural" theory of knowledge goes on to argue that it is still possible to deduce or to infer some explanation of the relation of cognition to the object from what the natural sciences enable us to know, although not immediately, about nature as a whole.

To this, Husserl objects: "Seeing does not lend itself to demonstration or deduction" (31; 38). Concerning what is a matter of seeing, it is absurd to "draw conclusions from existences of which one knows but which one cannot 'see' " (31; 38). Husserl gives this illustration: "A man born deaf knows that there are sounds, and that sounds produce harmonies . . . but he cannot intuit such things and in intuiting grasp the 'how' of such things" (30 modified; 38). When Husserl maintains that, by limiting itself to immanence and by reducing all transcendence to a nonoperative level, phenomenology liberates the theory of knowledge from its perplexities, he merely states that the theory of knowledge has to be based at the outset on a 'seeing' and to remain constantly based on it. The bracketing of transcendence is by no means the exclusion of objects out of the field of the theory of knowledge. It is the exclusion of the unseen, including all the absurd attempts to demonstrate, on the basis of the unseen, something that is, in principle, open to a 'seeing' only.

Phenomenological immanence is therefore much broader and of a different sort than the immanence found in the natural theories of knowledge. It is of another sort because, on the one hand, it is 'pure' and unmixed with transcendent elements and because, on the other hand, it gives access to essences and not to factual occurrences. It is broader because at the outset it is relational and not closed upon its internal flux.

When the natural theory of knowledge reflects on knowledge, it treats its themes in an impure manner, because in its approach to them it has recourse to procedures, laws, and concepts that are not required by the matters themselves (i.e., that are not seen by the theoretician within the phenomena), but imported or borrowed from pregiven natural sciences. In other words, although the natural theorist of knowledge claims to limit his investigation to whatever is seen within the sphere of immanence, he does not really maintain this principle, but decides beforehand that this sphere is composed only of factual occurrences because the natural sciences assure him that reality is composed of facts explainable by other facts. Therefore his reflection is blind toward what it is supposed to reflect upon and his sphere of immanence is thoroughly intermingled with transcendence. Phenomenological reflection frees its sphere of immanence from this confusion.

Freed from any *metabasis eis allo genos,* the immanence which the phenomenologist considers as the given is not limited to a succession of factual occurrences. What is offered to a phenomenological seeing is not the event of this or that *cogitatio.* Instead it is the essential manner in which *cogitationes* are given as examples of a kind, their essential mode of given-ness. If immanence were limited to mental events, phenomenology would be nothing more than psychology. But its goal, Husserl insists, "is not to explain cognition as a psychological fact; it is not to inquire into the natural causes and laws of the development and occurrence of cognitions" (25; 32). Rather, its task is to offer to a direct seeing the essence of the *cogitationes* which the mental events exemplify—as in the case of this perception, that imagination, or that judgment.

Thus purified and essentialized, this sphere of immanence is freed from the limits imposed by the natural theory of knowledge. For a relationship immediately reveals itself as belonging to the intuitively given essence of every *cogitatio.* Every *cogitatio* is essentially related according to its specific modality to a *cogitatum* that it claims to intend and attain. This relat-edness does not have to be explained mediately, for it is given immediately to the very *cogitatio* of which it is an essential trait, rather than as a complement or supplement.

Two further stages are thus anticipated in the stage devoted to the *ep-oche*: the eidetic reduction and the analysis of intentionality.

3. The reduction which is here called "epistemological reduction" is the topic of the third lecture. Husserl begins by recalling the result of the *epoche.*

We have indubitably secured the whole realm of the *cogitationes.* The being of the *cogitatio,* more precisely the phenomenon of cog-nition itself, is beyond question and it is freed from the riddle of transcendence. These existing things are already presupposed in the statement of the problem of cognition. The question as to how transcendent things come into cognition would lose its sense if cognition itself, as well as the transcendent object, were put in question. It is also clear that the *cogitationes* present a sphere of *absolute immanent data; it is in this sense that we understand "im-manence."* In the "seeing" pure phenomena, the object is not out-side cognition or outside "consciousness," it is being given in the sense of the absolute self-givenness of something which is simply "seen." (33 modified; 43)

The "reduction," again referred to as the "epistemological reduction," is designed first of all to defend pure immanence against any contamination by transcendence. We have already seen that the equation "absolutely seen = actually contained in the mind as a fact" was the definition of immanence in the "natural" nonphenomenological theories of knowledge, and was the basic reason for the abysmal puzzlement entailed by them. The reduction aims at overcoming once and for all this deceptive equation. The reduction is needed precisely "in order to prevent the evidence of the Being of the *cogitatio* from being confused with the evidence that my *cogitatio* is, with the evidence of the *sum cogitans,* and the like" (33 modified; 43). This sentence clearly indicates that in the Husserlian sense, "the Being of the *cogitatio*" does not consist in its factual occurrence, in the fact that it is present. It consists rather in the presentation, the absolute givenness, of its essence. *Existence here means essence.* That the *cogitatio* is factually present is not of interest to the phenomenologist at all, but only to a naturalist of a certain kind (i.e., the psychologist). More precisely the fact that *my cogitatio* exists, that it belongs to me, i.e., its existential "mineness," its individuation, this fact never turns into a characteristic of the phenomenon in the phenomenological sense. Husserl writes:

> If I, as a human being employing my natural mode of thought, look at the perception which I am undergoing at the moment, then I immediately and almost inevitably apperceive it (that is a fact) in relation to my ego. It stands there as a mental process of this mentally living person, as his state, his act; the sensory content stands there as what is given or sensed, as that of which I am conscious; and it integrates itself with the person in objective time. Perception, and any other *cogitatio,* so apperceived, is a *psychological fact.* Thus it is apperceived as a datum in objective time, belonging to the mentally living ego, the ego which is in the world and lasts through its duration (a duration which is measured by means of empirically calibrated timepieces). This, then, is the phenomenon which is investigated by the natural science we call "psychology." (34 modified; 44)

Hence it is not essential to the pure immanent *cogitatio* that it should exist, that it should belong to an existing ego and that this ego should be in the world. In general, individual existence, mineness, Being-in-the-world, the temporality proper to the one who says "I"—these features are transcendent, they must be excluded from the phenomenon in the phenomenological, purely immanent, sense of the word. It is for the natural attitude and its way of thinking that the *cogitatio* is linked to individual existences that are in the world and are given within a certain timespan.

Husserl therefore presents us with an alternative: Being in the transcendent and nonabsolute or relative sense and Being in the immanent and absolute sense. In the first case Being means: to occur as a fact. In the second case, it means: to exhibit an essence. We have to choose: Either (*a*) consciousness is the conscious act of a singular entity which, in fact, is in the world and has certain duration (in which case we remain engulfed in the natural attitude, and this ultimately leads us to psychologism and anthropologism); or (*b*): being-conscious is the pure givenness of the essence of *cogitationes* (but these are without intrinsic relation to the facticity of the ego that is in the world and exists for whatever time is granted to it). Between these two meanings of Being, we have to choose.

In addition to striking at the mineness of *cogitatio* and at the existential facticity to which mineness is linked, the reduction also strikes at the existential facticity of the objects aimed at in the *cogitationes*. If I consider, for example, this particular *cogitatio*, let us say this perception as a pure, immanent, and reduced phenomenon, I can indeed attain to the pure contemplation of the phenomenon of perception on the basis (*Fundierung*) of this or that actual perception that I am having *hic et nunc* of this tree, this field, this street. But the question is not whether this tree, this field, this street really exist, nor whether the perception of these things is actually taking place within me. What must be offered to contemplation is perception, as such, in its essence.

> *Thus to each psychic lived process there corresponds through the device of phenomenological reduction a pure phenomenon, which exhibits its intrinsic (immanent) essence* (taken individually) *as an absolute datum.* Every postulation of a "non-immanent actuality," of anything which is not contained in the phenomenon, even if intended by the phenomenon, and which is therefore not given in the second sense, is bracketed, i.e., suspended. (35; 45)

This essence, universal by definition, can be contemplated by means of an "eidetic abstraction," i.e., of an ideation that is neither inductive nor deductive, but thoroughly intuitive. It is in relation to this essence and not on the ground of actual events that we must pose the famous problem of the relation of knowledge, particularly of perceptive knowledge, to its objects. Indeed, the intuitive inspection of the essence of each *cogitatio* reveals in it a specific openness to a specific correlate. Here again the actual existence of a concrete correlate, the existence of a tree over there, is not what we are talking about. Instead what we are dealing with is the essential relation of the perceptive *cogitatio* to its specific correlate, the perceived-as-such in its essence. Such an essential relation can be intuited within the pure phenomenon, it is an absolute datum. "When at the same time nothing is presupposed regarding the being or non-being of objective actuality," it appears within "those absolute data" exhibited by the "reduced" *cogitationes* that "if these data are *related* to objective actuality via their intentions, this *relatedness* is an intrinsic character *within* them" (35 modified; 45).

Even if I raise questions about the existence and reaching the object of this relation to transcendent things, still it has something which can be grasped in the pure phenomenon. The relating-itself-to-transcendent-things, whether it is meant in this way or that way, is still an inner feature of the phenomenon. (36; 46)

Because the pure phenomenon—displayed in the reduced *cogitatio*—is an essence, pure immanence is an *eidetic* field. But because a relating-oneself-to-the-transcendent, as well as a claim to posit the transcendent as existing, essentially belong to the *cogitatio*, pure immanence also forms a transcendental field. In other words, it is a field in which we find conditions for validity. Indeed, what is given to contemplation within the pure phenomenon in which the relatedness to something transcendent inheres, comprises both the sense (*Sinn*) of the specific intention consisting of this relatedness and the condition of possibility for its validation. Husserl asks:

Since I have to cancel out any previous acceptance of the intended transcendent objects, where else could I investigate both the *meaning* of this intending-something-beyond, and also, along with this meaning, its possible *validity,* or the meaning of such validity? Where else but the place at which this meaning is unqualifiedly given and at which in the pure phenomenon of relation, corroboration, justification the meaning of validity, for its part, comes to absolute givenness. (36; 46–47)

In this context, Husserl evokes an objection that manifestly originates in the natural attitude. In that attitude, one might object to the phenomenologist: 'Your phenomenological approach aims at being scientific, but there is no science that does not lead to the establishing of objects existing in themselves, i.e., to transcendent objects. Now, this very transcendent existence is precisely what you have suspended in your reduction; consequently the judgments you attempt to make after the reduction, have no scientific value. They are purely and simply "subjective" and involve nothing but the reality of the "Heraclitean flux" (37; 47) of your mental processes. In other words, from this position it could be objected that, at most, your propositions are judgments of perception in the Kantian sense, but they are not at all judgments of experience.' The allusion to Kant is precisely what allows Husserl to deflect the objection. For the natural attitude (in spite of its passing mention of Kant) fails to acknowledge the "indispensable distinction" between the transcendental and the empirical. Such a distinction, even though Kant "did not arrive at the ultimate significance of the distinction," is reappropriated by Husserl. Husserl claims that it is precisely not at the level of empirical subjectivity that phenomenology finds its ground, but at the level of "transcendental apperception, consciousness as such" (38; 48). However this apperception has for the phenomenologist "a completely different meaning, one which is not at all mysterious" (38; 48).

Indeed, the synthetic unity that defines transcendental apperception in the Kantian sense is not given to a 'seeing,' it cannot be intuited. In Kant, only space and time, the *a priori* forms of sensibility, are pure intuitions, purely given to an immediate seeing, whereas the *a priori* concepts or categories together with the *a priori* principles of the understanding are not intuitively given, are not offered to a seeing, and therefore remain mysterious. By characterizing phenomenological immanence by the notion of transcendental apperception, now freed from the Kantian obscurity, Husserl in a single stroke acknowledges that (*a*) this immanence is a field of *a priori* conditions of possibility and of validity and (*b*) that these conditions can be integrally offered to a seeing which is in no way empirical. In relation to Kant, a metamorphosis of the *a priori* has occurred. It is not only space and time that have the value of pure *a priori* intuitions, but also all the *cogitationes* and their *cogitatum,* the various moments of each, along with the predicative and logical forms in which they are expressed. Thus we have a domain of universal entities (*Allgemeinheiten*), of "universal objects," of "universal states of affairs" (41; 51) which can be characterized as *a priori* inasmuch as they are "essences" absolutely given to a totally pure seeing and in no way presuppose the mediation of any extrinsic support from what is neither contained nor seen in purified immanence. This domain is *a priori* (*a*) because it is composed of immediately given essences, also (*b*) in the *transcendental* sense of a critique of theoretical reason (it makes visible what allows, within limits which also are made clear, a knowledge of transcendence), and (*c*) of practical reason (it brings to sight what makes possible any ethical evaluation).

At this juncture we are able to define more precisely the notion of phenomenological immanence. As Husserl indicates in the summary of the movement of the five lectures, the step taken in the second phase "makes clear to us in the first place that *actual immanence* (*reelle Immanenz*)—and the same is true of *actual transcendence* (*reelle Transendenz*)—is but a special case of the *broader concept of immanence as such*" (6 modified; 9). In Husserlian terminology, the adjective '*reell*' means: actual or positive. Actual immanence is the mental flux or the stream of experiences actually felt by a given consciousness. But, after the reduction, we do not accept as obvious that what is absolutely given and what is actually immanent "are one and the same" (6; 9). To be sure, when after the reduction I contemplate—in a pure *Schauen*—a *cogitatio,* no longer as a factual occurrence but as a general essence, my seeing is still a mental act. It is mine and belongs to the positive flux of my actual conscious experiences. It is then possible to say that this seeing and intuition of a *cogitatio*, taken in its general essence, or "this act of cognizing the universal," is "something singular," "something which at any given time, is a moment in the stream of consciousness." But precisely "the universal itself, which is given in evidence within the stream of consciousness is nothing singular but just a universal, and in the actual or positive (*reell*) sense it is transcendent." Yet, this "universal is absolutely given" (i.e., in an immanent manner offered to a seeing), but it is "not actually (*reell*) immanent" (7; 9). Though transcendent in the *reell* sense, it is not at all so in the phenomenological sense; it is in no way accepted as existing without being seen. "Consequently, the idea of phenomenological reduction acquires a more immediate and more profound determination and a clearer meaning. It means not the exclusion of the *reell* transcendent" (7 modified; 9) (because then the exclusion would mean exclusion of the universal, since the universal even when aimed at in a singular act is not actually contained as a part in the stream of consciousness within which the act takes place), but "the exclusion of the transcendent in general as something to be accepted as existent, i.e., everything that is not evident givenness in its true sense, that is not absolutely given to pure 'seeing' " (7; 9).

4. The third phase in phenomenology consists in exploring eidetic and transcendental immanence. As Husserl insists at the beginning of the fourth lecture: "The singular cognitive phenomenon, coming and going in the stream of consciousness, is not the object of phenomenological statements" (44 modified; 55). The subject matter of phenomenological statements is a "generic" cognitive phenomenon. Once reduced, that is, detached from its singular occurrence and considered from what allows it to be "seen," the *cogitatio* is an absolute "generic" givenness. It is an eidetic datum, an essence. From actual immanence, the reduction allows us to shift to eidetic immanence.

But this purified sphere of immanence is intrinsically intentional:

Cognitive mental experiences (and this belongs to their essence) have an *intentio*, they refer to something, they are related in this or that way to an object. This activity of relating itself to an object belongs to them even if the object itself does not. And what is objective can have a certain kind of givenness in appearance, even though it is not contained in a *reell* manner within the cognitive phenomenon and moreover does not exist as a *cogitatio*. To clarify the essence of the cognitive phenomenon and to bring to self-givenness the connections of essence which belong to it, this involves examining both these sides of the matter; it involves investigating this relatedness which belongs to the essence of cognition. (43 modified; 55)

In other words, both the *intentio* of the cognitive phenomenon and what is *intended* by it qualify as absolute givenness: both the *intentum* and the *intentio* are immanent in the phenomenological sense. But if this *intentum* is called "objective," it is not in the usual and "natural" sense of the word, as when I say that my perception presents an object to me now (which means that my perception informs me that there is a tree, a field, a road over there). The object in that sense (the existence of something over there) has been reduced. But the reduction of the existential position of the object is precisely what allows me to contemplate intuitively the generic way in which the object presents itself, in which it appears, its way of being-given. It is this way of appearing (not the fact of being) which is the phenomenological *intentum*. The *intentum* is one of the two sides of the intentional relation. The other side (the *intentio*) and the relation itself are not given as singular, but as universal moments of the intentional relation.

Two questions can be raised. The first is: How are these two sides and the relation that links them given as universalities? They are given on the basis of something singular. The *intentio* "perception of" is given in its universal properties on the basis of a singular perception of something. We already know that the elevation from the level of the singular to the level of the universal is an "eidetic abstraction." This abstraction, also called "ideation," initiates a break from the singular only in order to intuit the universal through the singular. The universal exceeds the singular, it is in a position of surplus with regard to the singular, but only on the basis of the singular can it be phenomenologically seen. The relation between singular and universal, in this case, is called a relation of *Fundierung*. Thus, on the basis of the particular perception that I now have of this or that thing over there, I can phenomenologically grasp that perception, taken in its *intentio*, is essentially intuitive and that it belongs to perception essentially, i.e., universally, to be oriented toward the fulfillment of an *intentio*, that is, to be an intention of fulfillment.

The second question is: What is the extension of the sphere of the absolutely and universally given? The answer is already implicit in what has been said above. The absolutely given includes all the constituents of both sides of the intentional relation. But a precision is required as far as the *intentum* is concerned. Not only can every kind of *intentio* be absolutely 'seen' in its specific universality, but its specific *intentum* (at which the considered *intentio* aims) can be seen too. Not only all the specific *cogitationes*, but also their *cogitata* can be seen. The examples given by Husserl are sufficient to suggest the breadth of the field of investigation formed by those *cogitata*. First, he mentions the sensible universals, e.g. a specific coloration (for instance "redness") as such can be intuited in its generic character on the basis (*Fundierung*) of some particular red. Then, he mentions sensible relations, e.g. the relation of resemblance, which can be intuited as an ideality on the basis of the consideration of a specific similarity, (for instance the relation that obtains between two samples of the color red). In both cases, a sense (*Sinn*) is given to intuition: the sense "red," the sense "resemblance." But Husserl insists that phenomenology is concerned with the entire sphere of cognitive phenomena (their "many forms and types" all considered in their *eidos,* and also in their "essential relations" and their "teleological connections"): this entire sphere can be given to a "pure seeing and ideation" (45; 57). These phenomena are offered to seeing along with their specific *cogitata,* so that on both sides, "phenomenology proceeds by seeing, by clarifying, and determining meaning (*Sinn*), and by distinguishing meanings" (46; 58). In this clarification, all the categories and structures which determine the various types of objectivity can be intuited in a pure manner; this includes not only the sensory categories which determine perceptive objectivity (color, extension, form, etc.), but also the categorial forms by which we articulate what we perceive. "The categorial forms . . . find expression in words like "is," "not," "same" and "other," "one" and "many," "and" and "or," and in the forms of predication and attribution, etc." (56; 71). Included also are "the basic concepts and propositions (*Grundbegriffe und Grundsätze*) which function as principles governing the possibility of "objectivizing" science" (46; 58). The allusion to these principles evokes the Kantian categories and principles of pure understanding, and suggests once again a connection with the transcendental problematic of Kant's *Critique of Pure Reason.*

The move that founds phenomenology and gives it its guiding Idea revitalizes Kant's project with the help of the eidetic method. "This method," says Husserl, "belongs essentially to the meaning of the critique of cognition and so generally to every sort of critique of reason (hence also evaluative and practical reason)" (46 modified; 58). In Kant, the critique of theoretical reason aims at determining the conditions of possibility for knowledge and its objects. But for Kant, only mathematics and physics deal with objects. Mathematics for Kant is cognitive to the extent that it restricts itself to a construction of concepts within time and space as *a priori* intuitions. And experimental physics is cognitive insofar as it deals with the empirical content of space and time, as a content which is articulated a priori by the categories and principles of pure understanding. In Husserl, we no longer have this limitation of knowledge to mathematics and physics. The a priori realm, as far as knowledge is concerned, is no longer limited to the a priori conditions of mathematical entities and of physical objects. The phenomenological reduction shows that it makes sense to say that perception, for example, (which was relegated by Kant, except for what concerns the position of existence, to the realm of subjectivity) as well as imagination also have their objects. And because the phenomenological transcendental field is broader than the Kantian transcendental field, it can ground, as sciences, disciplines that were not scientific in Kant's view, e.g., psychology or history and even the Geisteswissenschaften in general.

In addition to revitalizing and enlarging Kant's project, phenomenology is also in continuity with Kant as far as metaphysics is concerned. In Kant, the critique of theoretical reason opens the way to a metaphysics of nature. Likewise the critique of practical reason opens the way to a metaphysics of morals. Although now expanded, this metaphysical aim is also reappropriated by Husserl, who writes:

> Whatever, in addition to the critique of reason, is called philosophy in the strict sense, is intimately related to this critique: hence metaphysics of nature and metaphysics of spiritual life as a whole (des gesamten Geisteslebens), and thus metaphysics in general in the widest sense. (46 modified; 58–59)

> Pure immanence, as the transcendental field open to a pure eidetic seeing, is the field of an investigation that is both critical and metaphysical. The phenomenological investigation is critical when it determines, on the basis of an eidetic seeing, the specific validity of each type of cogitatio. It is metaphysical when it determines, on the basis of this critique but also in a pure seeing, the categories and structures that characterize Being as a whole. The Idea of Phenomenology seems to accept as certain, i.e., purely self-given to a pure seeing, that Being as a whole is divided in two ontological realms: nature and Spirit. Hence, "metaphysics . . . in the widest sense" is composed of metaphysics of nature and of metaphysics of spiritual life.

We have thus achieved a full characterization of phenomenological immanence. The eidetic sphere of essences and essential structures determine each type of intentionality on its two sides, the side of the intentio and the side of the intentum. Immanence is also a transcendental sphere in the sense given to the word in Kant's philosophy because in it categorial and axiomatic conditions for the validity of each type of intentionality are given. Moreover this sphere is transcendental in the metaphysical sense of the word because in it ontological categories and structures of Being as a whole (both the realm of nature and the realm of spirit) are exhibited. This sphere of pure immanence is *a priori*. In each of the avenues that it opens to research, it offers itself wholly to a seeing that borrows nothing from any presupposed, presumed or inferred existence, extrinsic to its realm. The reduction brackets such extrinsic existence and retains only the existence of the *cogitationes*. But as soon as the *cogitationes* are taken as the specific focus of research, their existence, i.e., their actual occurring here and now, is of no interest to the phenomenologist and is therefore also bracketed. What is phenomenologically relevant is the generic essence of each *cogitatio* with its intentional and transcendental features. And such an essence may be seen on the basis of a *cogitatio* which does not actually occur but is merely imagined.

Hence phenomenological reduction does not entail a limitation of the investigation to the sphere of actual, positive (*reell*) immanence, to the sphere of that which is actually contained within the absolute this of the *cogitatio*. . . . It entails a limitation to the sphere of things that are purely self-given, to the sphere of those things which are not merely spoken about, meant, or perceived, but instead to the sphere of those things that are given in just exactly the sense in which they are aimed at or meant, and moreover are self-given in the strictest sense—in such a way that nothing which is meant fails to be given. In a word, we are restricted to the sphere of pure evidence. (48–49 modified; 60–61)

Within this sphere of pure evidence, it turns out that pure immanence, because of its eidetic and transcendental properties, is in a position of excess, or surplus, vis-à-vis the actual immanence with which the psychologist is concerned. Envisaged as an actual immanent occurrence, the *cogitatio* is a closed, atomic entity, deprived of any intrinsic openness to an object, and, consequently, deprived of any intrinsic capacity for truth. But if considered in its immanent purity, the same *cogitatio* turns out to be intrinsically open; it bears in itself a relatedness to an object, which means a specific claim to validity, to verification. Likewise, the actual immanent *cogitatio,* for example perception, is deprived of any consciousness of time, since at all times it is encapsulated within a mere now-moment. By contrast the reduced *cogitatio* gives itself to the pure phenomenological seeing as pervaded by an internal consciousness of time, in the form of "the retention that is necessarily bound up with every perception" (52 modified; 67). Finally, the actually immanent *cogitatio* is devoid of any internal capacity for ideation, of any view of the generic, or of any categorial intuition. Not so with the phenomenological immanence. This reduction enables one to see that even such a simple *cogitatio* as the perception of a thing is pervaded by ideation and categorial intuition. Husserl writes:

> In the perception of an external thing, just that thing, let us say a house standing before our eyes, is said to be perceived. The house is a transcendent thing, and forfeits its existence after the phenomenological reduction. The house-appearance, this *cogitatio,* emerging and disappearing in the stream of consciousness, is truly given. In this house-phenomenon we find a phenomenon of redness, of extension, etc. But is it not also evident that a house appears in the house-phenomenon, and that it is just on that account that we call it a perception of a house? And what appears is not only a house in general, but just exactly this house, determined in such and such a way and appearing in that determination. Can I not make an evidently true judgment as follows: on the basis of the appearance or in the sense of this perception, the house is thus and so, a brick building, with a slate roof, etc.? (57 modified; 72)

By focusing on a specific example of a *cogitatio,* this passage condenses the whole issue of the reduction. To be sure, it seems to endow the phenomenological operation with an excessive facility, to ignore its complexity, perhaps even to confuse the singular and the universal. Moreover, shortly thereafter, Husserl denies that "everything perceived . . . would be evidently given" (58; 73). Nevertheless this text brings out the full import of the reduction because the bracketing that it describes, in relation to what it calls transcendence, is presented as the condition for a true return to what had been, at the outset, discarded in appearance only.

What is bracketed here as transcendent, or more precisely as "transcendent existence," is not the concrete manner in which what is perceived in an everyday fashion gives itself to perception, it is not the things perceived *qua* perceived, but *qua* facts, which the so-called "natural" attitude views as moments inscribed in the regulated connection of a totality of facts. From this bracketing, the result is not that the perception I have, the perception of this house, disappears. On the contrary, it now gives itself to be apprehended in its appearing, in other words—since the appearing is eidetic—to be apprehended in its essential features. Such a perception is a *cogitatio.* This term (as it is now used) refers both to the side of *intentio* and to that of *intentum.* The *intentum* here given in a purely immanent manner is the appearing *of* the house. This appearing, also called a phenomenon, contains features such as redness, extension, form, functional relations between parts: walls, roof, etc. These features can become, by virtue of *Fundierung,* the object of an ideation (I can apprehend eidetically redness as such) or categorial intuition (I can eidetically apprehend the relationship between whole and parts). But in reverse (and it is here that a true return begins to take place), the universals that stand in a position of surplus or excess vis-à-vis the strict singular sensorial data (exclusively considered by the empirical psychologist) play for my perception a *constitutive* role in the very appearing of that house. Thus, in that appearing, they have a foundational role. They make it possible in its physiognomy. In this sense the eidetic intuition of them is also a transcendental apperception. This transcendental apperception founds my concrete perception, in such a fashion that I am entitled to say both (*a*) that I am seeing what I am describing and (*b*) that I am describing what I am seeing. This means that I have an empirical seeing of what I am saying with universal terms that express possible correlates of an eidetic seeing. It also means that the linguistic account of what I perceive is connected with a seeing that combines empirical and transcendental levels. The bracketing of the empirical sphere, a bracketing which opens the way to the eidetic, implies—because the eidetic has a transcendental function—a return to the empirical sphere, no longer defined by the sum of the regulated facts considered by the psychologist. In such a return to the empirical sphere, what is at stake is nothing less than truth. Husserl insists on the fact that the investigation of the immanent sphere of essences is conducted with the objective of uncovering the validity, i.e., the truth specific to each type of intentionality. This validation presupposes a return from the transcendental to the empirical, because the truth of the former founds that of the latter. It is in this sense that Husserl could affirm with regard to perception, as early as Lecture Two, that "this perception is, and remains, as long as it lasts, something absolute, something here and now, something that in itself is what it is, something by which I can measure as by an ultimate standard what being and being given can mean and here must mean, at least, obviously, concerning the sort of being and being-given which a "here and now" exemplifies" (24; 31). In other words, the phenomenological intuition of the essence of perception gives an *a priori* norm against which I can measure the claim of any perception to be valid, i.e., to perceive truly what it claims to perceive. The same phenomenological intuition shows that this norm contains two sides: (*a*) the side of its *intentio* as intention of fulfillment, and (*b*) the side of its *intentum* (for example as the bodily presence given through the *Abschattungen* or profiles and exhibiting universal properties of sensible as well as categorial kind).

Transcendental immanence is therefore the foundation of the specific truth of all empirical *cogitationes*. And this is why it compels us to reject the framework within which psychology treats cognitive phenomena: in such a framework, perception (for example) is nothing but an event that occurs in me, and the relation of this event to something external is not given within the event. Thus the relation of perception to something perceived is supposed to be incidental, like a supplement to the event of perception, a supplement which therefore has to be explained from the outside, starting with the totality of the regulated facts that are supposed by the natural attitude to define the 'world,' or nature as a whole.

The above commentary is another way of saying that the sphere of pure immanence is the sphere of *constitution*. Constitution, which is the main topic of the fifth Lecture, is neither the creation of beings *a nihilo* nor is it the shaping of entities out of a pregiven matter. It does not designate an activity by which consciousness would let its objects emerge into existence nor an activity by which consciousness would give objects to itself. Neither does it designate some univocal and centrifugal giving operation of consciousness. Rather, the term refers to a correlation between a giving by consciousness, a specific *intentio,* and a self-givenness of the *intentum,* to which the *intentio* is related. It is one and the same thing to say that consciousness constitutes its objects and to say that objects constitute themselves in front of consciousness. In this double giving, consciousness does not bring its correlates into being but makes them appear or lets them be given by themselves in the way they are intended by consciousness. What is at issue in this correlation is a giving of meaning (*Sinngebung*), not a matter of existence. The person who lives in the natural attitude posits existing beings, his own existence and that of all the beings of the world. The person who contemplates the reduced sphere of immanence purely does not posit existing beings; this person discovers meaning, the sense of each intention, and the sense, or the manner of appearing, of the *intentum* to which it is related.

That is why Husserl can conclude with the following words:

Originally the problem concerned *the relation between subjective psychological experience and the actuality grasped therein, as it is in itself*—first of all actual reality, and then also the mathematical and other sorts of ideal realities. But first we need the insight that the *crucial problem* must rather have to do with the *relation between cognition and its object,* but in the *reduced* sense, according to which we are dealing not with human cognition, but with cognition in general, apart from any existential assumptions either of the empirical ego or of a real world. We need the insight that the truly significant problem is that of the *ultimate bearing of cognition,* including the problem of objectivity in general, which only is what it is in correlation with possible cognition. Further, we need the insight that this problem can only be solved within the sphere of pure evidence, the sphere of data which are ultimate norms because they are absolutely given. (60; 75–76)

2. The Heideggerian Reappropriation

Husserl apparently wrote the text of the five lectures in a sort of fever—the fever attending the discovery of a monumental task—and for the benefit of advanced students already convinced by the *Logical Investigations* that phenomenology was the revival of philosophy. Because it is a foundational text, *The Idea of Phenomenology* reveals at once, in a very vivid way, the fertility of Husserl's phenomenological approach and also areas of darkness in the midst of the new light shed by it.

No one was better able than Heidegger both to take advantage of the master's discoveries and to reveal the dark spots in the Husserlian concept of phenomenology. The lecture courses offered by Heidegger in Marburg, before the publication of *Sein und Zeit*, express both his tribute to those discoveries and his awareness of the presence of points of obscurity. Among these lecture courses, the course on *The History of the Concept of Time*, offered in the summer of 1925, which in many ways is a sort of first draft of the 1927 master work, provides a very clear survey of both the discoveries and the dark spots. The first pages of *The History of the Concept of Time* contain long preliminary developments that both praise and criticize Husserl on "the meaning and the task of phenomenological research."

Naturally this preliminary part does not contain any mention of Husserl's lectures on *The Idea of Phenomenology* because at the time the stenographic copy of Husserl's text had not been transcribed. Heidegger grounds his account on those works of Husserl then available in print, i.e., the *Logical Investigations*, the paper on *Philosophy as a Rigorous Science*, and the first volume of *Ideas*. Yet it will not be artificial to carry out the task of elucidating the 1907 Husserlian lectures—whose movement we have tried to retrace—in the light of Heidegger's account and conversely of elucidating Heidegger's lecture course in the light of Husserl's *Idea of Phenomenology*. Indeed, all the discoveries to which Heidegger pays a tribute in his 1927 lecture course can be found in Husserl's 1907 lecture course, where they also leave the reader with a feeling of uneasiness concerning the same blind spots, about which Heidegger raises questions.

According to Heidegger, at least three decisive discoveries were made by Husserlian phenomenology: I. intentionality, II. categorial intuition, and III. the original sense of the *a priori*.

I. Concerning the first discovery, Heidegger stresses that Husserl discovered that "intentionality is a structure of lived experiences, not just supplementary relation" (37; 47–48).[4] More precisely, he discovered (thereby overcoming the uncertainties of Brentano who brought "into relief intentionality as such, as a structural totality") that "the basic constitution of intentionality" resides in "a reciprocal belonging-together of *intentio* and *intentum*" (46; 61–62). In the first section of this essay, I have attempted to show that this discovery is at the core of *The Idea of Phenomenology,* and how it overcomes the perplexities entailed by the "natural" theories of knowledge. Over against these theories, Husserl insists in the first Lecture that "cognition, according to its essence, is *cognition of objectivities, and it is this through its immanent sense,* by virtue of which it relates itself to objectivities" (*The Idea of Phenomenology,* 15 modified; 19).

II. The second discovery celebrated by Heidegger is *categorial intuition.* Husserl is credited by Heidegger with showing that "there is a simple apprehension of the *categorial,* i.e., such constituents in entities which in traditional fashion are designated as *categories* and were seen in crude form quite early [in Greek philosophy, especially by Plato and Aristotle]." But Heidegger insists that the discovery is "above all the demonstration that this apprehension is invested in the most everyday of perceptions and in every experience (48; 64)."

According to Heidegger, four themes will help us elucidate this inclusion of categorial intuition in the most modest of intentionalities, the perception of things. The *first* theme is the identifying fulfillment of the intentional presuming, or intending. Such presuming or intending, empty at first, reaches fulfillment when what it aims at or intends (i.e., its intentional correlate), at first devoid of any intuitive givenness, achieves this givenness in the form of a state of affairs given in an original manner to intuition, i.e., to perception. When one considers the sequence of the initial empty intending and the intuitive seeing that provides it with a fulfillment, it appears that the seeing is an act of identification (*Identifizierung*). The act brings to coincidence the empty intentional presuming of the beginning with what is "primordially intuited" in perception. But more deeply than

---

4. *History of the Concept of Time,* Prolegomena, trans. Theodore Kiesel (Bloomington: Indiana University Press, 1985). As previously, we will first give the page number in the English edition, then in the German original, unless otherwise specified. When one number is given, this number refers to the German pagination. (Trans.)

this identification is a demonstration (*Aufweisung*) in the sense that perception shows in an authentic, primordial mode, in its identity, what had initially only been presumed. Such an identification, understood in both meanings of the word—the production of a matching-out and the display of identity—is the act which Husserl calls "evidence." Heidegger stresses the originality of this concept of evidence in opposition to the mythological view incorporated in the traditional logic and theory of knowledge. Evidence, for the traditional view, is a feeling whose intensity alone signals the presence of an object, a feeling which, moreover, functions as a supplement in only one class of lived experiences: in judgments. Intentionality completely rids us of such mythology. Evidence, as a property of intentionality, is no longer a feeling whose intensity will betray the presence of truth. Rather, it is the manifestation by intentionality of its intended correlate.

Such an evidence, Heidegger insists, is at the same time regional and universal (68). It is regional in the sense that each type of intentionality aims at a specific fulfillment and, consequently, has its own evidence, i.e., its specific mode of bringing to a seeing the intentional correlate to which it is essentially connected. For example there is perceptive evidence of which the mathematical evidence cannot be the norm: two different regions of intentionality are involved here, neither of which should be allowed to absorb the other. But evidence is also universal in the sense that it is "a function of all the acts which give their objects, and then, of all acts (evidence of willing and wishing, of loving and hoping). It is not restricted to assertions, predications, judgments" (51; 68).

Recall the themes of Husserl's five lectures. His analysis of the perception of the house served as an example of regional evidence. On the other hand, it was the universality of evidence that was envisaged by Husserl in the words: "*Überall ist die Gegebenheit*" (Everywhere there is givenness, *Die Idee der Phänomenologie*, 74). But Heidegger praises the Husserlian discovery of the regional character and the universality of *Aufweisung* as the concretization and the radicalization of the old Scholastic definition of truth (*adaequatio rei et intellectus*). Here his own reappropriation of Husserl is intimated: "The demonstration (*Aufweisung*) of the presumed in the intuited is identification (*Identifizierung*), an act which is phenomenologically specified in terms of intentionality, directing-itself-toward" (51; 69). This amounts to giving a concrete phenomenological interpretation to the old concept of truth as adequacy. This concept, Heidegger says, has always had a double meaning, depending on whether it designated the *res* or the cognitive act. This double meaning remains present in the phenomenological interpretation of truth as identification (*Identifizierung*). On the one hand, this identification is concerned with the *intentum,* and thus means the being identical of the presumed and of the intuited. On the other hand, the identification is connected with *intentio,* and in this case designates the very act of identifying, or the correlating of an act of presuming and an act of intuition (or intentional directing-itself-toward). Yet, deeper than this being identical or deeper than a coincidence, there is the manifestation or demonstration of the intuited entity. "As the originally intuited, it provides the demonstration, it gives the identification its ground and legitimacy (53; 71)." At this point we move from the concretization to the radicalization. The fact that *Aufweisung* is both regional and universal means that phenomenological truth has a field broader than the acts of assertion and predication. "Phenomenology thus breaks with the restriction of the concept of truth to relational acts, to judgments. The truth of relational acts is only one particular kind of truth, the truth which characterizes the objectifying acts of knowing in general" (55 modified; 73).

The *second* theme that helps to clarify the inclusion of categorial intuition in the simplest type of intentionality is the link between *intuition* and *expression.* We just found that the entire field of intentionality is characterized by truth. Likewise the same field is characterized by expressedness, but an expressedness which extends beyond predicative propositions. Heidegger writes:

> *Assertions are acts of meaning,* and assertions in the sense of a formulated proposition are only specific forms of expressness, where expressness has the sense of expressing lived experiences or comportments through meaning. It is essentially owing to phenomenological investigations that this authentic sense of the expressing and expressness of all comportments was made fundamental and placed in the foreground of the question of the structure of the logical. This is not surprising when we consider that our comportments are in actual fact pervaded through and through by assertions, that they are always performed in some sort of expressness. It is also a matter of fact that our simplest perceptions and constitutive states are already expressed, even more are interpreted in a certain way. What is primary and original here? It is not so much that we see the objects and things but rather that we first talk about them. To put it more precisely: we do not say what we see, but rather the reverse, we see what *one says* about the matter. (56; 74)

It is therefore a specific feature of the world that it is determined and apprehended through expressedness. Categorial intuition is implied in the intrinsic expressedness of each apprehension. Here too, perception provides a clue. When I give expression to my perception by saying: "this chair is yellow and upholstered," I do not merely *announce* that I have a perception, I *communicate what* I perceive. "A perceptual assertion is a communication about the entity perceived in perception and not about the act of perception as such" (57; 77). This raises the question: "Can the assertion which I make in a concrete and actual perception be fulfilled in the same way that an empty intention or presuming is fulfilled by a concrete perception?" (56 modified; 75). In other words, since in the end the act of fulfillment is a demonstration, the question is to know whether "the perceptual assertion which gives expression to the perception [is] demonstrable perceptually (*Wahrnehmungsmässig aufweisbar*): . . . Are the 'this', the 'is', the 'and' perceptually demonstrable in the subject matter?" (57; 77). Obviously I cannot see the 'this', the 'is' and the 'and' as I see the thing. Those words express "*a surplus of intentions (Überschuss an Intentionen)* whose demonstration cannot be borne by the simple perception of the subject matter" (57; 77). I can see the yellow color of the chair, but I cannot see its *being*-yellow as I can see its color. At this point, Heidegger recalls the teaching of the Sixth *Logical Investigation* (continued in *The Idea of Phenomenology* as previously seen) and says in full agreement with Husserl: "*Being,* Kant already said, *is not a real predicate of the object.*" Hence there are components of the statement which are in excess of what is objectively given in the perceived *res.* One could therefore believe, Heidegger says, that these components are strictly subjective and result from a reflection of consciousness upon itself; one can think of this reflection in terms of an "immanent perception" as did the British empiricists (Locke) or in terms of the data of "the internal sense" as did Kant. But Heidegger insists that these two options are precisely what is eliminated by the Husserlian discovery of categorial intuition. Against these varieties of idealism, "phenomenology has demonstrated that the non-sensory and ideal cannot without further ado be identified with the immanent, conscious, subjective" (58; 79). Even though they are in surplus vis-à-vis the sensorial, the components of the statement, far from expressing subjective data, express "a special kind of objectivity" (59; 80).

Although these components cannot be shown in a strictly sensory intuition, they can be exhibited in a demonstration of a higher order, i.e., in a categorial intuition. This intuition is an intentional act which consists in apprehending a category. That act is always founded (*fundiert*), in the sense that it presupposes actual perceptions upon which it depends, that are simple, direct, and of a single—yet complex—level. But the founded act of categorial intuition, as a founded act, is not a formal repetition, at the level of ideality, of the founding act. Instead, categorial intuition allows us to see "how even simple perception, which is usually called sense perception, is already intrinsically pervaded by categorial intuition" (60; 81). It is by virtue of such founded acts that the objects of perception "come to explicit apprehension precisely in what they are" (62; 84).

At this juncture the first two themes highlighted by Heidegger in the Husserlian doctrine of categorial intuition (the identifying function of intentionality and the surplus character of categorial intuition vis-à-vis the sensory datum here and now) are articulated in relationship to one another. The act of identification is not only the matching of a presumed and an intuited, or of a presuming and an intuition. It involves the bringing into view, the unveiling of an intentional correlate which is now exhibited for what it is. But in this unveiling, which provides access to the truth of the *intentum*, a surplus is involved, i.e., the surplus revealed in categorial intuition. Thus it could be said that truth, in the sense of a monstrative unveiling, only occurs in the movement of passing beyond or of transcending what is presently given, *hic et nunc*, as a factual occurrence.

Two additional themes allow Heidegger to clarify further the impact of categorial intuition: the categorial act of synthesis and the categorial act of ideation. In the examination of those acts, the perception of things also provides the first clues.

Let us consider the *third* theme. The *act of synthesis* is what allows me to distinguish a property in an object, while attributing it to the object, for example the yellow color of that chair. To distinguish and detach such a property amounts to singling out and highlighting this characteristic as a "moment" of the thing. Such a singling and highlighting is an analysis of the thing. Yet while raising this characteristic to prominence, I relate it to the totality of the thing, which means that a synthesis accompanies the analysis. The act of synthesis is a double act: it detaches the components of a totality and, from the detached moments, it returns to the totality. In this act, the correlating is what comes first and the correlated terms become explicit by virtue of it. Husserl calls the intentional correlate of this categorial act a state-of-affairs, more precisely a relation-within-the-thing-itself (*Sachverhalt*). This *Sachverhalt*, expressed according to the structure *S is p*, is not a *real* part of the thing (the chair) such as its legs or its back. Instead, this *Sachverhalt* is of an ideal nature and stands in a position of excess vis-à-vis the real components of the chair. Yet this relation-within-the-thing is intuitively grasped in the categorial act of synthesis. This act is founded (*fundiert*), Heidegger insists, on the basis of a prior relationship to a matter antecedently given. Yet the act of categorial intuition is what allows "this matter and this alone [to] show itself explicitly in the state of affairs (*Sachverhalt*)" (64; 87). What is decisive, according to Heidegger, is that

by way of understanding what is present in categorial intuition, we can come to see that the objectivity of an entity is really not exhausted by this narrow definition of reality, that objectivity in its broadest sense is much richer than the reality of a thing, and what is more, that the reality of a thing is comprehensible in its structure only on the basis of the full objectivity of the simply experienced entity. (66; 89)

The last theme that clarifies categorial intuition is the *act of ideation.* Ideation is involved in the act by which an essence is intuited in its universality; this can be a sensory universal ('yellowness', or 'redness', for example) or a category in the traditional sense ('substance' or 'causality'). Like any categorial act, insists Heidegger, the act of ideation is founded: it rests upon the perception of this red or that yellow or upon the apprehension of this or that body as a substance. It is on the basis of a certain number of cases of red that I form the categorial intuition of redness. It is on the basis of a certain number of perceived houses that I form the categorial intuition of what a house is. Categorial intuitions, thus founded, are therefore the result of an "eidetic abstraction." But the *idea* or *eidos* which the phenomenologist now takes as his explicit theme is not a philosophical construct. Instead, phenomenological thematization reveals that "each concrete apprehending . . . also already includes the ideal unity of the species, although not explicitly" (67; 91–92). In other words, phenomenological analysis reveals that perception, instead of being the reception of strictly individualized data, is universalizing from the outset. It implies "that concrete intuition expressly giving its object is never an isolated, single-layered sense perception, but is always a multi-layered intuition, that is, a categorially specified intuition" (68; 93). It would therefore be a misunderstanding, Heidegger says, to interpret ideation along the line of the Kantian dichotomy of sensibility and understanding, the former being receptive of a pure matter and the latter productive of a pure form. Constitution, he insists, is not productive. It consists in *"letting the entity be seen in its objectivity"* (71; 97).

Concerning each of the four themes praised by Heidegger in the Husserlian discovery of categorial intuition, it is significant that he notices a fourfold correspondence with Aristotle's thought. In his opinion, the *Aufweisung* revivifies the Aristotelian conception of truth. The link revealed by Husserl between intuition and expression for him revivifies the Aristotelian concept of *logos apophantikos*. Also, the Husserlian notion of act of synthesis revivifies the link, stressed by Aristotle, between *synthesis* and *diairesis*. Finally ideation revivifies the Aristotelian conception of abstraction.

It is significant too that the Husserlian discovery of categorial intuition is presented by Heidegger on the one hand as a "concretion" of the "basic constitution of intentionality'' (72; 98–99), and on the other hand as what puts "philosophical research in a position to conceive the *a priori* more rigorously and to prepare for the characterization of the sense of its being" (72; 98).

III. The third discovery celebrated by Heidegger is what he then calls "the elaboration of the sense of the *a priori*" (72; 99). When dealing with this discovery, Heidegger does not quote any specific text from Husserl. Moreover, he says that

> this discovery can be characterized more briefly, 1) because despite some essential insights into phenomenology itself, the *a priori* is still not made very clear, 2) because the *a priori* is by and large intertwined with traditional lines of inquiry, and 3) above all because the clarification of its sense presupposes the understanding of what we [viz. Heidegger] are seeking, *time.* (72; 99)

This is a way of suggesting that the Husserlian discovery of the *a priori* was insufficient. Yet Heidegger credits Husserl with liberating the *a priori* from the limits assigned to it by Kant. Kant basically agrees with the Cartesian notion of the preeminence of subjectivity, specifically cognitive subjectivity. Thus his *a priori* is "a feature specifically belonging to the subjective sphere . . . *before* it oversteps the bounds of its immanence" (73; 100). By contrast, Husserl has shown that "the *a priori* is not limited to the subjectivity, indeed that in the first instance it has primarily nothing at all to do with subjectivity" (74; 101). Indeed the doctrine of categorial intuition shows that there is an *a priori* in the field of the ideal and an *a priori* in the field of the *real*, or of the thingly content (color, materiality, spatiality). Thus it shows that the *a priori* is "something in the being of the ideal and in the being of the real, which is *a priori* and structurally earlier" (74; 101). The *a priori*, therefore, is not a characteristic of the subjective sphere, it is a "title for Being" (74; 101), it is "a feature of the being of entities" (75; 102). However it is not clear that Husserl fully realized the implications of his discoveries or that he was able to avoid the same ruts into which his modern precursors had fallen. The very words in which Heidegger assesses the importance for him of the Husserlian discovery of the *a priori* suggest this: "The *a priori* is not only nothing immanent, belonging primarily to the sphere of the subject, it is also nothing transcendent, specifically bound up with reality (*Realität*)" (74; 101). Yet, as we have pointed out, it was precisely in terms of immanence and transcendence that Husserl himself presented his discovery of the field of phenomenology.

Hence, the fact that Heidegger no longer sticks to the transcendence-immanence framework indicates clearly that his praise of Husserl is accompanied with reservations that must be investigated closely if we want to understand what he considered to be the areas of darkness in Husserl's phenomenology. That there are such areas of darkness, Heidegger makes clear in his presentation of the first of Husserl's discoveries:

> Intentionality is not an ultimate explanation of the psychic but an initial approach toward overcoming the uncritical application of traditionally defined realities such as the psychic, consciousness, continuity of lived experience, reason. But if such a task is implicit in this basic concept of phenomenology, then "intentionality" is the very last word to be used as a phenomenological slogan. Quite the contrary, it identifies that whose disclosure would allow phenomenology to find itself in its possibilities. (47; 63)

In other words, if it were the case that the Husserlian exploration of intentionality was accompanied with the continuing acceptance of a certain number of traditional unquestioned notions, then we would be justified in applying to Husserl himself what he says of Descartes in the five Lectures: "For [him], to discover and to abandon were the same" (*The Idea of Phenomenology,* 7; 10). Now, in spite of the stress put by Husserl on the pure seeing of the matters themselves and on the necessity of avoiding all noncritical presuppositions, we can wonder whether these presuppositions did not affect each and every step of Husserl's approach, starting with *The Idea of Phenomenology.*

Let us consider the preliminary step. At the very outset, the notion of "natural attitude" poses some difficulties. Husserl speaks as though it characterizes the comportment of each and every individual in everydayness, as well as the comportment of the scientist. To this, Heidegger raises the legitimate objection:

> For man's way of experience vis-à-vis the other and himself, is it his natural mode of reflection (*Betrachtungsart*) to experience himself as *zoon,* as a living being, in this broadest sense as an object of nature which occurs in the world? In the natural way of experience, does man experience himself, to put it curtly, zoologically? (113; 155)

Is this characterization of man's spontaneous manner of experience phenomenologically seen in the phenomenon, or is it a determination projected by the philosopher on the basis of a "well-defined theoretical position, in which every entity is taken *a priori* as a lawfully regulated flow of occurrences in the spatio-temporal exteriority of the world?" (113; 155–56). At this point, is not the very fact that ordinary experience should be termed an "attitude" significant? For an attitude is nothing spontaneous, it is a posture, or a comportment, that one adopts deliberately.

"One must so to speak "place oneself into" (sich hineinstellen) this way of considering things in order to experience them in this manner. Man's natural manner of experience, by contrast, cannot be called an attitude" (113; 156). Therefore the so-called natural attitude can be suspected of being artificial. For it corresponds more to the way modern science has considered nature since Descartes than to man's everyday manner of experience.

Indeed, Husserlian phenomenology begins with the bracketing of what it calls the "natural attitude." However, this bracketing may well be suspected of having been motivated by what it suspends. What is bracketed is an attitude that is only interested in sequences of spatio-temporal events taken from within the globally regulated totality of nature. This attitude is supposed to apply to man's everyday experience, to the theoretical comportment of the modern scientist in his exploration of nature, and finally to the position of the theoretician of knowledge who adopts the theoretical comportment of the modern scientist. The epoche was motivated by the perplexities encountered in this third modality of the natural attitude. It consists in suspending the theoretical stance of the modern scientist in regard to nature and in rejecting this stance as a ground for the theory of knowledge. The epoche claims therefore to introduce a radically new dimension in opposition to the dimension it brackets. However, the bracketing maintains at least two characteristics taken from what it suspends. What is suspended, we just saw, is less a spontaneous comportment than a theoretical position. The epoche reintroduces what it suspends because of its admission that the new dimension (intentionality) is first and foremost cognitive and thus falls under the exclusive jurisdiction of a theory of knowledge. In addition, it reintroduces what it suspends because for Husserl, world and nature are thought as synonymous: there is no concept of world in Husserl other than that of a totality of spatio-temporal events regulated by laws. Finally, the epoche reintroduces what it suspends because it implies that to be an entity, including one endowed with intentionality, is simply to occur among events of this type. Thus, it cannot be denied that the immanent sphere opened by the epoche implicitly preserves the notion of a succession of natural occurrences. For where could the notion of a "flux of lived experience" or "stream of consciousness" originate, if not in the concept of nature adopted in and by the supposedly natural attitude?

To be sure, the sequence of events called the "stream of lived experiences" is the object of an ever-repeated reduction, since the phenomenological seeing is not focused on those experiences as events but as intentional acts. Once reduced, the Erlebnis is no longer an occurrence which happens and is simply a matter of fact; reduced, it is an essential correlation. Yet if every essential correlation is based on an experience whose ontological status is simply that of an occurrence, it remains to be seen how the sphere of immanence, pure and reduced as it then claims to be, might have an ontological status other than the sphere of transcendence. Is it not significant, in this regard, that the only definition of metaphysics given by *The Idea of Phenomenology* deals with the distinction between nature and spirit, that is to say between two ontical regions, and that the ontological question of the Being of these two regions is never posed? Such a silence implies that Being has the same meaning in each case, and therefore that the question of the meaning of Being does not need to be raised. Does not the very distinction between nature and spirit, if construed as ultimate, presuppose that metaphysics can be satisfied with the Cartesian distinction between *res extensa* and *res cogitans,* a distinction reiterated in Kant, in Hegel, and in neo-Kantianism? In a nutshell, does not this very distinction indicate that, in Husserl, "the thematic field of phenomenology is not derived phenomenologically by going back to the matters themselves but by going back to a traditional idea of philosophy" (107; 147)?

At any rate, we can grant Heidegger the point that the ontological status of Husserlian intentionality remains *indeterminate.* This is what he proposes to demonstrate on the basis of the four characteristics of pure consciousness given by Husserl (102–108; 140–148).

1. If the being of consciousness is characterized by *immanence,* the latter term remains ontologically indeterminate since it consists in an ontical relation of inclusion between two beings, the reflecting being and the reflected one.

2. If we say that consciousness, as an *absolute* datum, is "absolute being," we indicate by this wording that consciousness will not unveil itself indirectly or symbolically, but directly. And this determination is not more ontological than the previous one because it limits itself to characterizing the way the reflected entity is apprehended by the reflecting one. Thus it does not consider consciousness as a being in its way of being, but only as a possible object for reflection.

3. If we add that the property of being absolutely given signifies that consciousness *"nulla re indiget ad existendum,"* this third determination again would not be more ontological than the previous ones (1 and 2). For, in agreement with Cartesian doubt, it signifies that negating the existence of the world does not eliminate immanence, and it means that no transcendent being can claim to be real and exhibit its essence without a reference to consciousness. This determination therefore only involves an ontical relation between the region "consciousness" and the region "transcendent reality." It considers consciousness not in its Being, but in relation to its

priority in the order of the constitution of any possible objectivity. The very fact that the *a priori* is limited, in the wake of Descartes and Kant, to a formal priority of the subjective realm over the objective one, proves the ontological deficiency of this ontological definition of consciousness.

4. The fourth determination which characterizes consciousness as '*pure being*' concerns "even less than the other three a characterization of the being of the intentional, that is, of the entity which is defined by the structure of intentionality" (106; 145). For consciousness is characterized as pure only "to the extent that it . . . is no longer regarded in its concrete individuation and its tie to a living being" (106; 145). In other words, it is not pure "to the extent that it is *hic et nunc* real and mine, but instead purely in its essential content." Its being is pure inasmuch as, far from being real, it has the ideality of an essence, of an "intrinsically detached structure" (146).

The examination of these four determinations of consciousness shows that Husserl's delimitation of the thematic field of phenomenology and his use of the notion of Being for that purpose were not guided by an ontological concern. What guided him instead was a scientific project, mapped on the idea (Cartesian in origin) of an absolute science whose site is in consciousness. Hence, in many respects, the presence of a specifically modern tradition seems to have blocked the way to the "things themselves," in spite of Husserl's motto. What is more, the very manner in which this access to the "things themselves" is conceived by Husserlian phenomenology (from the moment it intends to be grounded on the region of pure consciousness) betrays a position of ontological neglect. The mode of access is the phenomenological reduction. The Husserlian reduction, in its very concept, implies an exclusion of Being. For the *epoche* affects "the real consciousness of the factually existing man." This "real experience" must be bracketed in order to allow us access to pure consciousness. The injunction "to disregard . . . and dismiss the reality of consciousness as such" (109; 150) is required by the reduction, so that "in its methodological sense as a discarding, then, the reduction is in principle inappropriate for determining the being of consciousness positively" (109; 150).

But there is more. The reduction not only forces us to neglect the actual existence of our lived experiences, but also to abstract from their individuation, from the property that each has of being mine. It is only in their *quid*, in their *Wasgehalt*, that the reduction seeks to consider them. The reduction is eidetic precisely by focusing on this *quid*, or on the *essentia* to the neglect of the *existentia*. It therefore postulates that "the what of any entity is to be defined by disregarding, by abstracting from, its existence." But if it should turn out, Heidegger objects, "that there were an entity whose what, whose essence is precisely to be and nothing but to be'' (110; 152), then the Husserlian eidetic seeing would be "the most fundamental of misunderstandings" (110; 152).

Such an entity is precisely the one that we are, the being to which Heidegger assigns the denomination not of an adjective, but a verb, *Dasein.* That is because its essence is to exist, not in the sense of occurring in the present as any other natural occurrence (connected and related to nature as a regulated totality), but in the sense of being in fact thrown into an intrinsic relation of openness to a having-to-be, or *Zusein.* Such an existing is strictly individuated, since it is the ownmost of every one. Because mineness determines it in its ownmost, Heidegger charges the Husserlian phenomenological reduction with three flaws.

At the outset the reduction has decided that neither *facticity,* nor *openness* to a having-to-be, nor *mineness* belong to the essence of the intentional entity. By canceling at the outset those three features for intentionality, Husserl neglected in principle the mode of being of the being endowed with intentionality, that is, the intentional being. More precisely, to the question of the Being of the intentional, the Husserlian reduction had responded in advance by positing that there is no other meaning to the word "Being" than that of "a real worldly occurrence just like any natural process" (111; 153). Heidegger can therefore summarize the results of his ontological questioning of Husserl's approach as follows:

In elaborating intentionality as the thematic field of phenomenology, the question of the being of the intentional is left undiscussed. It is not raised in the field thus secured, pure consciousness; indeed, it is flatly rejected as nonsensical. In the course of securing this field, in the reduction, it is expressly deferred. And where the determinations of being are brought into play, as in the starting position of the reduction, it is likewise not originally raised. Instead, the being of acts [the intentional acts which for Husserl are the *cogitationes*] is in advance theoretically and dogmatically defined by the sense of being which is taken from the reality of nature. The question of being itself is left undiscussed. (113–14; 157)

The Heideggerian reading has thus identified two fundamental neglects in the Husserlian return to the matters themselves: the neglect of the being of the intentional and the neglect of the meaning of "Being." These two neglects go hand and hand. First, the exploration of the phenomenological field in Husserl's sense (i.e., pure consciousness, taken in its intentional structures) demands that the phenomenologist suspend the existence of the being endowed with intentionality. Secondly, the suspension now affecting the natural attitude shares with the latter the presupposition that there is no other meaning to "Being" than that of an occurrence in the totality of nature. Why then should the question of the meaning of Being be raised, if its meaning is taken for granted?

Do these considerations amount to a claim that Heidegger considers as ontologically deficient, and to be discarded, the Husserlian distinction between transcendence and immanence whose importance I attempted to highlight in the unfolding of *The Idea of Phenomenology*? I do not think so. To be sure, the Husserlian demarcation between Being in the transcendent sense (of a factual occurrence) and Being in the immanent sense (of the exhibiting a pure intentional essence) is tantamount to dissociating existence and intentionality. Accordingly Heidegger correctly points out that while Husserl seems to speak about Being, his demarcation never inquires what the word "Being" means in each case. On this point, he recalls a crucial sentence of *Ideen I* (for which we can find equivalents in *The Idea of Phenomenology*):

> The doctrine of the Categories must take its start unreservedly from this most radical of all distinctions of Being (*Seinsunterscheidungen*)—Being as *Consciousness* and Being as 'declaring' itself in consciousness, or as 'transcendent' Being, a distinction which, as clearly apparent, can be drawn in all its purity and properly justified only through the method of phenomenological reduction (*Ideen I*, 141)[5]

Heidegger protests: Is it not remarkable that "one should claim to conquer the most radical distinction of being without actually inquiring into the being of the entities that enter into the distinction"? (*History of the Concept of Time*, 114 modified; 158). And later: "How is it possible that a form of research whose principle is 'to the matters themselves' leaves the fundamental consideration of its most proper matter (*Sache*) unsettled?" (115; 159).

Yet Heidegger acknowledges that in the Husserlian dissociation of immanence and transcendence, an impulse (*Ansatz*) was given "which points in the direction of determining the being of the intentional out of itself" (115; 159). In that dissociation, the demarcation of phenomenology from naturalism is at issue. This demarcation is connected with the objective of

---

5. *Ideas, General Introduction to Pure Phenomenology*, trans. W. R. Boyce Gibson (New York: Collier Books, 1962), p. 194.

focusing the research on intentionality as such, in all its various modalities. Such modalities are called by Husserl "acts," and were reduced in naturalism (psychologism in particular) to "appendages of a material thing" (116; 160). Heidegger agrees with Husserl on the point that it is necessary to demarcate phenomenology from naturalism in order to gain access to the Being of intentionality. But at stake in his debate with Husserlian phenomenology is the issue of whether Husserl had managed to secure this demarcation clearly and radically enough. It is the insufficiency of the demarcation that strikes him in the steps taken by the Husserlian approach.

The Logical Investigations denounce the naturalistic confusion between the laws of thought and the natural laws of psychic events, thus establishing a distinction between the real event of judgment and the ideality of that upon which it judges. But this demarcation does not consider anything other than the ideality of what is judged, and thus leaves indeterminate the reality of the act of judging, i.e., the ontological status of that intentionality. Consequently it leaves open the possibility of aligning the Being of the intentional act with that of natural processes.

When a little later, under the influence of Dilthey's efforts to replace natural psychology with a personalist one, Husserl poses the distinction between the transcendent and the immanent (the former characterizing nature and the latter consciousness), again we have a demarcation. The import of this demarcation was analyzed above in our discussion of *The Idea of Phenomenology.* Heidegger first noticed the same demarcation in Husserl's 1910 essay on *Philosophy as a Rigorous Science,* then in *Ideen I.* Yet according to him, this distinction was not oriented toward the question of Being, at least not in any way more significant than the distinction opposing real and ideal. What is of interest to Husserl when he speaks of the Being of immanence, or of consciousness, or of intentionality, is the possibility that these notions will acquire the status of scientific objectivity. And even when he claims that the unity of the person is in principle different from that of the thing-like realities of nature, it is not the Being of the person which interests him, but the immanent structure of consciousness.

Finally, Husserl's contrast in *Ideen II,* which Heidegger studied in manuscript form, between the "personalist attitude" and the "naturalist attitude" suggests an ontological indeterminacy. First, the question that guides Husserl in his inquiry about this contrast is not that of the Being of beings, but that of the constitution of various types of objectivity (material nature, animal nature, and spiritual world). The same holds for the mode of access to the person defined as an individual spiritual entity. The mode of access in personalist attitude is simply an *inspectio sui,* which in the previous writings defined the immanent reflection on the ego's lived experiences. Finally (and this is most crucial) the unity of experiences that is supposed to be constitutive of the individuation of the person is based on the model of the concept of man as *animal rationale*.

It might be because Husserl took this concept as obvious that he conducted his analysis of the person as if the person were made up of different layers: a material substratum, a living body (*Leib*), a psychic dynamism, a spirit. According to Heidegger, Husserl speaks as if "the being of the full concrete man in his totality could be *assembled* from the being of the material substrate, of the body, and from the soul and the spirit" (125 modified; 173). For Heidegger, it is clear that in such a composition we are not presented with "the being of the person . . . in a primary way" (124; 172). Instead we face the experience of a "natural reality," of a "worldly thing present here in the forefront" (*eines vorhandenen Weltdinges*), of a "reality of the world which constitutes itself as transcendence in absolute consciousness" (125; 173–74), and to which a certain number of properties relative to matter and life are simply added.

Thus, in Heidegger's view, each stage in Husserl's phenomenology confirms the persistence of a double neglicence, the neglect of the Being of the entity endowed with intentionality and the neglect of the meaning of Being. Heidegger insists that those two forms of neglect go hand in hand. It is precisely because it was postulated that there is no other meaning for Being than occurring as a thing in the world understood as nature (which means that there is no other meaning for Being than that of *Vorhandenheit*) that the question of the meaning of the Being of the intentional being is avoided.

But it would be wrong to believe that this critical reading imposed questions on Husserlian phenomenology that are incompatible with its own. Let us remember that the master work of fundamental ontology, *Sein und Zeit*, asserts in the presentation of "the question of the meaning of Being," that "the following investigation would not have been possible if the ground had not been prepared by Edmund Husserl, with whose *Logical Investigations* phenomenology first emerged" (62; 38). This is tantamount to saying that, in spite of Husserl's neglect and his objective of an absolute science, the ontological aim is not absent at all from his phenomenology. As for the question of the ground and what it consists in, *Sein und Zeit* gives no indication. There is an exception in the text in praise of Niemeyer, to which we shall return later, but—except for that—it was not until forty years after the publication of *Sein und Zeit* (and Heidegger's last seminar) that we would realize what such ground was. This last seminar made clear that, in Heidegger's view, Husserl had established this ground in his *Logical Investigations*, specifically with his phenomenological retrieval of Kant's thesis on Being in the sixth *Investigation*. But Husserl had ultimately left the ground unexplored.[6] Kant's thesis on Being is the following: Being is not a real predicate. This means that Being is not an ontical property, that it is not to be included among the series of properties which determine the *realitas*, or the essence of beings. In other words, Being is not a being. Husserl reappropriates Kant's thesis in a framework that is no longer Kantian but specific to phenomenology. This framework is the doctrine of categorial intuition. Whereas for Kant there is no intuition of categories, especially of Being as a category of modality, the repetition of the Kantian thesis in the new framework means that we have an intuition, an immediate view of Being, inasmuch as it stands in "surplus" or "excess" vis-à-vis the ontical properties of beings. The Husserlian retrieval of Kant's thesis on Being provided Heidegger with the "ground" for his investigation of the meaning of Being, that is, the "ground" for his fundamental ontology. For this Husserlian retrieval means that we understand Being and, therefore, that the key to the intelligibility of Being has to be found in the being that we are, namely in a being who understands the difference between Being and beings.

With regard to the Husserlian origin of that ground, the Heideggerian *History of the Concept of Time* (1925) is just as discreet as *Sein und Zeit*. But precisely because Heidegger's critical reading of Husserl in *The History of the Concept of Time* makes up half of the lecture course and is much more detailed and explicit than in *Sein und Zeit*, it allows us to cast new light on the critical role of a debate with Husserl in the genesis of fundamental ontology.

We saw that Husserlian phenomenology is held together (*a*) by the fundamental distinction between what he calls transcendence and immanence, and (*b*) by the mode of access to that distinction, the phenomenological reduction. By virtue of the phenomenological reduction, our interest shifts from the natural attitude which only looks to transcendence and for which, therefore, there are only natural events. The ontological status of such events is that of an occurrence within the regulated totality of nature, a status which in the Heideggerian terminology is called *Vorhandenheit*. It goes without saying that fundamental ontology does not repeat this distinction as such: The very term "immanence" disappears from its vocabulary, and the term "transcendence" no longer applies to nature but to the being that we are *because* this being extends beyond beings to grasp their Being

---

6. For an analysis of the seminar see my book *Dialectic and Difference*, ed. Robert Crease and James T. Decker (Atlantic Highlands: Humanities Press, 1985), pp. 91–113.

and more deeply to grasp its own Being. However fundamental ontology is also held together by a fundamental distinction, the one which separates the everyday mode of being from the ownmost mode of being.

It would be too simple to pretend that Heidegger's demarcation is entirely free from the Husserlian demarcation and retains no trace of it. To be sure, the everyday mode of being is no theoretical attitude, as was the natural attitude in the Husserlian sense. The everyday mode of being is not a matter of knowledge, but of preoccupation, of practical circumspection dealing with entities available or usable for this or that end, entities characterized by their *readiness-at-hand*. Yet, even though such comportment cannot be limited to knowing natural occurrences, it is the ultimate source and foundation of the understanding of Being as *Vorhandenheit*, and is thus analogous to the understanding involved in our natural attitude according to Husserl. On the other hand, the ownmost mode of being in Heidegger is very different from Husserlian immanence revealed by the *inspectio sui* of reflection. Such a mode of being is not immanent, but ec-static. It is not contemplative, but resolute, disclosing the openness to the most individuated capacity-for-Being in the moment of resoluteness. Nevertheless, this mode of being is characterized in terms of 'selfhood' and exhibits itself in a specific mode of reflection called *"augenblickliches Sichselbstverstehen."* One might object that the mode of access to Heidegger's demarcation is not the phenomenological reduction. We recall that Heidegger criticized the Husserlian reduction for neglecting the Being of the intentional entity, and more generally for suspending Being for the sake of pure eidetic essences. Moreover the reduction is not mentioned once in *Sein und Zeit*. But in the roughly contemporary lecture course called *The Basic Problems of Phenomenology*, the reduction is presented as an essential component of the phenomenological method, in the sense in which Heidegger intends to develop it. To be sure, the Heideggerian reduction is no longer "a method of leading phenomenological vision from the natural attitude of the human being whose life is involved in the world of things and persons back to the transcendental life of consciousness and its noetic-noematic experiences, in which objects are constituted as correlates of consciousness," as was the case for Husserl. Instead the Heideggerian reduction means "leading phenomenological vision back from the apprehension of a being, whatever might be the character of that apprehension, to the understanding of the being of this being (projecting upon the way it is unconcealed)" (21; 29).[7]

Heidegger's and Husserl's reductions obviously are considerably differ-

---

7. *The Basic Problems of Phenomenology*, trans. Albert Hofstadter (Bloomington: Indiana University Press, 1982).

ent, but what they have in common is the fact that both are based on a fundamental demarcation and distinction. Whereas the Husserlian reduction views the fundamental distinction as one opposing transcendence and immanence, the Heideggerian reduction views the fundamental distinction as obtaining between the understanding of Being as *Vorhandenheit* (an understanding to which everydayness is associated) and the understanding of Being in the sense of existing in the ownmost.

The Heideggerian distinction does not relinquish the Husserlian demarcation so much as it radicalizes it. This radicalization was guided by the seriousness granted to Husserl's declarations of principle and his call for a distinction between "being as consciousness" and "transcendent being," which Husserl terms "the most radical of all the distinctions of Being" (cf. supra). Since Heidegger wants to take such a declaration seriously, he must lift the indeterminacy affecting Husserl's usage of the term "Being" everywhere in his text. Yet in his attempt to lift the indeterminacy, Heidegger shares with Husserl the principle that gaining access to "the things themselves" (even if, for Heidegger, the "things" are not the various ways of appearing of objects, but the various ways of Being of beings) requires returning to a unique center of intelligibility, which is the Self (*Selbst*). This 'self'-centeredness is Husserl's legacy.

Someone might object that the Heideggerian demarcation (existence versus presence-at-hand) still amounts to discarding the Husserlian distinction because what is questioned is no longer consciousness, but Dasein. Dasein, not consciousness, is the "ground" upon which phenomenology now builds. But precisely, it is not by rejecting Husserl, but by radically exploiting what he considered to be the three fundamental discoveries of Husserlian phenomenology that Heidegger was able to explore and conquer that "ground." And in his use of Husserl's discoveries, Heidegger radicalizes the very movement by which Husserlian phenomenology removed itself from naturalism in order to reach the purity of the Self. In other words, what we face here is a metamorphosed reappropriation of the Husserlian demarcation between transcendence and immanence.

During the Marburg years, Heidegger repeatedly said that fundamental ontology was nothing but a radicalization of the innermost possibility of phenomenology. In much later texts devoted to an explanation of his itinerary, he also repeatedly said that fundamental ontology had received its impetus from Brentano's thesis *On the Manifold Meaning of Being in Aristotle*. Being is predicated in many ways. "Latent in this phrase is the *question* that determined the way of my thought: what is the pervasive, simple, unified determination of Being that permeates all of its multiple meanings?" Or, put differently: what is "the common origin" of the four ways in which, according to Aristotle, Being can be expressed, i.e., Being as property, Being as possibility and actuality, Being as Truth, Being as schema of the categories.[8] In other words, fundamental ontology started to gather its articulation only by presupposing that the multiplicity of meanings mentioned by Aristotle, whose origin the Greek thinker never sought, is no pure semantic dispersion, but refers to a unique center of intelligibility, from which the four senses derive "an intelligible harmony" (ibid.). Where should we look for that center? How can we gain access to it? Such are the preliminary and formal questions to which Heidegger, by virtue of his apprenticeship with Husserl, was enabled to supply an incipient, though preliminary and formal, answer: This center is ourselves, and the access to ourselves is phenomenological seeing.

What does it mean to say that "we" are that center? And what does phenomenological seeing consist in? This "we," in Husserlian phenomenology, is intentional immanence, taken in its manifold species (perception, imagination, judgment, evaluation, etc.). And the seeing that is entailed by intentional immanence is focused upon the noetic-noematic correlations that are essentially involved in each kind of intentional act.

Intentionality, in the Husserlian sense, is what takes us, as conscious beings, into the locus of all *a prioris,* i.e., of all the conditions of possibility for any meaning whatsoever. When Heidegger, at Marburg, maintains that Husserlian intentionality should not be the final word, but the indication of a task, he expresses not a rejection of Husserl but rather a determination to take seriously what Husserl discovered at the heart of intentionality, i.e., the surplus status of *Sachverhalte,* of ideas and categories with regard to the flux of occurrences to which the natural attitude limits itself. According to Heidegger, this was Hussserl's crucial discovery. In his homage to Niemeyer, written in 1963, Heidegger recalls that, during his formative years with Husserl (1919–1923), "the distinction which is worked out there [in the sixth Logical Investigation] between sensuous and categorial intuition revealed itself to me in all its scope for the determination of 'the manifold meaning of Being'."[9] His long debate with Husserl essentially consisted in using the Husserlian discovery of categorial intuition to overcome the ontological indeterminacy that affected the Husserlian concept of intentionality. If our intentionality contains not only the character of excess and supplement for an articulated complex of *Sachverhalte* (of ideas, of categories, which alone are capable of manifesting our *intenta* as

8. William Richardson, *Heidegger: Through Phenomenology to Thought* (The Hague: Martinus Nijhoff, 1967), p. x.

9. *On Time and Being,* trans. J. Stambaugh (New York: Harper Torchbooks, 1972), p. 78.

what they are in their *realitas*), but also the character of excess of the category "Being," then it should be stated that it is a fundamental characteristic of the intentional entity to make manifest beings not only in their *realitas,* or beingness, but also in their Being. At this time Heidegger agreed with Husserl that the Being of nature, including the Greek sense of *phusis,* is that of a simple occurrence in a flux of events. In other words, the mode of being of nature is *Vorhandenheit.* His disagreement originated in the refusal to transpose this mode of being to the Being of intentionality. The Husserlian discovery of categorial intuition means for Heidegger that intentional being does not occur purely and simply as a natural sequence of events. Indeed intentional being is open to beings other than itself, which means that it extends beyond their occurrence toward their beingness and stretches even beyond their beingness, or essence, to reach their Being. For all these reasons the mode of being of the intentional entity must be radically demarcated from *Vorhandenheit.* Husserl himself seems to express the necessity for such a demarcation when he asserts that no distinction of being is "more radical" than the one obtaining between transcendence and immanence.

But he does not determine immanence ontologically. To the question as to what the Being of intentionality is, Husserl provides an equivocal answer: On the one hand it is a stream of occurrences (the *Erlebnisse*), and on the other hand a set of eidetic structures. In other words, we have on the one hand *Vorhandenheit,* and on the other hand pure essences detached from any existence. Moreover, Husserl's answer is not driven by an ontological goal, but by a cognitive one. The issue for him is the distinction between contingent particularity and necessary universality. But if it is true that, ultimately, the intentional being is open not only to the *realitas* of beings but to their Being, then the study of intentionality belongs not to the theory of knowledge, but to ontology. More precisely the answer to the question "What does it mean to know, for an intentional being?" must be inscribed within the framework of an answer to a deeper question: "What is Being in the case of a being that understands beings and their Being?" One can object that to answer the deeper question by speaking of transcendence where Husserl talked of immanence does not show deference in the least for the master. Indeed a certain impertinence cannot be ruled out. Yet does not the medieval word "transcendence" express the very excess that lies at the core of the Husserlian doctrine of categorial intuition? One might object that this interpretation does not take Aristotle into account: after all, even if Husserl suggests the necessity of an ontologization of the intentional being and opens the way to it by his doctrine of categorial intuition, he never investigated this problem. It could even be said that he turned away from it, if, as Heidegger points it, he came very close to repudiating his famous sixth *Logical Investigation* after the publication of *Ideen I.*[10] These objections are not without justification. It is undeniable that a reappropriation of Aristotle played a considerable role in the Heideggerian ontologization of intentionality. But it would be inappropriate to conclude that this ontologization consisted generally in pitting the ancients against the moderns, and in particular Aristotle against Husserl.

When Heidegger's relationship to the Greeks is mentioned, today, at least three themes are usually considered. The first has to do with Pre-Socratic thought. In a nutshell, we can say that, after reaching a certain point in his itinerary, Heidegger urged us to view the most evocative words and concepts of the Pre-Socratics (*aletheia, phusis, logos*) as designations for Being. Among these notions, *aletheia* serves as a guide. It invites us to think of Being as an ambiguous process of manifestation that reserves or withdraws itself from the very beings which it brings to manifestation. Thus we have the theme of the *withdrawal of Being* as a constitutive feature of Being. Meditating on this withdrawal requires a distancing from another notion of *aletheia*. The tradition of philosophy has conceived of *aletheia* in terms of the nonambiguous notion that came to the forefront with Plato: it conceives of truth as the correct adjustment of the seeing of *nous* focused on the clarity of *eidos*. With the Platonic doctrine of truth, philosophy institutes itself as an onto-theology which obliterates the intrinsically ambiguous or polemic nature of Pre-Socratic *aletheia*. Instead it instigates an ontical hierarchy, from sensible to intelligible beings, to the Ideas, to the most eminent being and highest Idea (which are all capable of appearing in full clarity). Hence the meditation on the constitutive withdrawal of Being is interwoven with a second theme: Metaphysics, as onto-theology, instituted itself by *an obliteration of the withdrawal of Being,* toward which Pre-Socratic thinking pointed. But this second theme is linked to a third. This obliteration of the withdrawal of Being (constitutive of metaphysics) is not the sign of a fault, or mistake, made by metaphysicians, starting with Plato—an interpretation against which Heidegger warns us. It is, on the contrary, the guise under which Being advents for Western man. The history of metaphysics up to the present (i.e., up to the age of generalized technology) is the history of Being itself, which in each epoch offers itself while also concealing itself. But the current epoch (of the *Gestell,* as the total and limitless manipulation of beings, and as the nihilistic completion of the age of subjectivity) shows the most complete obliteration of Being in its withdrawal.

Hence there is a third theme: The history of Being is the *history of the*

---

10. See "My Way to Phenomenology," in *On Being and Time,* p. 79.

forgetfulness of Being. But we are forced to admit that in the constellation of theoretical terms regulating the first Heideggerian interpretation of the Greeks, i.e., in fundamental ontology, none of these themes could be accommodated. Indeed, at the time of fundamental ontology, Heidegger did not detect *any discontinuity* between the writings of the Pre-Socratics and those of Plato and Aristotle. Consequently, fundamental ontology did not in any way attempt to regress beyond metaphysics toward a more meditative thinking, in the wake of a reflection on the Pre-Socratics. It attempted in contrast to *achieve metaphysics* by bringing the meaning of Being to conceptual clarity. In the framework of this attempt, the history of metaphysics was not considered as increasing the obliteration of Being, but instead as the *maturation of the science of Being.* In such a framework, the emergence of subjectivity plays a capital role because it is within ourselves that the key to that science is to be found.

Accordingly, when during the period of fundamental ontology Heidegger used Aristotle to ontologize the intentionality wich had been discovered by Husserl, his objective was not at all to oppose Aristotle to Husserl. Neither in the letter to Richardson nor in the homage to Niemeyer is there any mention of such a confrontation. Both texts, instead, call attention to an overlapping relationship between the thought of Aristotle and the thought of Husserl. In short, both texts seem to say: The more I took an interest in Husserl, the more I became interested in Aristotle. And when we take into account not only the retrospective assessment made by Heidegger fourty years after the genesis of fundamental ontology but also his reading of Husserl at the time of that genesis, we realize that, in each of the Greek themes and inspirations retrospectively valued as foundational for fundamental ontology, Husserl's work is less rejected than affirmed and continued [*prolongé*].

The letter to Richardson asserts that three decisive insights (*Einsichten*) allowed fundamental ontology to be launched as a project. Heidegger says that the first of these intuitive discoveries took advantage of "the direct experience with the phenomenological method acquired by discussions with Husserl in order to secure the conquest of the concept of phenomenology as *logos* of *phainomenon,* such as it is defined in Section 7 of *Sein und Zeit.* The second consisted, by means of a renewed study of Book IX of the *Metaphysics* of Aristotle and of Book VI of the *Nicomachean Ethics,* in grasping truth as unconcealing (*aletheuein*). The third discovery consisted in realizing that presence, i.e., a mode of time, is the fundamental characteristic of Being."

The homage to Niemeyer does not mention the third discovery, but brings an important precision to the first two. Apropos of the first one,

Heidegger indicates that "the step-by-step training in phenomenological seeing" with Husserl was fruitful for his interpretation of Aristotle and allowed him to gain "a transformed understanding of Aristotle" ("My Way to Phenomenology," p. 78)[11]. He adds that his attempt at gaining a renewed understanding of "the determination of the manifold meaning of Being," had been facilitated by the Husserlian doctrine of categorial intuition, which functioned as a revealing agent.

The second discovery discussed in the letter to Richardson is presented as exclusively Aristotelian, but a precision is added in the homage to Niemeyer: It was in the preparation of his seminar on the *Logical Investigations* that Heidegger discovered "at first rather led by surmise than by founded insight" that "what occurs for the phenomenology of the acts of consciousness as the self-manifestation of phenomena is thought more originally by Aristotle and in all Greek thinking and existence as *aletheia.*" ("My Way to Phenomenology," p. 79)

Let us put aside for a while the issue of the third discovery, the question of time, and consider for the moment the first two issues. It is clear that, according to the presentation made by Heidegger in these retrospective texts, the first two discoveries were the result of an overlapping of Husserl's text and Aristotle's. More precisely, an overlapping of the sixth *Logical Investigation* and Aristotle's text. We are therefore led to seek signs of the evidence of such an overlapping and to determine successively its scope in the two discoveries.

It is not immediately apparent that the phenomenological concept outlined in Section 7 of *Sein und Zeit* contains the evidence of an overlapping of Husserl and Aristotle. Indeed, even though the pages from Section 7 claim to follow the motto, "Back to the things themselves," and credit, in passing, the *Logical Investigations* with preparing the ground for the investigation carried out in *Sein und Zeit,* they use the terminology of Aristotle, and not of Husserl. This paragraph deals with Aristotle's attention to *logos* and to *phainomenon* and his assertion that *logos* is apophantic, i.e., that its function is to let things be seen. Accordingly, the phenomenon is what shows itself directly, but also what can pass itself off as what it is not. Hence the word "phenomenology," strictly speaking, means the attitude that will allow every being to display itself and to be seen from within itself. However we should not, Heidegger warns, be limited to such a formal definition by means of which the clarification of any being from the consideration of how it displays itself would claim to be "phenomenology." A phenomenon, in the phenomenological sense, is what "proximally and

---

11. *On Time and Being,* trans. Stambaugh, p. 78.

for the most part" does not show itself at all, but on the contrary remains invisible within what "proximally and for the most part" shows itself, even though the invisible constitutes the phenomenon in its meaning and its foundation. Such a phenomenon is the Being of beings: Being that extends beyond all ontical determinations of beings, Being as transcendence pure and simple. Heidegger insists that this notion stimulated the inquiries of both Plato and Aristotle. Because Being offers itself to a seeing, phenomenology is the method of ontology. Because Being is the central theme of philosophy and because the cardinal problem of philosophy is the meaning of Being, phenomenology must be the science of Being, i.e., ontology. It is in that capacity alone and beyond the "actuality [of phenomenology] as a philosophical movement"[12] that ontology will fulfill the possibilities of phenomenology. At first sight, these remarks claim allegiance more to the Greeks than to Husserl, more to the ontological objectives of the former than to the cognitive objectives of the latter.

But a more careful study reveals that what really occurs in Section 7 of *Sein und Zeit* is an overlapping of Husserl and the Greeks. *Logos* as apophantic is indeed an Aristotelian theme, but it is no less Husserlian. We have already noted that the 1925 lecture course *The History of the Concept of Time*, in its probing of the structure of the logical realm, credited the sixth *Logical Investigation* with the discovery of the authentic meaning of expressedness. Expressedness is not the communication of lived experiences, but the manifestation of the Being of the objects to which the logical lived experiences are referred. It is Husserlian, as much as Aristotelian, to insist with the *Metaphysics* that: "It is when we know the *to ti en einai* that there is a science of the particular."

It is a distinction originating in the Platonic doctrine of Ideas, and one accepted by Aristotle, that the phenomenon, in the sense of what displays itself intrinsically, should encompass not only the way beings have of exhibiting themselves in the ordinary apprehension we have of them, but also the Being of those beings. Aristotle, it is true, refuses to conclude that it implies a demarcation between two regions, the first sensible, the second intelligible. But this distinction between an entity and its Being is perfectly Husserlian too. When Section 7 of *Sein und Zeit* adds that the phenomenon in the sense of phenomenology is not what shows itself in everydayness, but rather what the everyday mode of understanding hides while presupposing, Heidegger is also referring to Kant and Kant's distinction between sensible intuition and pure intuition (space and time). But the retrospective hints made in the letter to Richardson and in the homage to Niemeyer allow us to

---

12. *Being and Time*, trans. John Macquarrie and Edward Robinson (New York: Harper and Row, 1962), English p. 63; German p. 38.

suspect that he was not so much aiming at Kant's distinction as at Husserl's. The distinction between sensible intuition and categorial intuition, which is absent in Kant, designates an intuitive *logos,* analogous to the Aristotelian *"apophantic* logos," i.e., an intuitive *logos* exhibiting not only the categories characterizing beings in their beingness, but also the category "Being." Finally, when Section 7 stipulates that Being is the "transcendent pure and simple" and that its manifestation is transcendental, the formulation seems to be indebted to Aristotle and is certainly in conformity with the terminology of the commentaries of the Medievals. Nevertheless here again there is an overlapping because it is within ourselves that the manifestation of Being, its "transcendental truth" (a Kantian and Husserlian formulation just as much as a medieval one) has its site. We might even assert that at this point the overlapping encroaches upon the moderns. We would never find in Aristotle and the ancients the confirmation of the status given by Heidegger to Dasein: "ontological priority over every other entity" *(Being and Time,* 62; 37–38). Instead, the language as much as the actual movement of reflection assigned by Heidegger to philosophy seems to be in strict conformity with the style of the moderns, from Descartes to Husserl, via Kant and Hegel. Such a movement of reflection is contained in the affirmation that "universal phenomenological ontology . . . takes its departure from the hermeneutic of Dasein, which, as an analytic of *existence,* has made fast the guiding-line for all philosophical inquiry at the point where it *arises* and to which it *returns" (Being and Time,* 62; 38).

What about the second discovery, that of *aletheia*? Here at last, it seems harder to suggest that there was an overlapping of Husserl and Aristotle: From truth as unconcealing to truth as indubitable evidence, is there not a mutation? Yet, the homage to Niemeyer mentions nowhere that, concerning truth, Husserl is adrift whereas Aristotle is close to the origin. On the contrary, this text says that it is thanks to the *Logical Investigations* that Heidegger discovered that Aristotle grasped the issue of truth "more originally" than Husserl. This is a strange overlapping: Although less so than Aristotle, Husserl is still original, his originality being undeniable in the *Logical Investigations.* Once more, it is the Husserlian doctrine of categorial intuition that Heidegger has in mind. Recall that in the 1925 *History of the Concept of Time,* Heidegger detects the import of Husserl's theory in the regionality and universality of the act of identification, understood as the manifest seeing of the coincidence between the intentional act and what is grasped in and by it. The regional character means that each modality of intentionality (perception for example) has a specific manner of bringing to a seeing the *intentum* which corresponds to that modality. The universality of *Aufweisung* means that intentionality as such is unveiling. This means that consciousness as such (not judgment alone) is a bearer of truth and that there are pre-predicative truths. These points are constant features in Husserl's teaching. But Heidegger claims that, concerning the issue of truth, Husserl also "thinks the matters from the origin." Thus even though Husserl uses the old language of correspondence—*adaequatio*—and the Cartesian term of evidence, the essence of truth for him is unveiling and its site is the intentionality of consciousness as such and not judgment alone. The 1925 lecture course on *The History of the Concept of Time* is very clear on the subject. Heidegger says: "Without being explicitly conscious of the [fact], phenomenology returns to the broad concept of truth whereby the Greeks (Aristotle) could call true even perception as such and the simple perception of something" (55; 73). In other words, this amounts to saying that like Aristotle, Husserl thinks that *psuche* is unveiling and that "it is in a certain way all beings" (*De Anima*, III, 431, b, 21–22, quoted in *Being and Time*, 34; 14). If Aristotle thinks the issue of truth "more originally" than Husserl, it is because *psuche* is for him a principle of life, or of existence as such. Consequently the unveiling or *aletheuein* is not the privilege of any *cogito*, no matter how broadened it is, but pervades every human comportment. Thus if Aristotle is closer to the primary source of the "things themselves," it is because, in Heideggerian terms, he thinks the unveiling act in relation to Dasein, and not in relation to *Bewusstsein*.

Hence one can claim that some preeminence was given to Aristotle over the moderns. However during the period of fundamental ontology, the acknowledgement of that preeminence did not at all imply Heidegger's alignment with the ancients against the moderns. What this ontology wants to discover is the very center of the different meanings of Being. Such a discovery came to the forefront in the analytic of Dasein, which is the being that understands Being. The understanding of Being has two forms: one occurs in everydayness and is not truly our own; the other one is ownmost.

In a later chapter we shall attempt to show that this distinction (between a mode of unveiling specific to preoccupation, i.e., practical circumspection, on the one hand and a mode of unveiling specific to care, i.e., resoluteness, on the other hand) was worked out by Heidegger from an original reappropriation of the Aristotelian distinction between *poiesis* and *praxis*, a distinction which is at the core of the two Aristotelian treatises mentioned in the letter to Richardson. But the fact, undeniable for me, that such a reappropriation took place, in no way implies that what he reappropriated has to be understood in an Aristotelian way. In order to determine in its ultimate depth the Being of beings, Aristotle's questioning is not directed toward the being that we are, a being affected by the movement of being born and perishing. Instead, it is directed toward what in nature has always been and will ever be what it is. In other words, the Aristotelian *sophia* is not at all centered on *praxis*, that is, on the very existence of mortals, but on the eternal characteristics of the imperishable bodies. It was not therefore by virtue of a Greek attitude, but of a modern one, that Heidegger turned the being that we are into the ground of first philosophy, from which one could investigate the center of the meaning of Being. And if it is true that the ground of fundamental ontology once depended upon the *Logical Investigations,* we do not see how it could be totally independent from the Husserlian *Sinngebung.*

Let us now return to the third discovery, that of time. Can we speak here of an overlapping of Husserl and Aristotle? At first sight, the question seems absurd because fundamental ontology claims to demarcate itself both from the Aristotelian theory of time and from the Husserlian investigations on internal time consciousness. But on closer inspection, what takes place is less a double rejection than a double radicalization. The Aristotelian definition of time as "that which is counted in the movement which we encounter within the horizon of the earlier and the later" is not, in fundamental ontology, the object of a refutation, but of a "positive reappropriation" (*Being and Time,* 473; 421). This is tantamount to assigning the traditional concepts to their proper place by showing how they originate in the comportment of Dasein. Fundamental ontology considers that the comportment in which the Aristotelian definition of time originates is everyday preoccupation, which is animated by a specific mode of seeing, the practical circumspection of everyday surroundings. Aristotle, Heidegger claims, implicitly and uncritically bases his definition of time on this comportment. One of the tasks of fundamental ontology is to overcome that naivete, and to take into account and thematize the ontological existential presupposition of the Aristotelian definition. As soon as it is led back to its presupposition, i.e., to everyday preoccupation and circumspection, the time Aristotle talks about should be expressed in the following way: "This time is that which is *counted* and which shows itself when one follows the travelling pointer, counting and making present in such a way that this making-present temporalizes itself in an ecstatical unity with the retaining and awaiting which are horizonally open according to the 'earlier' and 'later' " (*Being and Time,* 473; 421). It is clear from these words that Heidegger existentially reappropriates the Aristotelian concept of time in a language that is closely akin to the one in which Husserl describes the "internal consciousness of time." Thus it is with Husserl's help that Heidegger is able to lead the Aristotelian concept of time back to its original and existential source. To be sure, neither Husserl nor Aristotle was capable of moving beyond the "everyday" understanding of time. But at least it is Husserl who helps us decipher what in Dasein is the condition for that understanding, with the notion of a temporalization enacted by the intentional being.

On this point, it is significant that when Heidegger explains the Aristotelian notion of *ousia* in terms of presence, he uses the Husserlian term *Gegenwärtigung*, or presentification, which applies to the noetic comportment that grasps *ousia* (*Being and Time*, 48; 26). He even goes so far as to imply, without stating it explicitly, Husserl's relative superiority on this point:

> The Greeks have managed to interpret Being in this way without any explicit knowledge of the clues which function here, without any acquaintance with the fundamental ontological function of time or even any understanding of it, and without any insight into the reason why this function is possible. On the contrary, they take time itself as one entity among other entities. (*Being and Time*, 48; 26)

It is hard to see how Husserl could be accused of the same confusion. In addition, in the 1928 lecture course on *The Metaphysical Foundations of Logic* and in one of the few passages containing an express mention of Husserl's *Phenomenology of Internal Time-Consciousness*, Heidegger unmistakably acknowledges his debt to Husserl. We read: "With regard to all previous interpretations, it was Husserl's service to have seen these phenomena [of the now, the next and the before] for the first time, with the aid of the intentional structure." He suggests that the limitation of that discovery is to have conceived intentionality as a knowledge of objects, albeit immanent, comparable to the temporal occurrence of a sound. But apart from this limitation, one may say of the Husserlian discovery of temporalization: "That which Husserl still calls time-consciousness, i.e., consciousness of time, is precisely time, itself, in the primordial sense" (*The Metaphysical Foundations of Logic*, 204; 263–64).[13]

Someone might object that the overlapping of Husserl and Aristotle only concerns understanding in the fallen, improper mode and that this overlapping ultimately plays no role in the Heideggerian conquest of authentic temporality. I would suggest instead that the radicalization of the Aristotelian concept of time facilitated by Husserl was accompanied by a radicalization of the Husserlian consciousness of time facilitated by Aristotle. Care has a higher status than preoccupation. Preoccupation relates Dasein to beings whose mode of being is not Dasein's own. Care relates Dasein to its ownmost potentiality-for-Being. The time of care is in no way reducible to the time of preoccupation, which is nothing but the fall

---

13. *The Metaphysical Foundations of Logic*, trans. Michael Heim (Bloomington: Indiana University Press, 1984).

of the former. This opposition cannot be adequately described in terms of the Husserlian intertwining of retention, protention, and presentification. Husserl's analysis was insufficient because he argues in terms of consciousness of objects, not in terms of existence or of ways of being. Now, as we saw, it is because Aristotle understood unveiling not in relation to consciousness but in relation to existence, that Heidegger credits him with grasping the source of the phenomena more radically than Husserl.

Consequently, we can wonder whether something in Aristotle could not have put Heidegger on the way to the discovery and the articulation of authentic temporality, i.e., the ec-static unity of self-precedence, of repetition, and of the moment of vision. Not in the *Physics*, of course, but rather in the treatise in which Aristotle describes our comportment and to which Heidegger in Marburg gave the status of "an ontology of Dasein": the *Nicomachean Ethics*. In the latter text Aristotle distinguishes two fundamentally temporal comportments: *poiesis*, or fabrication, and *praxis*, or action properly speaking. But he stresses that past, present, and future are not articulated in the same manner for each comportment. *Poiesis* is a movement which, each time, has its past and its future outside of itself. The production of a product is absolutely not the beginning of its fabrication, and this production has an end that falls outside of itself: the product. In contradistinction, *praxis*, that is, existence itself, is a movement that at each point includes its past and decides on issues regarding the end (*telos*) that it contains in itself: acting well. However Aristotle did not thematize the time of *praxis*. Yet the *Nicomachean Ethics* clearly outlines the structure of an existential temporality, thereby enabling Heidegger to discern in time a triad other than the Husserlian triad.

Perhaps the light cast on these various overlappings can now explain how Heidegger in Marburg could, without contradiction, claim two things: that compared to Husserl, he was only an apprentice, and that the real master of phenomenology was Aristotle.

Appendix to Chapter 1

Voice and Phenomenon in Heidegger's Fundamental Ontology[1]

In *Sein und Zeit*, Husserl is mentioned only a few times, either in the text proper or in several footnotes at the bottom of the pages; Kant is mentioned more frequently; Aristotle even more so than Kant. Not only are the references to Husserl scarce and discreet, but their substance too seems hardly worthy of much attention. Some of them give nothing but a very general expression of gratitude to a master and pathfinder. Others merely indicate to the reader that a certain number of analyses conducted in the analytic of Dasein can be compared to—or should I say confronted with—specific Husserlian analyses. In both cases, these allusions leave the reader yearning for more. In general, they make points the reader is willing to grant without difficulty, for example that phenomenology achieved its "breakthrough" (*Durchbruch*) in the *Logical Investigations,* that Husserl deserves to be acclaimed as the one who established the "ground" (*Boden*) on which the investigations of fundamental ontology became possible (62; 38),[2] that Heidegger's approach is indebted to Husserl for "having taken a few steps toward the things themselves" (489 modified; 39 note), and that there is "nothing constructivistic" in Husserl's '*a priorism*,' which is fundamentally an attempt at "reawakening the meaning of authentic philosophical empiricism" (490 modified; 50 note). Yet because these remarks limit

---

1. This text first appeared in French in *Revue philosophique* 2 (1990), a collection of essays in homage to Jacques Derrida. It was not part of this collection as it was originally published in French in 1989. The author has included it in the English version.

2. We first give the page number of the English text, then the page number in the original German text. The first page number here corresponds to *Being and Time*, trans. John Macquarrie and Edward Robinson, (Harper and Row); the second to the page number in the original *Sein und Zeit*.

themselves to considerations of method, and very general ones at that, they do not show precisely how fundamental ontology might claim for itself a Husserlian legacy. Furthermore when precise themes and texts are considered in the middle of specific analyses, the references aim either at pointing out a deficiency in Husserl's problematic (e.g., all the analyses of personality in *Philosophy as a Rigorous Science* and in *Ideen II* are flawed in that they do not raise the question of "personal *Being*" (73; 47)), or they provide the reader with some sort of information so cut and dried that one cannot imagine just how to use it. Such is the case in particular with the references to Husserl's name in Sections 17 and 34 of *Sein und Zeit*. A note within Section 17, the section entitled *Reference and Signs*, indicates that "for the analysis of *Zeichen* and *Bedeutung*, the reader is referred to the first *Logical Investigation*" (490 modified; 77 note). A note within Section 34, the section entitled *Being-there and Discourse*, again mentions that "concerning the theory of *Bedeutung*, the reader is referred to the first *Logical Investigation*, but also to the fourth and the sixth" (492 modified). In addition, the note maintains that "for a more radical conception of the problematic" one can consult *Ideen I*, Sections 123 and following.

But without a guide to their use, these allusions remain enigmatic. At least, by virtue of their repetition, they indicate clearly the importance Heidegger ascribed to the Husserlian theory of *Bedeutung*, particularly in the form that it takes in the first *Logical Investigation*, the text whose argumentation Jacques Derrida's essay *La voix et le phénomène*³ investigates with unsurpassed rigor and penetration. What lies hidden behind Heidegger's interest in the first *Logical Investigation*? Does he make reference to it only so that the reader will soon realize how far the analytic of Dasein has moved away from it? Or, on the contrary, is it Heidegger's intention that the reader will discern between the first and the second something akin to a legacy? If we were limited only to the text of *Sein und Zeit*, these questions would remain without answer because of the book's reserve [*discrétion*] on these issues. But the situation changes when we consider the less reserved lectures delivered around the time of the publication of the treatise (1927).

Indeed we read in the Marburg 1927 summer lecture course on *The Basic Problems of Phenomenology*:

> Only in recent times has this problem of the sign been pursued in an actual investigation. In the first of his *Logical Investigations*

---

3. *La voix et le phénomène* (Paris: Presses Universitaires de France, 1972). *Speech and Phenomena*, trans. David B. Allison (Evanston: Northwestern University Press, 1973).

Ausdruck und Bedeutung (expression and meaning), Husserl gives the essential determinations concerning sign (*Zeichen*), mark or symptom (*Anzeichen*), and designation (*Bezeichnung*)—taking all of them together in distinction from *Bedeuten*.[4] The sign-function of the written as opposed to the spoken is altogether different from the sign-function of the spoken as opposed to what is *Bedeutet* in speech (*Rede*), and conversely altogether different from the function of the written, of writing, as opposed to that which is aimed at in it. Implicit here are a multiplicity of symbolic relations (*Symbolbeziehungen*) which are very difficult to grasp in their elementary structure and require extensive investigations. Some inquiries of this kind are to be found, as supplements to Husserl's investigation, in *Being and Time* (Section 17, *"Verweisung und Zeichen,"* "Reference and Signs"), the orientation there being toward principles. Today the symbol has become a favorite formula, but those who use it either dispense with any investigation as to what is generally meant by it or else have no suspicion of the difficulties that are concealed in this verbal slogan. (185–86; 263)[5]

Thus the meaning of the note of Section 17 of *Sein und Zeit* is clarified. Far from inviting the reader to conclude on his own that Heidegger only intends a demarcation, this page of *The Basic Problems* expresses the acknowledgement of a Husserlian legacy in fundamental ontology. This legacy is connected to the fact that the definitions laid out by the first *Logical Investigations* are "essential" in Heidegger's eyes and, more precisely, that it is essential to distinguish *Bedeutung* from sign, mark, and designation.

The passage we just quoted claims in essence that Section 17 of *Sein und Zeit*, which is said to complete the Husserlian investigation, relies on the same "essential" distinction. Yet, and this restriction is far from evident, the previously mentioned section (17) is said to contain an "orientation toward principles," which by implication is lacking in Husserl's approach. In other words, what is suggested by this page of *The Basic Problems* is the fact that Heidegger's reappropriation of Husserl's "essential distinction" is inscribed in an ontology of Dasein, which is absent from Husserl's works.

Finally, this page suggests by the same token that what is said of *Rede* (discourse) in *Sein und Zeit* and of *Bedeutung* (of which discourse is the site

---

4. Hofstadter, the translator, adds the linguistic explanation: this is "[t]he verbal noun for meaning or signifying, whose principal substantive form, *Bedeutung*, is then to be read as significance or meaning."

5. *The Basic Problems of Phenomenology*, trans. Albert Hofstadter (Bloomington: Indiana University Press, 1982).

and by which it is animated), far from distancing itself from the first Logical Investigation, affirms and continues [prolonge] it in the direction and "orientation toward principles" required by the ontology of Dasein. We are therefore invited to consider that the note found in Section 34 is not inserted simply for the sake of information but contains also the acknowledgement of a Husserlian legacy.

My goal here is not to trace the evidence of this legacy from indications found in Sections 17 and 34, but rather to inquire into the persistence of this legacy at the time when the "orientation toward principles" adopted in the analytic of Dasein unfolds into the analysis of the deepest form of Rede, i.e., Gewissen, which we should positively resist translating as "moral conscience." It seems to me that the terms of this inquiry are laid down in another lecture course from the Marburg era, the Prolegomena to the History of the Concept of Time, which presents the double advantage of being a sort of first version of Sein und Zeit (especially of Sections 17 and 34) and also of highlighting the specific points on which the research conducted therein may lay claim to a Husserlian heritage. In its preliminary section, this lecture course credits Husserl with three decisive discoveries: intentionality, categorial intuition, and the originary meaning of the a priori. The second discovery is intimately related to our present goal and will help us to determine the terms of our inquiry.

Generally speaking, the preliminary part of this lecture course presents instances of mutual overlapping between Husserl's teaching (especially in the Logical Investigations) and Aristotle's. For the most part, this overlapping takes place with respect to the notion of Rede, which is a word commonly used by Husserl and which, in Heidegger, is used as the German equivalent of logos in Aristotle.

It is said in De Interpretatione (4, 17a, 1 ff.) that every logos is semantikos, but not apophantikos. Heidegger's commentary reads:

> Every logos, or discourse, is semantikos, inasmuch as discourse in general "bedeutet," means something, "shows something in the sense of a Bedeuten (signifying) which yields something understandable (Verständliches) (84; 116).

But the only apophantic logos is the one that is theorein, seeing, he says.

There are, therefore, two levels in the hierarchy of manifestation. Whether it be semantic or apophantic, every discourse shows (zeigt) something understandable and Bedeutung consists more generally in this showing. But it is one thing to manifest what is understandable as does wish, greeting, solicitation, prayer; it is another to let what is thus shown be seen in itself. To these two levels of manifestation, one of which yields something understandable in general whereas the other lets something be seen as it is, correspond two levels of *Bedeutung*: the first is limited to delivering something understandable in general; instead of being thus limited, the second displays the thing in its proper mode, it is *"sacherfassenden,"* a seeing of the thing itself (See *Gesamtausgabe*, 20, pp. 115–116).

There is no doubt that a powerful intuitionist inspiration sustains this reading of Aristotle. Specifically, it determines the Heideggerian interpretation of *phone*, voice. Aristotle suggests that "in its concrete performance, discourse assumes the form of speaking, vocal utterance in words" (84; 115). Heidegger insists that we must understand that "this feature (*phone*, *Stimme*, voice) however does not constitute the essence of *logos*. On the contrary, the feature of *phone* is defined from the authentic sense of *logos* as *apophainesthai*, from what discourse [*Rede*] truly [*eigentlich*] is and does—pointing out and letting something be seen" (84; 116). There is a link between voice and phenomenon, such that the phenomenon rules over the voice and the voice reaches what is ownmost in itself when it can be limited to gathering the phenomenon in the ownmost. Because Heidegger associates the *De Interpretatione* and the first of the *Logical Investigations* (see *The Basic Problems of Phenomenology*, 185; 263) by thus citing them together, we can wonder whether the "essential distinctions" made by Husserl might not guide Heidegger's reading of the Aristotelian text; in other words, whether these distinctions might not determine his characterization of the semantic and the apophantic.

Leaving this aside for now, we may acknowledge that the intuitionist inspiration plays a central role in Heidegger's analysis of the decisive discovery made by Husserl, a topic on which he comments at length: *kategoriale Anschauung*, categorial intuition. *Anschauen* in German is the equivalent of the Greek *theorein* which, as we noted above, is present at the core of the Heideggerian characterization of the Aristotelian *logos*. *Anschauung* is an equally central term in Husserl's theory of discourse and is one of the focal points on which the inquiry pursued by Jacques Derrida is the most insistent. By contrast, on this point, Heidegger subscribes without hesitation to the Husserlian analysis. Let us consider this issue more closely.

The Husserlian notion that *Rede* (discourse) is first of all enunciative, that it is essentially made of assertions and therefore falls within the philosophical competence of a logic in the sense of an *Erkenntnislehre*, forms a thematic totality which Heidegger is far from endorsing as such. *Sein und Zeit* maintains that assertion is not at all an originary mode of discourse and that discourse is primordially interpretative in nature. First and foremost, discourse consists in apprehending states of affairs *as* having this or that meaning, so that assertions are nothing but a derivative mode of interpretation (see Section 33). Even though the criticism leveled at the privilege given to assertion and the demonstration of its derivative character in relation to interpretation (*Auslegung*) are not formulated as such in the 1925 course, they are foreshadowed in the insistence with which Heidegger maintains that discourse is a possibility of the being of Dasein and therefore that "the sense of a *scientific logic* is the elaboration of this *a priori* structure of discourse in Dasein (*diese apriorischen Daseinsstruktur*), the elaboration of the possibilities and kinds of interpretation" (264; 364). Contrary to what Husserl thought in the *Logical Investigations,* therefore, logic is nothing ultimate. It refers back to the ontology of Dasein. Ontology is the ultimate discipline.

But substituting the primacy of the ontology of Dasein for the primacy of *Erkenntnislehre* in Husserl changes nothing in Husserl's teaching on *Bedeutung* (formulated in the doctrine of categorial intuition), even though it displaces its center of gravity. According to this doctrine, inasmuch as it means something (*bedeutet*), discourse (*Rede*) depends on a complex set of idealities—forms and categories which (in spite of their position of excess or surplus vis-à-vis any given content offered to sensible perception) are nonetheless offered to an intuition that is ideal, and no longer sensible: the so–called categorial intuition. Ultimately therefore, the *Bedeutungen* that discourse expresses are based on the intuitive seeing of these idealities. It is thanks to their *Anschauung* that discourse is capable of expressedness. Heidegger writes: "It is essentially owing to phenomenological investigations that this authentic sense of the expressing and expressedness of all comportments was made fundamental and placed in the foreground of the question of the logical." And he adds:

This is not surprising when we consider that our comportments are in actual fact pervaded through and through by assertions, that they are always performed in some form of expressedness. It is also a matter of fact that our simplest perceptions and constitutive states are already *expressed,* even more, are *interpreted* in a certain way. What is primary and original here? It is not so much that we see the objects and things but rather that we first talk about them. To put it more precisely: we do not say what we see, but rather the reverse, we see what *one says* about the matter (56 modified; 75–76).

At the deepest level, to say something is to see something. On this point, these lines stress that, for Heidegger, the teachings of Husserl and Aristotle overlap one another. They also allow us to understand why the note of Section 34 of *Sein und Zeit* credits Sections 123 and following of *Ideen I* with a superior sort of radicality. The reason is that in these sections Husserl considers expression in its purity, that is, as a logical *Bedeu-*

tung that is "unproductive" and limited to expressing a pre-expressive meaning given to intuition (See Jacques Derrida, *Speech and Phenomena*, 72 ff.; 83 ff.).[6] Heidegger's remarks cited above do not mean that what should be seen according to Husserl is identical with what should be seen according to Heidegger. Indeed these remarks subtly intermingle allegiance with reappropriation, and therefore bring about a displacement of the center of gravity. Where Husserl talks about "acts" of *Bedeutung*, Heidegger speaks of "comportments," thus displacing the site of phenomenological research: it is no longer centered on *cogitationes*, but on ways of comporting oneself or existing. Where Husserl speaks of expression, Heidegger speaks of interpretation, thus suggesting by the same token that deeper than the knowledge conveyed by "acts" of *Bedeutung* in Husserl's sense lies the understanding (*Verstehen*) that animates our entire way of existing. These movements of displacement suggest that intentionality, the first of Husserl's discoveries termed "decisive" by Heidegger, could not now be repeated as such, because intentionality specifically designates the structural relation of a *cogitatio* to its *cogitatum*.

Likewise, Heidegger cannot accept as such the third of Husserl's decisive discoveries, the *a priori*. In order to understand why not, we must now enter into the specifics of his debate with Husserl's doctrine of categorial intuition. Among the categorial intuitions mentioned in the *Logical Investigations*, one stands out as having superior theoretical importance for Heidegger concerning the project to which he had subscribed from the outset: the question of the meaning of Being. For not only do the *Logical Investigations* state that "Being is not a real predicate," and confirm Kant's thesis, but also maintain that "Being" is given to a categorial intuition, a thesis that obviously is no longer Kantian. "Being is not a real predicate" means that it is not in any sense a being, and that it is not in a continuity of predicates which determine the quiddity of what is. In his last seminar (1973), Heidegger acknowledged that he had secured the "ground" of fundamental ontology[7] thanks to the notion that "Being" is given to categorial intuition. Because for Heidegger the *Bedeutung* "Being" is the most fundamental of all *Bedeutungen* and—in the theory of categorial intuition of the *Logical Investigations*—is granted a position of surplus or excess, Heidegger is tempted to transform simultaneously the three Husserlian discoveries that he finds decisive. First, the metamorphosis of intentionality: deeper than intentionality, he finds the openness of Dasein to beings

6. *Speech and Phenomena*, trans. David B. Allison (Evanston: Northwestern University Press, 1973).

7. See Jacques Taminiaux, *Dialectic and Difference*, trans. Robert Crease and James T. Decker, (Atlantic Highlands, N.J.: Humanities Press, 1985), pp. 91–113.

inasmuch as they are, therefore to the Being of beings and more importantly to the Being of Dasein. Second, the metamorphosis of categorial intuition: if "Being" is not a *Bedeutung* among others, but the first *Bedeutung*, it follows that what is most profound in this discovery is the understanding of Being. Third, the metamorphosis of the sense of the *a priori*: for the same reason, if Being is the first *Bedeutung*, then the *a priori* cannot be limited to the noetic–noematic correlations that have their site in immanence in the Husserlian sense. What we face in the *a priori* is rather "a title for Being," a character of the "ontological structure of entities" (*History of the Concept of Time*, 74; 101–102). But these three transformed discoveries are intertwined, and an intuitionist inspiration inextricably welds them together, when Heidegger insists that intuition is "the way of access to the *a priori*," which is "in itself demonstrable in a simple intuition" (*in einer schlichten Anschauung an ihm selbst aufweisbar*) (ibid.). Even if we admit that these three metamorphoses mean in essence that Being is the phenomenon of phenomenology, we still have to determine to which *logos* (*Rede*), itself an intuitive seeing as previously indicated, this phenomenon corresponds. And because to *logos* in the proper sense (i.e., as *apophainesthai*) corresponds a voice (*phone, Stimme*), the question is to determine which "voice" is present in the *logos* involved in the seeing of the phenomenon of Being.

But now we ought to make a distinction that is not without relationship to the first *Logical Investigation*, nor to the teaching of Aristotle. We have already seen that Heidegger holds as essential Husserl's distinction between *Bedeutung* and sign, indication, and designation. We suggested that for him this distinction corroborates the Aristotelian distinction between the apophantic and the semantic. Now, if it is true that the primordial *Bedeutung* is Being and that Being offers itself for understanding to the being that we are, the theory of *Bedeutung* cannot have any other "root" than the ontology of Dasein, of the being who understands Being (*Being and Time*, 209–210; 166). We know that this ontology acquires its structural support from the distinction opposing authenticity to inauthenticity, existing for the sake of oneself to everyday existence. I have tried to show elsewhere that this distinction—ontological in Heidegger—draws its inspiration from the Aristotelian distinction between the comportment of *praxis* and the comportment of *poiesis*.[8] On closer inspection, this distinction is not without connection to the distinction between the apophantic and the semantic. For according to the *Nicomachean Ethics*, *praxis* is authentically itself only when it is concerned with its own manifestation, with its own radiance,

---

8. See Chapter 4 of this book: "The Reappropriation of the *Nicomachean Ethics*: *Poiesis* and *Praxis* in the Articulation of Fundamental Ontology."

when it aims at its own excellence, when, therefore, it is *hou heneka*. As such, it is fundamentally apophantic. *Poiesis,* on the other hand, is an activity which, instead of having its end within itself, has it outside of itself in a work, such that once in existence, it is nothing but a means to future ends (*pros ti* or *tinos*). As such, it is fundamentally semantic, and its telos, its work, unceasingly escapes it in such a way as to be inscribed in an endless cycle of references. This topic is treated in Section 17 of *Sein und Zeit,* "Reference and Signs."

This section focuses on the activity of *poiesis,* absorbed in the production and the manipulation of utensils in our everyday environment. It establishes that the sign is not at all a thing present–at–hand in front of us (*vorhanden*), which would maintain its status as a thing in its relationship of manifesting another thing. On the contrary, the sign is nothing but a particular case of ready–to–hand (*zuhanden*) and therefore the manifesting reference that characterizes it is founded upon a deeper reference, i.e., "usefulness for," which is the ontological characteristic of the ready–to–hand in general. Because this deeper reference (*um zu*; *pros ti* in the Aristotelian text) is constitutive of the *Zuhanden,* it is the ontological foundation of the sign, and "itself cannot be conceived as a sign" (114; 83). However, as opposed to other ready-to-hand beings, the sign has the privilege of highlighting and promoting a global overview of the surrounding world with which we are in daily intercourse, and to which our preoccupation, as well as *Umsicht* or circumspection animating it, are related. "Signs always indicate primarily 'wherein' one lives, where one's concern dwells, what sort of functionality is linked with the concern" (111 modified; 80). Thus we discover that functionality (*Bewandtnis*), which is a relation allowing us to be close to this (*bei*) by means of that (*mit*), ontologically characterizes the reference constitutive of the ready-to-hand in general. And every ready-to-hand is nothing but a moment in the totality of a functional contexture. But Section 18 indicates that the totality of these functional involvements "goes back ultimately to a "towards-which" in which there is no further involvement: this "towards-which" is not an entity having the kind of Being belonging to what is ready-to-hand within a world; rather, it is an entity whose Being is defined as Being-in-the-world, and to whose state-of-being worldhood itself belongs. This primary " "towards-which" (. . .) is a "for-the-sake-of-which" (*Worum-willen*). But the "for-the-sake-of" always pertains to the Being of *Dasein,* for which, in its Being, that very Being is essentially an *issue*" (116–17; 84). *Worumwillen* is the Heideggerian equivalent of the Aristotelian *hou heneka* of *praxis.*

But, in addition to its reappropriation of a crucial distinction of the *Nicomachean Ethics,* the analysis conducted in these two Sections (17 and

18 of *Sein und Zeit*) also reappropriates Husserl's distinction between sign, indication, and designation on the one hand, and *Bedeutung* (now displaced, of course, from its former location in consciousness) on the other hand, in a reappropriation which also incorporates Aristotle's distinction between the semantic and the apophantic. It is by virtue of *Worumwillen*, i.e., being-in-the-care-of-oneself, and in function of it alone, that there can be *Bedeutung* in the strict sense, as opposed to the references characteristic of signs and the ready-to-hand in general. More profound than the references in which everyday Dasein becomes absorbed and loses itself, there is the reference of Dasein to its can-be in the ownmost mode as opposed to its can-be in the inauthentic mode. Properly speaking, *Bedeutung* consists in the fact that Dasein "in a primordial manner . . . gives itself both its Being and its potentiality-for-Being as something which it is to understand with regard to its Being-in-the-world" (120 modified; 87). This self-giving of self-understanding is what originarily constitutes *Bedeutung*. For Dasein *Bedeutung* consists in giving itself to "be-deuten," that is, to "make clear" to itself its own Being, being for the sake of itself (*umwillen seiner*). On the basis of this originary self-giving clarity and in the wake of a sequence of steps that bring about a gradual distancing from primordial *umwillen* ("for-the-sake-of"), we can have a clarification of the characteristics of *Um-zu* ("in-order-to"), of *Da-zu* ("toward-which"), of *Wo-bei* ("next-to-which"), and of *Wo-mit* ("by-means-of-which"), in short of the contexture of functional relations familiar to the everyday comportment of Dasein, characterized by what Heidegger calls *Bedeutsamkeit,* significance. But this significance that propagates itself within the environment and animates the contexture or the totality of functional involvements, even though from the outset it is familiar to Dasein, is yet secondary to and derivative from the primordial "self-referential" *Bedeutung*. It is this primordial *umwillen seiner* which initially brings about clarity (*be-deutet*) and which, in the final analysis, alone "matters" (another meaning of the German word *bedeutet*).

Our question fundamentally is to determine whether and how, following the Husserl of the first *Logical Investigation* from which he accepts "the" essential distinction, Heidegger attributes an intuitive nature to this primordial *Bedeutung*. The fact that this *Bedeutung* is self-referential does not entail that it is intuitive. And in the first place, the very fact that this *Bedeutung* is ruled by *Verstehen,* by a type of understanding, seems to indicate that its nature is not intuitive, that it does not manifest itself to an originary intuition. Indeed, the analysis of *Verstehen* carried out in Section 31 of *Sein und Zeit,* which is implicitly announced in Section 18 (120–121; 87), claims that fundamental ontology "has deprived pure intuition (*dem puren Anschauen*) of its priority" (187 modified; 147). Could the praise of the doctrine of categorial intuition and, in particular, of the intuition dealing with Being be considered a perfidious or malign compliment? In no way. By rejecting the preeminence of *Anschauung,* Heidegger intends only to mark a distance from what, starting in Aristotle and still present in Husserl, used to correspond, as a noetic correlate, to the "ontological privilege of the *Vorhanden*" (ibid.). Whether it is inscribed in the Aristotelian *nous,* or in the Husserlian *Bewusstsein,* such an intuition would only correspond to a limited meaning of Being: *ousia* or *Vorhandenheit,* presence-at-hand. Such *Anschauung* cannot correspond to Being in the sense of the existence of Dasein. But it does not follow from this distancing that the Being for the sake of which Dasein is as it is, cannot be presented to a seeing. The project of an ontology of Dasein as phenomenology would collapse in its very concept—presented in the famous Section 7 of *Sein und Zeit*—if this Being were not capable of showing itself as a phenomenon and being offered to a seeing. To be sure, the substitution of *Verstehen,* understanding, for *Anschauung,* intuitive contemplation, entails that potentiality is prior to actuality: to understand is to project, to open oneself to one's can-be, and "as can-be, understanding has itself potentialities, which are sketched out beforehand within the range of what is essentially disclosable to it" (186 modified; 146). But if the preeminence of potentiality over actuality eliminates the traditional privilege of intuition (*Anschauung*), the privileged status of seeing remains. Heidegger writes:

> In its character of project, understanding goes to make up existentially what we call Dasein's 'seeing,' . . . a seeing which is directed upon Being as such, for the sake of which (*umwillen dessen*) Dasein is each time as it is. The sight which is related primarily to it and in totality to existence, we call *Durchsichtigkeit,* transparency" (186 modified; 146).

This mode of seeing, as such intuitive by nature, or this metamorphosized *Anschauung,* is at the core of the Heideggerian *Bedeutung,* considered in its deepest sense.

If the ontology of Dasein—the only being that understands Being—is not to become merely the construction of a philosopher and if—thanks to Husserl and beyond the letter of his teachings—it is to revive "the meaning of authentic philosophical empiricism" (see the first page of this appendix and *Being and Time,* 490; 50 note), then we must attribute to every Dasein, on the ontical level, the mode of seeing at the core of the originary *Bedeutung*—thanks to which the ownmost can-be is offered for understanding. Such an attribution is provided by the phenomenon of *Gewissen. Gewissen* means con-science (*cum-scientia*), knowledge of the Self within and with itself, intimate science [*science intime*].

A detailed analysis of Sections 54 to 60 of *Sein und Zeit* would take us beyond the limits of this essay. Let me confine myself to features that repeat and continue [*prolonge*] the first *Logical Investigation,* along the axes developed in *La voix et le phénomène,* which unfortunately I will be able to present here only in outline.

Jacques Derrida stresses that the status of ideality in Husserl is assigned to something that can be indefinitely *repeated.* Its ultimate form is the living present as self-presence of transcendental life. This self-presence derives from a fundamental difference, in their very parallelism, between the transcendental ego and the worldly ego, the latter proceeding from the former and—by means of the transcendental reduction—constantly capable of being freely converted into the former. The possibility of this transformation [*conversion*], that is to say the preservation of ideality and of every presence, depends on the privilege of the voice, the phenomenological voice, "this spiritual flesh which continues to speak and to present itself to the self—*to hear itself*—in the absence of the world" (16; 15–16). This silent and solitary voice, which has nothing to do with signs, indications, and expression and even monologue, is the pure appearing of ideality in the indivisibility of the *Augenblick,* the blink of an eye, the instant.

If, as we have shown, up to this point the ontology of Dasein considers as essential and reappropriates the teaching of the first *Logical Investigation,* it would not be surprising if the same axes discovered in Husserl's text by Derrida could be found also in Heidegger's text. We might even suspect that they will resurface at the very moment when the analytic describes the attestation within Dasein of its ownmost ontological understanding, i.e., the attestation of the categorial intuition given priority and metamorphosized by Heidegger: the intuition of the *Bedeutung* "Being." This attestation is *Gewissen.* Can the axes only sketched above be detected in Heidegger's analysis of conscience?

To be sure, what is at stake at the core of the analytic of Dasein is no longer the possibility of an unlimited repetition of idealities in general. What is at stake, instead, is the possibility of the repetition of Being inasmuch as Being is nothing real, or is no being. More precisely, what is at stake is the possibility of a repetition of Being in the ownmost sense, as opposed to Being in an inauthentic and derivative sense, the latter being the fall of the former. *Gewissen* ensures the possibility of such a repetition and does so endlessly. Furthermore *Gewissen* validates this repetition in the pure element of *solus ipse,* i.e., the Self-sameness of Dasein. But this Self, as ownmost can-be, is nothing but a "modification" (Section 54) of the "they." The repetition, therefore, is supported both by a strict parallelism between the "they" of the everyday and public world and Dasein's ownmost can-be, and by a radical difference opposing the two. The free conversion between the first and the second is a possibility shown or attested by *Gewissen,* in that it ensures for each Dasein the possibility of the reduction in the new Heideggerian sense, where phenomenological seeing is converted into the vision of the project constituting the understanding of Being. The possibility of this reduction requires that a privilege be given to the voice that animates *Gewissen*. The voice of *Gewissen* is the ultimate essence of discourse, for the same reasons that constituted the privilege of the voice in the first *Logical Investigation*: solitude, silence, presence to self, pure appearing. In addition, the privilege of the voice is here reinforced because, in each of these reasons, we are dealing only with the ownmost can-be and no longer with cognitive idealities in general, or with noetic-noematic relations. Not only does the call of *Gewissen*, as the fundamental mode of discourse, go beyond all communication, all expression, and finally all monologue, but also it concerns in its very structure nothing but the *Self*: it is from the Self that the call emanates, it calls Dasein to face its own Self, it summons it silently but exclusively to its ownmost potentiality-for-Being, and the call presents Dasein with nothing else for it to hear (Section 56). At this juncture, we find the most intimate connection between phenomenon and *logos*, because what this voice gives for hearing, it also presents to a seeing. The call does nothing but open and disclose; it is through and through *Erschliessung*, disclosing (ibid.).

Finally, let us consider the privilege of the instant. Of course, it can be more appropriately said of Heidegger's phenomenology of ec-static temporalization than of the Husserlian descriptions of the internal consciousness of time, that in it "we recognize an irreducible non-presence as having a constituting value, and with it . . . an insuperable non-primordiality" (6–7; 5).[9] Ec-static temporality undermines the privilege of the present to the extent that it is essentially oriented [*déportée*] towards the retrieval of a past in the self-anticipation of a future that will never be present since it is the very death of the temporalizing individual. It is, then, all the more paradoxical to witness the reemergence—in the midst of the description of this movement, which one is inevitably tempted to call "*differance*" for a variety of reasons—of an unexpected theme: the "peak of the instant," the indivisibility of the *Augenblick*, the "blink of an eye" which, as Derrida shows, provides Husserl with the means of an originary intuition, i.e., of the "absence and uselessness of signs," therefore of "non-signification as the 'principle of principles' " (60; 66). We know from Section 60 of *Sein und Zeit* that the intimate science of *Gewissen* confirms within Dasein itself a primordial openness and truth that is resoluteness. But resoluteness is disclosing only in the "moment of vision" (*Augen-blick*) thanks to which Dasein takes upon itself its ownmost can-be (see p. 338).

---

9. *Speech and Phenomena*, trans. Allison.

It is not immediately apparent that the entire constellation of topics that determine metaphysics (e.g., totalization, foundation, mastery) should gravitate around this "moment of vision," because it seems to concern first of all the individual only. In fact, however, the moment of vision is the ultimate focus on which fundamental ontology, as the science of the manifold meanings of Being, relies. In this moment of vision, at the time of *Sein und Zeit* Heidegger seeks the key to the entire deconstructed history of metaphysics. This is why the introduction to the last Marburg lecture course, which is the first to stress that "philosophy can be characterized only from and in historical recollection" adds immediately afterwards that "this recollection (*Erinnerung*) is only what it is, is only living in the self-understanding taking place in the moment of vision" (*im augenblicklischen Sichselbstverstehen*) (*Gesamtausgabe*, Bd. 26, p. 9).

In its principle, therefore, fundamental ontology privileges reduction over deconstruction. Its deconstruction is not exposed to an outside, to a "differance," to a semantic dispersion. The age-old texts that it scrutinizes are in no way undecipherable and enigmatic, and like the Hegelian path of *Erinnerung*, they merely lead us back to the apophantic certainty of self-presence.

2

Kant's Thesis on Being and the Phenomenology of Perception[1]

For a long time, Heidegger's commentators noticed and deplored the absence of a phenomenology of perception in *Sein und Zeit*, which is a work nevertheless insistently phenomenological. For example, in his preface to *La structure du comportement*,[2] Alphonse De Waelhens suggested that Merleau-Ponty's work was filling a lacuna in the problematic of *Sein und Zeit*, by bringing the analysis of Being-in-the-world into the primary field of perception neglected by Heidegger.

The publication of the lecture courses given by Heidegger at Marburg, particularly *The Basic Problems of Phenomenology*[3] (a course given shortly after the publication of *Sein und Zeit*), has occasioned a reappraisal of this criticism. These lectures, in fact, develop what is truly a phenomenology of perception and therefore prove that the problem was never neglected by Heidegger. However, the essence which they assign to perception is such that it cannot truly manifest Being-in-the-world. In other words, these lectures suggest that, at the period of *Sein und Zeit*, the Heideggerian concept of perception was such that it could not have the value of a primordial experience, but only of a derivative and narrowing experience of Being-in-the-world. They suggest therefore that the analysis of Being-in-the-world could not grant any privilege to perception.

---

1. This essay was first published in French in *Etudes d'anthropologie philoso-phique* (Louvain-la-neuve, 1984), pp. 221–263.

2. *La structure du comportement* (Paris: Presses Universitaires de France, 1947), *The Structure of Behavior* (trans. Alden Fisher, Boston: Beacon Press, 1963).

3. *The Basic Problems of Phenomenology*, trans. Albert Hofstadter (Bloomington: Indiana University Press, 1982). We will continue to indicate first the page number of the English translation, then the page number of the German original.

In this essay, we shall first present Heidegger's concept of perception, then we shall attempt to explore its presuppositions, and finally, we would like to consider its subsequent evolution in Heidegger's itinerary.

I

Let us first consider the analysis of perception developed in *The Basic Problems of Phenomenology*. It is inscribed within the framework of a "phenomenologico-critical" discussion of several traditional theses on Being. The first thesis to be considered is Kant's: "Being is not a real predicate." The examination of this thesis leads Heidegger to propose his phenomenology of perception. Let us follow his examination in order to shed light on his phenomenology of perception.

After recalling that the Kantian thesis was articulated for the first time in the precritical essay, *Of the Unique Possible Foundation for a Demonstration of the Existence of God,* and then repeated in the *Critique of Pure Reason* in the section on the Transcendental Dialectic entitled "Of the Impossibility of an Ontological Proof of the Existence of God," Heidegger makes a remark on terminology. It is immediately clear that this remark introduces the phenomenological dimension of his inquiry into the meaning of the thesis:

Kant is speaking of the proof of the *existence of God*. He speaks similarly of the *existence of things* outside us, of the *existence of nature*. This concept of existence, Dasein, corresponds in Kant to the Scholastic term *existentia*. Kant therefore often uses the expression 'Existenz,' 'actuality' *(Wirklichkeit)*, instead of 'Dasein.' In contrast, our own terminological usage is a different one, which, as will appear, is grounded in the nature of the case. For what Kant calls existence, using either *Dasein* or *Existenz,* and what Scholasticism calls *existentia*, we employ the terms *Vorhandensein*, 'being extant,' 'being-at-hand,' or *Vorhandenheit*, 'extantness.' These are all names for the way of being of natural things in the broadest sense. As our course proceeds, the choice of these expressions must itself be validated on the basis of the specific sense of this way of being—a way of being that demands these expressions: things, extant, extantness, being-at-hand. In his terminology Husserl follows Kant and thus utilizes the concept of existence, *Dasein,* in the sense of being extant. For us, in contrast, the word 'Dasein' does not designate as it does for Kant, the mode of being of natural things. It does not designate a way of being at all, but rather a specific being which we ourselves are, the *human Dasein.* We are at every moment a Dasein. This being, the Dasein, like every other being, has a specific way of being. To this way of the Dasein's being we assign the term '*Existenz,*' 'existence;' and it should be noted here that existence or the expression 'the Dasein exists' is not the sole determination of the mode of being belonging to us. We shall become acquainted with a threefold determination of this kind, which of course is rooted in a specific sense in existence. (28; 36–37)

It is clear that this lengthy terminological comment expresses much more than a lexical convention. In the same fashion as *Sein und Zeit,* it suggests that because the Kantian understanding of Being operates only at the level of *Vorhandenheit,* i.e., of the mode of being of the things of nature, it is to some extent blind to the existential mode of Being of the being that we are, and therefore reveals itself as not founded in the things themselves. This passage also announces that it is on the basis of a "threefold determination" of the mode of being unique to us, i.e., existence—a phrase that immediately calls to mind the threefold dimension of the ecstases of temporality—that we should clarify phenomenologically the meaning of what Kant calls indiscriminately *Dasein, Existenz, Wirklichkeit,* and call into question the privilege that he uncritically bestows upon it. Finally the passage quoted indicates that this "phenomenologico-critical" clarification will distinguish its approach from that of Husserlian phenomenology which, like Kant, construes Being as *Vorhandenheit.* The Introduction to *The Basic Problems* had already outlined with clarity in each of its propositions the need for such a demarcation, especially when it stressed that phenomenological reduction in the Heideggerian sense is in fact quite different from the Husserlian reduction:

For Husserl, phenomenological reduction, which he worked out for the first time expressly in the *Ideas toward a Pure Phenomenology and Phenomenological Philosophy* (1913), is the method of leading phenomenological vision from the natural attitude of the human being whose life is involved in the world of things and persons back to the transcendental life of consciousness and its noetic-noematic experiences, in which objects are constituted as correlates of consciousness. *For us,* phenomenological reduction means leading phenomenological vision back from the apprehension of a being, whatever might be the character of that apprehension, to the understanding of the being of this being (projecting upon the way it is unconcealed). (21; 29)

But do these lines have any sort of connection whatsoever with perception? We shall see that they do because the analysis of Kant's thesis will demonstrate that perception is inscribed at the core of Kant's understanding of Being in the sense of what Heidegger calls *Vorhandenheit*.

Kant's thesis presents itself as a negative judgment: Being or existence is no real predicate. It dissociates Being or existence from reality. An understanding of the thesis in its negative formulation requires therefore a clearer specification of the Kantian concept of reality. Contrary to current usage, reality in the Kantian sense is not actual existence, but thingliness, *re*-ality (*Sachheit*),[4] the tenor of the thing, the totality of determinations or predicates that give a *res* its character of whatness (*Wasgehalt*), or quiddity (*Quid*). It is from this characteristic that existence is distinguished. In their thingliness, a hundred possible thalers are identical to a hundred existing ones: in both cases the tenor of the concept is the same. And to say that a thing exists is not to add any predicate to those that determine its thingliness; existence does not augment the tenor of the concept of the thing. Of course, we use the word "is" to attribute to a thing those predicates that determine its reality, but this "is" in the sense of the copula must be clearly distinguished from the "is" by which one expresses that a thing exists. In the first case, we only link a subject to its predicates without asking the question of whether such an entity exists, as when we say that bodies are extended, whether or not actual bodies exist. It does not follow however that Being in the sense of the copula is any more a real predicate than Being in the sense of the judgment of existence. Being in the sense of the copula does nothing but posit the relation of a predicate to a subject and this "simple position" is not itself a predicate of the subject, it adds nothing to the reality (i.e., thingliness) of the subject. Being in the sense of the copula is called "simple position" because it is limited to positing the relationship of a property or characteristic to a thing: A is B or C. These properties or characteristics alone can be called real predicates.

But granted that Being cannot be a real predicate (either in the sense of the copula, or in the sense of a judgement of existence), what then is existence—in positive terms—according to the Kantian interpretation? The differentiation established by Kant between the judgment of existence (A is) and the predicative synthesis (A is B) offers a first positive clue for answer-

---

4. We shall follow Hofstadter's spelling and typography for the term "reality." Because our everyday understanding of this term must be clarified phenomenologically, the French text often uses new coinages such as "*ré-ité*" (sometimes corresponding to Hofstadter's "thingliness") for the substantive and "*ré-al*" for the adjective. It would be possible, although ultimately confusing, to italicize the Latin stem *re-* in such compounds. (Trans.)

ing the question. Whereas the predicative synthesis unites a real [*réal*] predicate to a subject, the judgment of existence (A exists), synthetically connect this concept to an object, that is to say to an actually existing thing, which henceforth is *posited absolutely,* without adding anything to the concept, to the *realitas* of A. *Existence is tantamount to absolute position:* such is the first positive determination of Kant's thesis. Such an absolute position posits a relation of the actually existing object to its concept, and to the entire *realitas* expressed by the concept. The clarification of the Kantian concept of Being or existence thus reveals that Being equals position, and existence equals absolute position. Is this clarification satisfactory? Kant notes in the *Beweisgrund* that "this concept [existence, being] is so simple that nothing can be said in explication of it, except to take careful note that it must not be confused with the relationships things have with their distinctive marks" (Kant, *Beweisgrund,* pp. 77–78, quoted in *The Basic Problems,* 42; 57). This seems to suggest, Heidegger remarks, that the concept of Being is directly accessible to an extremely simple understanding. But it is precisely this understanding that must be broadened by investigating Kant's explanation: Being equals position. This is the task undertaken by the phenomenological analysis of the Kantian thesis.

We have just seen that in the absolute position expressed in the judgment of existence, "the object of the concept, the actual being corresponding to it, is put into relation, as actual, to the concept that is merely thought. Existence consequently expresses a relationship of the object to the cognitive faculty" (45; 61). In order to investigate Kant's explanation (Being equals position) we must clarify this relationship. Kant himself contributes to this clarification. Discussing "the postulates of empirical thought in general," he asserts "that the categories of modality [possibility, existence, necessity] have the peculiarity that, in determining an object, they do not in the least enlarge the concept to which they are attached as predicates. They only express the relationship [of the object] to the faculty of knowledge" (*Critique of Pure Reason,* B 266). Possibility expresses the relationship of the *realitas* to pure thought. Necessity expresses the relationship of the object to reason inasmuch as the latter is applied to experience. As for actuality, i.e., existence, it expresses the relationship to the empirical exercise of understanding or to what Kant also calls "the empirical faculty of judging." It is at this juncture that perception comes to the forefront. Kant characterizes this relationship to the empirical faculty of judging as follows: Existence, or actuality, only concerns "the question whether such a thing [as we can think it solely concerning its possibility] is given to us in such a way that the perception of it can possibly precede the concept" (B 272–273). More precisely, "the perception . . . which supplies the material to the concept, is the sole character of actuality" (B 273). It is thus perception that explains the specific character of what Kant calls *absolute position*. Perception is an operation of the faculty of knowledge or of cognitive subjectivity. It follows that the categories, or predicates, of modality add nothing at all synthetically to the *realitas* of the thing, and that they are something "merely subjective"; they "add to the concept of thing (of something real) . . . the faculty of knowledge" (B 273). To grasp a thing as existing is to add or attach *perception* to it. Such is the second—positive—determination of the Kantian thesis on Being.

In short, this thesis says: Existence equals absolute position, absolute position equals perception. The Heideggerian question aims at determining whether such a return to perception is sufficient to clarify the concept of existence. The response to this question requires a phenomenological articulation of perception. It is noteworthy that this phenomenological approach at the same time denounces the obscurity of the Kantian thesis and credits it with moving in "the right direction."

Indeed, the Kantian thesis is unclear. When Kant makes the following equation, existence = position = perception, we can easily object that understood as an existing comportment of an existing "I," perception could not be "existence" but could only be something existing; and that, understood as what is perceived, perception still cannot be identified with "existence," since in this case too it could only be something existing. In both cases, the Kantian thesis would mean that "existence" is something existing, i.e., a being, a *Reales*. In both cases the positive character of the thesis would contradict the negative one: Existence is nothing real which, reformulated in Heideggerian language, becomes: Being is no being. But let us adopt the most favorable reading of Kant's thesis. Let us suppose that by perception Kant understood neither the perceiving nor the perceived but the being-perceived (*Wahrgenommensein*) or perceivedness (*Wahrgenommenheit*). There is now no less obscurity than before. Can we say that the perceivedness of a being constitutes its "existence"? Can we say that something, this window for example, exists by virtue of a perception? Manifestly, the window does not gain existence "from the fact that I perceive it, but instead I can perceive it only if it exists and *because* it exists" (*Basic Problems*, 49; 66). Not only does perceivedness presuppose perceptibility but it requires and presupposes "the existence of the perceptible or perceived being." Perceivedness, or the uncoveredness of a being (*Entdecktheit*), cannot be identified with the existence of this being, or if we use Heideggerian terminology, with the *Vorhandenheit* of the *Vorhandenes*. Not only does the Kantian interpretation of existence as position = perception remain obscure in all these cases, but also taken in its most favorable sense, it remains questionable (*fragwürdig*) (49; 67).

However, Heidegger insists that in spite of this obscurity and of the problems that it entails, the Kantian attempt to clarify the meaning of existence moves in the "right direction" (49; 67). Taking the same route traced by Kant, and proceeding further, Heidegger proposes a positive elucidation of the concepts of existence and Being. As we just mentioned, perceivedness, or the discoveredness of beings, cannot be identified with the existence or the *Vorhandenheit* of these beings. In other words, since Kant says that perception = position, the positedness (*Gesetzheit*) of beings does not coincide with the Being of these beings. But the question is precisely to determine whether it was mere accident or whim (*Laune*) that led Kant (in the attempt to clarify Being, *Dasein*, actuality, existence) back to position (*Setzung*) and to perception.

If we succeed, therefore, in adequately elucidating the uncovering of things existent, perception, absolute position in all their essential structures, then it must also be possible to meet at least with existence, extantness and the like along the way. The question arises, How can we attain an adequate determination of the phenomena of perception and position, which Kant draws on for the clarification of actuality and existence? (50; 68)

Manifestly, this goal can only be achieved by overcoming the ambiguity and obscurity affecting the phenomena of perception and of position in Kant, and by revealing these phenomena for what they are. We will therefore have to turn our attention to what makes them possible, that is, to "what determines them as comportments of the being to whom they belong" (50; 69). To penetrate still further along the path already opened by Kant (in the right direction) it is first necessary to clarify these comportments.

It is at this juncture that Heidegger offers his own phenomenology of perception. His approach is to unfold the ontological constitution of perception as a comportment of the being that we are. Addressing the issue in a very Husserlian manner (in that it echoes Husserl's opposition to psychologism, but now directs the stakes of the endeavor toward the question of Being), Heidegger begins by rejecting as null and void the claim that psychology, as the inductive science of psychical facts, can be of any assistance in our endeavor. In the sciences, nature, whether physical or psychical, only answers questions that are put to it by the scientist. To be sure, the manner of asking questions can be changed, but any empirical research as such limits itself to confirming the fundamental *Fragestellung* which governs its movement. The fundamental *Fragestellung* and its way of thematizing beings cannot be grounded by any positive research. Because every empirical science is nothing but the science of a determined region of beings, it is in need of a preliminary delimitation of the ontological constitution of the beings it takes as its topic. Now this *Seinsverfassung* is not accessible to scientific research because it is itself not a being and thus requires an approach fundamentally different from the empirical one which is focused entirely on actual beings. Such an apprehension can only be found in philosophy, which is the science *not of beings, but of the ontological constitution of beings.* With regard to the ontological understanding to which it is implicitly committed, the empirical approach lives in a dreamlike state. And precisely because it presupposes the ontological constitution of beings only implicitly, it is by nature incapable of apprehending it in a concept. Because psychology needs the assistance of philosophy, it will not be able to fill in the gaps remaining in Kant's interpretation of existence as perception. It is not because the psychology of his century was a less exact science that Kant offers a concept of perception that remains ambiguous and obscure, but because his *a priori* foundation of perception is deficient (See *The Basic Problems,* Section 9, 49–55; 67–76). His flaw is an ontological one, not an empirical one.

Ultimately, Heidegger assigns to the *ontology of Dasein* the task of providing this *a priori* foundation and thereby of revealing the ontological constitution and the phenomenological essence of perception. The analysis of perception found in the *Basic Problems* aims at providing a first access to this ontology, which is also developed in *Sein und Zeit,* by stressing the very indeterminacy of Kant's thesis.

Taken in its negative dimension, Kant's thesis is unassailable: it means that Being is no being. Taken in its positive dimension, it remains indeterminate: by interpreting Being as absolute position, and absolute position as perception, it leaves the very concept of perception indeterminate. Does perception mean perceiving, the perceived, or perceivedness? Kant gives no clear answer, although he suggests that these three meanings belong in a unified way to perception. What thus remains unclear is "nothing less than the *constitution of the Being of perception in general,* that is, its ontological nature, and similarly, the *constitution of the Being of position*" (56; 77). Kant himself eliminates some of the obscurity when he suggests that the three meanings are associated in a primordial belonging-together. Heidegger writes:

> Possibly what is intended, which is separated into the three meanings, belongs originally to the unitary structure of what we have to understand as perception . . . This is in fact the case. What we concisely call perception is, more explicitly formulated, the perceptual *directing of oneself toward* what is perceived, in such a way indeed that the perceived is itself always understood as perceived in its perceivedness. (57; 79)

The Heideggerian phenomenology of perception investigates the specificity of this movement of *directing oneself toward,* characterized as it is by these three factors in their mutual belonging. When he speaks of perception as a "subjective synthesis" by means of which the thing is related to the faculty of knowledge, in his own way Kant expresses that perceiving is directed toward the perceived. This synthesis must now be considered. Heidegger reminds us that Husserl calls it "intentionality," a term used by the Scholastics to refer only to a voluntary activity and by Brentano to refer to all mental experiences, inasmuch as each of them has a specific way of directing itself toward something. Intentionality in the specific case of perception is what the *Basic Problems* attempt to elucidate, in the wake of Husserl's thought, but ultimately by going beyond his teaching.

As a characteristic of perception, intentionality means first that perception is perceiving-of, an *intendere,* an *intentio.* To any *intentio,* as relation-to, or orientation-toward, belongs a specific *Wozu* or *Worauf,* a specific *intentum.* The specific unity of these two moments (the *intentio* and the *intentum*) is what constitutes the structure and the intentionality specific to a particular mode of comportment. To elucidate perception is to elucidate its specific intentional structure. Heidegger warns us that such an elucidation is a difficult task: it can only be carried out successfully if we can demonstrate not only how this structure appears within the specific comportment of perception, but also *"how it is grounded ontologically in the basic constitution of Dasein"* (82). And such a task can be carried out only by being on our guard against the prejudices that "contemporary philosophy heaps upon intentionality," and against the ones—the most dangerous, the most insistent, and the most stubborn—arising from "the natural apprehension and interpretation of things by the Dasein's everyday 'good sense' " (59; 82).

Heidegger begins by denouncing one of these misunderstandings which are grounded "in the naive, natural view of things" (59; 82–83). According to the natural view, the relation of the perceiving *intentio* to the perceived *intentum* is the relation between a being, the extant thing over there, and an extant being here, the person who perceives: it is the relation between an object present-at-hand and a subject also present-at-hand. In other words, it is a relation, which is present-at-hand (*vorhanden*), between two terms present-at-hand (two *Vorhandene*) and which is present as long as both terms of the relation are present. For this natural conception, the intentional relation is something that happens to the "subject" because of the sheer presence-at-hand (*Vorhandensein*) of the object, and happens to the "object" because of the sheer presence-at-hand of the subject. This view reduces the "subject" to a being which is in itself devoid of intentionality and reduces intentionality to a merely sporadic occurrence depending exclusively on the presence of objects. This view then fails to recognize that the entity it calls the "subject" is, from the outset or *a priori*, constitutionally relational and that it exists in the mode of a relation-to, a being-directed-towards.

But it is no less confusing to assign to the subject itself the relational character, the orientation-towards, in short intentionality, if such an assignment ends up enclosing the subject within a "subjective sphere" whose "immanence," along with its components of "intentional lived experiences," is conceived in the wake of the Cartesian legacy as what alone is certain and indubitable.

> In themselves, it is said, intentional experiences as belonging to the subjective sphere relate only to what is immanent within this sphere. Perceptions as psychical direct themselves toward sensations, representational images, memory residues, and determinations which the thinking that is likewise immanent to the subject adds to what is first given subjectively. (62; 87)

This interpretation of intentionality does not explain at all how the beneficiary of immanence—the subject, the "I"—can relate to a transcendent world and transcend its own sphere, and what such a transcendence consists in. Heidegger points out that this second way of interpreting intentionality is widely accepted in phenomenological circles and among realist philosophers such as Nicolai Hartmann. As in the first misinterpretation of intentionality, "we close our eyes to the phenomena and do not give an account of them" (62; 86). The first conception was blind to the *intentio*, the second one is blind to the *intentum*. Because of its theoretical preconceptions, it closes its eyes to the phenomena or refuses to grant them the right to speak for themselves. Indeed, if one considers "natural perception without any theory, without any preconceived opinion about the relationship of subject to object and other such matters, and . . . interrogates this concrete perception in which we live, say, the perception of the window in this classroom" (63; 88), one must acknowledge that "to say that 'I am in the first place oriented toward sensations' is all just pure theory. In conformity with its sense of direction, perception focuses upon a being that is extant. It intends this being precisely as extant and knows nothing at all about the sensations it apprehends" (63 modified; 89). Therefore the question as to how an internal intentional experience reaches to the outside is thoroughly fallacious and "perverted." Such a line of questioning is pointless because the intentional comportment is related not to something subjective, or a representation, but to some present-at-hand entity (*Vorhandenes*). There is no need to ask how the so-called subjective sphere is transcended, how "the immanent intentional experience acquires transcendent validity; rather, what has to be seen is that it is precisely intentionality and nothing else in which *transcendence* consists'' (63; 89). But because the usual theory of intentionality fails to recognize the *intentum* of perception, and because it turns it into a subjective state instead of seeing it as something *vorhanden,* this theory also fails to grasp the *intentio.* It is led to subjectivize the *intentio* unduly. Hence we must admit that the intentional comportments themselves entail transcendence and the movement of transcending, and, consequently, we must abandon as pure construction—bound "to continually give occasion for further constructions"—the usual distinction (made by Husserl, as we know) between a subjective sphere of immanence and an objective sphere of transcendence: "From now on," Heidegger writes, "we cannot speak of a subject, of a subjective sphere, but we understand the being to which the intentional comportments belong as Dasein," i.e., as a being whose mode of being is existence and not *Vorhandenheit,* and which, precisely because it exists, has intentional comportments. This means that the mode of being of the being that we are is "essentially such that this being, so far as it is, is always already dwelling with the extant, the *Vorhanden"* (64; 90), and has always comported itself toward it. Understood as a comportment of Dasein, the intentionality of perception is therefore the movement by which the existing being that we are is directed toward beings that are *vorhanden,* or present-at-hand.

But in order to do justice to the totality of the phenomenon of perception, this phenomenology must also take into consideration what the analysis of the Kantian thesis calls "the perceivedness of the perceived." Obviously, this perceivedness concerns the *intentum* towards which the perceiving *intentio* orients itself. Let us consider the thing that I perceive right now. "In perceiving I am directed toward the window there as this particular functional thing" (68; 95). We quickly realize that such an example aims at distinguishing between perception in the narrow sense and a broader view, of a different kind, from which the former is extracted and contracted. For this broader view, the window is a piece of equipment marked by an instrumental characteristic *(Bewandtnis)* and endowed with properties linked to its specific function. "We can cover over the *instrumental* characteristics that in the first instance confront us in our natural commerce with such a thing as a window, constituting its utilitarian character, and consider the window merely as an extant *(vorhanden)* thing," as "pure natural thing" (68; 96) with properties such as hardness, weight, extendedness. This apprehension of natural things, having properties, is perception in the narrow sense, which covers up another, broader and more immediate type of seeing, called "circumspective foresight" in *Sein und Zeit.* But concerning the topic of perceivedness, the distinction between the two modes of seeing is not crucial. Whether seeing things consists in apprehending in them characteristics that constitute them as equipment and thus in understanding their *equipmental character,* or consists in apprehending in them purely material properties (after narrowing or covering up this first seeing), and thus in understanding their *thingliness,* in neither case is perceivedness among the apprehended determinations. Perceivedness is not among the characteristics that belong either to the equipmental character or to the thingly character of the thing. Perceivedness is not a "real predicate." It is not given-before-the-hand as the other characteristics. It is nothing *vorhanden* in the *Vorhanden,* it is nothing objective within the object. Can we say then that it is something subjective within the subject? This would amount to reintroducing the distinction between the spheres of immanence and transcendence, a distinction which (as we have seen) fails to reveal the phenomenon.

It is without a concern for the distinction between immanence and transcendence, loaded as it is with preconceptions, that we must approach the problem at issue: How does perceivedness somehow belong to the perceived without being in itself something present-at-hand and how, similarly, does it belong to Dasein without being something subjective? In other words, the issue is to determine how perceivedness concerns intentionality itself. It concerns both the intentional comportment (which consists in perceiving) and the perceived towards which such a comportment directs itself. The perceiving comportment consists in uncovering *(Entdecken)* what is given-before-the-hand, what is present-at-hand or extant. Its intentional movement of transcending is this very uncovering. Uncovering is the intentional sense of perceiving. Uncovering means removing from that towards which the comportment is directed what covers it up; it means allowing what comes before-the-hand to emerge into the open and thus offer itself to discovery in a condition of uncoveredness *(Entdecktheit).* "The mode of uncovering and the mode of uncoveredness of the extant obviously must be determined by the entity to be discovered by them and by its way of being" (70; 99). But how can such a determination, such a regulation by the being to be discovered, be possible if from the outset the perceiving *intentio* did not understand *Vorhandenheit,* extantness? At the heart of perceiving intentionality, i.e., at the heart of (and deeper than) the uncovering comportment of perceiving, there is the understanding of what it means to be given-before-the-hand. Such an understanding is open to *Vorhandenheit,* it is the capacity of remaining open to it, of being its *Erschlossenheit,* its disclosedness.

Understanding, or disclosedness of Vorhandenheit, is the *a priori* of any intentional comportment which, as uncovering comportment of perceiving, orients itself toward something *vorhandenes.* For an extant entity to be discoverable and perceptible, it is a requirement that *Vorhandenheit* should have manifested itself *a priori,* should have showed itself beforehand in a state of openness, offered to the understanding of the one who perceives. Such an understanding belongs to the perceiving comportment, that is, to the existence of Dasein. Because this understanding is always presupposed in any perceiving comportment, in any perceiving intentionality, we must say that "not only do *intentio* and *intentum* belong to the intentionality of perception but also does *the understanding of the mode of being of what is intended in the intentum*" (71; 101). Granted that perceivedness means the uncoveredness (*Entdecktheit*) of extant beings, we must admit that this perceivedness is made possible by the disclosedness of the Being of extant beings. "Not only does its uncoveredness—that it is uncovered—belong to the entity which is perceived in perception, but also the being-understood, that is, the disclosedness of that uncovered entity's mode of being." And Heidegger continues: "We therefore distinguish not only terminologically, but also for reasons of intrinsic content between the *uncoveredness* of a being and the *disclosedness of its Being*" (72; 102). This distinction, this difference between the uncoveredness of beings (their perceivedness) and the disclosedness of their Being, this difference between uncovered and uncoverable beings and their always already disclosed and unconcealed Being, this difference between beings and Being is the *ontological difference*. Hence the ontological difference is at the core of perceiving intentionality and regulates it.

We have seen above that the Kantian thesis contained an unquestionable negation (Being is no real predicate, in other words it is no being) and an obscure and indeterminate affirmation (Being is position or perception). We are now in the position to see how the phenomenological reappropriation of this thesis makes it possible—in the process of clarifying what the thesis states—to elucidate by the same token the link between the negative part and the positive one. Perception itself testifies that Being is no being because its uncovering orientation toward extant (*vorhanden*) beings and the display of their uncoveredness always presupposes the disclosedness of the Being of these beings, that is, the disclosedness of their *Vorhandenheit*, while this Being (*Vorhandensein*) itself is never a given being, never anything *vorhanden*.

II

In the previous section, we explored the phenomenological essence of perception. In this section, I would like to investigate its presuppositions. By presupposition, I mean what perception, according to Heidegger himself, presupposes as an uncovering comportment oriented toward something *vorhanden* in the light of its unveiled *Vorhandenheit*. This uncovering comportment presupposes nothing less than the constitution of Being (the ontological constitution) of the entity that we are ourselves, of Dasein. It is this constitution of Being that founds such a comportment. The phenomenological essence of perception would remain truncated and insufficiently elucidated if this comportment were not brought into relationship with the ontological constitution of Dasein. In spite of its condensed form, the analysis conducted so far gives us an important indication concerning the specificity of this relationship. For the analysis has stressed several times that perception, in the restricted and narrow sense of the simple consideration of what is given-before-the-hand, is secondary to and derivative of a broader seeing, which is never called "perception" by Heidegger, but which nevertheless is thoroughly a phenomenon of seeing. Understanding the relationship of perception, in the narrow and strict sense, to the ontological constitution of Dasein, amounts first to understanding that the comportment of seeing in the strict and narrow sense is derivative of a broader comportment of seeing. Heidegger demonstrates this relationship of subordination sometimes directly by describing our comportment or indirectly by deconstructing concepts inherited from the tradition. These two directions of investigation cannot be dissociated, for, in its attempt to uncover the forgotten origin of the traditional concepts, deconstruction constantly relies on the direct description of the comportment of Dasein. At the same time the description constantly carries on a dialogue with the tradition, either in order to find support in it, or to refute it. Let us examine how both axes in conjunction allow Heidegger to clarify the derivative character of perception in the narrow and strict sense as in relationship to a broader and more primordial comportment of seeing.

We need hardly recall that the Kantian thesis about Being has a negative component (Being is not a real predicate) and a positive one (Being = position = perception). Since *realitas* in the Kantian sense denotes precisely what the Middle Ages called *essentia,* the Kantian position refers back to the medieval distinction between *essentia* and *existentia* and invites us to question its origin. Medieval ontology maintains that both *essentia* and *existentia* are required as belonging to the constitution of the Being of all beings. This thesis has its roots in Aristotle. Questioning its origin amounts to exposing the hermeneutic horizon within which *existentia* and *essentia* were first apprehended. In the Middle Ages, *existentia* was also called *actualitas,* a word translated by Kant as *Wirklichkeit. Actualitas* refers back to the Greek *energeia.* Attention to the Latin or Greek words reveals that actuality refers to a way of being active, of acting (*Handeln*). In other words, it indicates that the extant being (what Heidegger calls *Vorhandenes*) "is somewhat referred by its sense to something for which, as it were, it *comes to be before the hand,* at hand, to be handled (*ein Handliches*)" (101; 143). This 'something' is obviously the being that we are,

Dasein, considered as an active being, "more precisely as creating and producing (*schaffendes, herstellendes*)." We can demonstrate that this reference is not based on terminology alone by showing that the concept of *essentia* (*ousia*)—considered within a constellation of associated notions in early Greek thought—refers to the productive behavior and thus shapes the primordial, albeit unformulated, horizon of the Greek understanding of the Being of beings. It is from within this horizon that it becomes possible to clarify the secondary, or derivative, character of perception in the strict and narrow sense of intuition of something *vorhanden*.

At the beginning of his genealogical study, Heidegger is careful to stress that two of the concepts used by the Greeks to characterize *ousia*, i.e., the concept of *morphe*, translated in Latin as *forma*, and in German as *Gestalt* or *Gepräge* (imprint), and the concept of *eidos*, which must be translated, he says, by aspect or look (*Aussehen*), have a relationship inverse to what they had in Greek ontology whenever they are considered as applying to perception in the narrow sense. For us, *eidos* depends on *morphe*, for the Greeks it was the reverse. "If we take a being as encountered in perception, then we must say: the look of something is based upon its imprint," upon its structure; its *eidos* is founded in its *morphe*. This proves that both of these determinations of *ousia*, of essence understood in the Greek sense, were not conceived in the first (*primär*) place by the ancients on the basis of "the order of the perception and perception itself" (106; 149), but rather in terms of a productive activity. From the perspective of production, the look (*eidos*) is the proto-type, the model—a consideration of which rules the process of shaping, forming and creating. The anticipated look, the proto-typical image, the archetype, the *Vor-bild* "shows the thing as what it is before the production and how it is supposed to look as a product" (107; 150). It is in relation to producing that the other notions that characterize *ousia* acquire for the Greeks their ontological sense. *Eidos* indicates the kind to which the thing belongs, what its origin is, what its *genos* is. When the Greeks speak of the nature of the thing, of its *phusis*, they mean its being produced, the *Erzeugung*, the *phuein* that makes it possible. When they speak of its contours, or its *horismos* or of its *teleion*, which the Scholastics translated as perfection, it is again in relation to productive activity that they understand these terms as the "finishedness of the thing." Even the word *hupokeimenon* is connected with production:

> To pro-duce, to place-*here, Her-stellen,* means at the same time to bring into the narrower or wider circle of the accessible, here, to this place, to the *Da,* so that the produced being *stands for itself* on its own account and remains able to be found there and to *lie-before there as something established stably for itself.* This is the

source of the Greek term *hupokeimenon,* that which lies-before.
That which first of all and constantly lies-before in the closest circle of human activity and accordingly is constantly disposable is
the whole of all *things in use,* with which we constantly have to
do, the whole of those existent things which are themselves meant
to be used on one another, *the implement that is employed* and the
constantly used products of nature: house and yard, forest and
field, sun, light and heat. What is thus tangibly present for dealing
with is reckoned by everyday experience as that which is, as a
being, in the primary sense. Disposable possessions and goods,
property, are beings; they are quite simply that which is, the Greek
ousia . . . Accordingly a *being* is synonymous with an *at-hand
[extant] disposable (vorhandenes Verfügbares).* (108–109; 153)

This comportment is the broader mode of seeing, the *Sicht* which at the
same time is pro-spective, or foreseeing, and circum-spective, or attuned to
an environment. The Greeks understood beings in function of this comportment. Even when they understood beings in the sense of what is already
purely and simply before-the-hand, we should realize that they meant that
which is "*before* all production and for all further production" (116; 163).
To be sure, the Greeks imposed on the philosophical tradition a mode of
access to beings that is not identical with this pro-spective and circumspective seeing. For it was they who imposed *theorein* in the sense of an
intuitive apprehension, of pure contemplation, in short of a perceiving relationship to a *vorhanden* pure and simple. Nevertheless, the productive origin of their most influential ontological concepts proves that *theorein* had
for them the status of a simple modification of seeing in the sense of the
Umsicht guiding productive comportment. More profoundly, pure seeing
into how a being stands in relation to itself is a prolongation of the movement belonging to productive comportment as such. Heidegger writes:

The sense of direction and apprehension peculiar to productive
comportment toward something involves taking that to which the
productive activity relates as something which, in and through the
producing, is supposed to be extant as finished in *its own self* . . .
In productive comportment toward something, the being of that
toward which I act in a productive manner is understood in a specific way in the sense of the productive intention. Indeed, it is
understood in such a way that the productive activity, corresponding to its own peculiar sense, absolves what is to be produced from
relation to the producer. (113; 159–160)

And further:

It is this understanding of what does not need to be produced, possible only in production, which understands the being of what already lies at the ground of and precedes everything to be produced
and thus is all the more already extant in itself. The understanding
of being in production is so far from merely understanding beings
as produced that it rather opens up precisely the understanding of
the being of that which is already simply extant. (116; 163–64)

Hence, because we find "in the specific intentional structure of production,
that is, in its understanding of being, a peculiar *character of discharge and
release* as concerns that to which this behavior comports itself" and because we have an understanding of it "as released for its own self and thus
as being in itself" (113–14; 160), it must also be said that perception, as
the pure intuition of what stands on its own account, is the extension of
production. But we must add immediately the restricting condition that, in
the pure consideration of what is before-the-hand, "Dasein comports itself
in such a way that it even desists from all commerce *with* [that] being, from
occupation with it" (118; 167) because perception "much more purely than
producing has the character of setting free" that to which it is related. One
can therefore say that Kant's thesis—Being is perception—is the literal
translation of Parmenides' sentence—*to gar auto noein esti te kai einai* (the
same is apprehending and Being)—but it should be added that "with Kant,
and already long before him, the stock of ontological categories handed
down from antiquity had become routine, deracinated and deprived of its
native soil, its origin no longer understood" (117; 166).

Only the ontology of Dasein allows us to apprehend radically this orig-
ination by showing "what function" productive comportment and the
purely perceiving comportment derivative from it, have for Dasein. In order
to grasp this function, we must consider these comportments with regard to
the Being of Dasein. This Being is existing, or existence. Existence therefore is what must now be elucidated. In a first approximation, we can
say that to exist is to be in the mode of a relationship to another entity, in
the mode of proximity to it, and that this relationship is such that the Being
of the other entity, as well as the Being of the relating entity, are both
understood and unveiled in and by this relationship. But precisely because
this relationship concerns at the same time the Being of the other entity
and the Being of the relating entity, an essential characteristic of the movement of existence consists in oscillating between what is ownmost and
what is not. It is an essential characteristic of the relationship that it tends
to be understood by means of a reflection, in the optical sense of the word,
of the Being of the entity that we are not, back upon ourselves. In order
better to discern this "enigmatic reflection," we must get closer to the

mode of being of Dasein, i.e., of existence, since such a reflection is made possible by existence.

The modern ontological distinction between *res cogitans* and *res extensa*, between the "I" and the "not-I," is of little help in determining existence in its specificity as opposed to the mode of being of the entity that we are not. It leaves indeterminate what it distinguishes for it recognizes only one type of Being: *Vorhandenheit*. Thus it is easy to see that from the outset this distinction relies on a construction founded upon the neglect of the phenomenal ground. For Heidegger, we have an example of such a construction in Fichte's famous sentence: "Gentlemen, think the wall, and then think the one who thinks the wall." From the outset, the requirement, apparently a simple and justified one, to think the wall does violence to the phenomenon: "For in our natural comportment toward things we never think a *single* thing, and whenever we seize upon it expressly for itself we are taking it *out* of a contexture to which it belongs in its real content: wall, room, surroundings" (162; 231). Fichte's injunction means: "Make yourselves blind to what is already given to you in the very first place and before all apprehending that is explicitly thinking" (162–63; 231). What is antecedently given in our natural intercourse with things, is a contexture of things, more precisely a contexture of equipment, since the closest things that we deal with are taken as tools. But these can only offer themselves to us insofar as they in turn refer to other tools, which form with them a functional complex (*Bewandtniszusammenhang*). This complex is not the result of the operation of equipment, but rather is presupposed as the foundation that allows tools to be what they are and to appear as such, i.e., the surrounding world always antecedently understood as the horizon within which they display themselves. But the various surrounding environments in turn presuppose the world and the world is neither the sum of the *Vorhandenes* nor of *Zuhandenes*, but the antecedently given horizon, which has always already been unveiled and from within which we understand all entities. It is always from within the world (i.e., as intraworldly) that entities offer themselves to us. Yet the world cannot be the sum of the intraworldly because it has a radically different mode of being. Indeed the world is nothing *vorhanden* nor *zuhanden*, but "a determination of Dasein's ontological constitution." Because Dasein's mode of being is existence, it must be said that the world "exists" (168; 239). Common sense will conclude that the world is something "subjective," a phenomenon "projected outside" by the subject "from the interior," in short a "projection." But this is not what the world is and the distinction between interior and exterior cannot apply to the world. The world is not the projection of a subject, but the project of a Dasein. Because Dasein has already projected itself and because the project that constitutes it, has already been cast-forth, we must say that the world itself is "cast-forth."⁵ With this casting-forth which the world is, "is unveiled that from which alone an intraworldly extant entity is uncoverable" (168; 239). It belongs to the essence of factical Being-in-the-world to be already alongside the intraworldly, and such Being-alongside-the-intraworldly-beings is founded in Being-in-the-world. Heidegger stresses that in order to understand the phenomenon of world and of Being-in-the-world, it is important "to contrast the difference between being-in-the-world as a necessary determination of the Dasein's ontological constitution and intraworldliness . . . as a possible determination of extant entities, of the *vorhanden*" (168 modified; 240). Let us investigate the status of this "possibility." We can surmise that it is not without some connection to the problem of perception—a topic that we shall consider below.

Intraworldliness is a "possible" determination that characterizes nature (where "possible" stands in contradistinction to "necessary"). When nature is unveiled (be it the physicist's nature or "in the sense in which we speak of 'the nature out-there,' hill, woods, meadow, brook, the field of wheat, the call of the birds" (169; 240)), it offers itself to us as intraworldly and can only offer itself in this way. But intraworldliness does not belong to its Being and concerns nature only inasmuch as nature has already unveiled itself to us. It is only because of this characteristic that intraworldliness can be called a possible determination of nature.

In commerce with this being, nature in the broadest sense, we understand that this being is as something extant (*Vorhandenes*), as a being that we come up against, to which we are delivered over, which on its own part already always is. It is, even if we do not uncover it, without our encountering it within our world. Being within the world *devolves upon* this being, nature, solely when it is *uncovered* as a being. Being within the world does not have to devolve upon nature as a determination, since no reason can be adduced that makes it evident that a Dasein necessarily exists. . . . Of nature *uncovered*—of that which is, so far as we comport toward it as an unveiled being—it is true that it is always already in a world; but being within the world does not belong to the *being* of nature. (169; 240)

---

5. It might be worth recalling Hofstadter's note concerning the translation of *vorher-werfen*, at the bottom of page 168 of *The Basic Problems*. It reads: "The phrase Heidegger uses, *sich Welt vorher-werfen*, also suggests that the world is thrown beforehand, in advance, and not 'forth;' it is pre-thrown, pre-cast; it is an a priori of the Dasein." (Trans.)

Nature can be, even if no Dasein exists and therefore even if there is no world.

However, there are some beings that are only as intraworldly. Such is the case of the entities we call historical, that is, "all the things that the human being, who is historical and exists historically in the strict and proper sense, creates, shapes, cultivates: all his culture and works" (169; 241). For such historical beings—and tools have to be counted among them—intraworldliness is a *necessary* characteristic. They presuppose a world, and because the world is only in relation to Dasein, these beings pre-suppose Dasein and the structure of Being-in-the-world specific to Dasein.

It is in this structure of Being-in-the-world that we must seek the pre-suppositions, i.e., the foundations of perceiving comportment, and it is to this structural determination that this comportment must be related. Thus in order to grasp this relation better, we must provide a detailed analysis of this structure. Two essential moments must be considered. The first is "the for-the-sake-of-which" Dasein exists (See first part of the subtitle Beta, 170; 242). It is the same thing to say that Dasein exists in the mode of Being-in-the-world and to say that it is "occupied with its own capacity to be" (170; 242). The second moment is "mineness" (*Jemeinigkeit*). This does not mean that Dasein is identical with itself, that it fuses with itself in the same way that every thing has the character of self-sameness; rather it means that Dasein is Self in its *ownmost* [*en propre*]. And because it is Self in its ownmost, it can also lose itself. To be a self in one's ownmost, means to chose oneself authentically. Hence, to understand oneself in the ownmost means to understand oneself "from the most proper and most extreme pos-sibilities of one's existence" (160; 228). In contradistinction, to exist in an inauthentic, improper, outward mode, means to leave one's own Being de-termined by others, or by intraworldly beings; it also means that under-standing oneself is conducted in terms of intraworldly beings, or is entirely absorbed in them. Such is the everyday self-understanding which, Heidegger stresses, remains in the *improper, inauthentic* mode. We shall later return to the description of this everyday self-understanding that reaches its self only from the consideration of intraworldly beings. For it will be legitimate to ask whether the description does not in the final anal-ysis call into question the distinction between the world and the intra-worldly, and even the distinction between ownmost authenticity and fallen inauthenticity. Such a line of questioning arises in the wake of Heidegger's reference to a specific mode of seeing, of a certain look—the gaze cast by Malte Laurids Brigge upon a wall different from the one envisaged by Fichte—a gaze Heidegger is careful not to call "perception."

In any case, even without considering the difficulties involved in this distinction, it will become increasingly clear that the demarcation between the proper ownmost and the improper inauthentic determines on the deepest level the quest for the ultimate presuppositions of the perceiving comportment.

This perceiving comportment was thematized with respect to its *structure* in the context of Heidegger's debate with Kant's thesis on Being. Let me recall the four points of that thematization:

1. perception is an intentional comportment whose specific orientation is turned toward something *vorhanden*, something present-at-hand; 2. this comportment is intrinsically uncovering, which means that in its very orientation it is open to the uncovered *vorhanden*; 3. this uncoveredness takes place in the light of Being, which means, in this case, in the light of presence-at-hand (*Vorhandenheit*) as the Being always already unveiled of the present-at-hand entities; 4. the light in which the uncoveredness occurs is the light of the ontological difference, i.e., the difference between Being and beings. However this structural analysis does not deal with the *foundations* of the perceiving comportment.

The detour we just took yields a first sketch of the foundations or presuppositions of the perceiving comportment. Based on a critico-phenomenological discussion in which Heidegger investigated the distinction—Greek in origin—between essence and existence, and then the modern distinction between thing and subject, this detour reveals first that the perceiving comportment (in the strict sense of a pure consideration of something *vorhanden*) is a modification of another comportment from which it has been excised or extracted. This other comportment is at the same time acting, foreseeing, and producing; it relates itself to beings that are ready-to-hand by virtue of the fact that the comportment is first of all related to a surrounding world (*Umwelt*) consisting in a functional totality (*Bewandtnisganzheit*). The detour also reveals that both comportments originate in Dasein, whose mode of being is existence, and that the fundamental determination of existence is Being-in-the-world. Finally it teaches us that Being-in-the-world is the ground of the specific intentionality of these comportments. Indeed anything *vorhanden* or *zuhanden*—toward which that intentionality is oriented—is something intraworldly whose uncoveredness presupposes the world and the unveiling of the world. Heidegger writes: "To intentionality, as comportment toward *beings*, there always belongs an *understanding of the Being* of those beings to which the *intentio* refers. Henceforth it will be clear that this understanding of the Being of beings is connected with the *understanding of world*, which is the presupposition for the experience of an intraworldly being" (175; 249–50).

Consequently, in order to elucidate the ultimate foundation of the intentionality of perceiving comportment and of the acting, foreseeing, and productive comportment, we must investigate the ultimate foundation of the understanding of Being, as opposed to beings, and of the understanding of the world, as opposed to the intraworldly. This leads us to investigate the condition of possibility of the understanding of Being, an understanding that belongs to the existence of Dasein.

This condition of possibility is temporality. It is not appropriate here to enter into the details of Heidegger's text. We will only attempt to highlight the relation of temporality to the perceiving comportment and to the acting, foreseeing and productive comportment. The temporality at stake here can only be approached by deconstructing the traditional concept of time as it had been presented by Aristotle; this traditional concept corresponds to the traditional and common conception of time as an irreversible and infinite sequence of "nows" unfolding from the not-yet to the no-longer. When this common understanding expresses itself, it says: now, later, before. Each of these expressions refers to Dasein and to its comportment. Inasmuch as it is expecting or waiting for something, Dasein says: "later." Inasmuch as it makes present or enpresents, it says: "now." Inasmuch as it retains or forgets, it says: "before" (257–61; 363–69). But if we look at the phenomenon more closely, when we say "now," or "later," or "before," we always mean a time *for* something, appropriate for something, or incongruous and out-of-season, hence bearing the character of *significance,* which is a character of the world in the existential sense; we also mean *datability* (now that this or that happens); we also mean spannedness, or interval (while this or that is happening), that is, a *tension;* finally in these expressions, each individual understands what others say and in turn expects to be understood by them; these expressions therefore denote *publicness,* as the capacity to be accessible to everyone. Such structural characteristics, unseen by the tradition, permit a more precise determination of expectation, retention, and enpresenting (261–64; 369–74). Thus determined, these three characteristics of temporality must next be apprehended in their origin and unity. "In their origin" means in connection with what is most properly characteristic of Dasein's Being. What is most properly characteristic of it is its ownmost capacity for Being—to which it is related and which it anticipates. Waiting is primordially—or existentially—to expect one's own capacity for Being. The advent to oneself in the light of that capacity for Being is what primordially defines the future. For Dasein primordial retaining or forgetting is its proper way of relating itself to its having-been. Having been belongs to its existence and because existence is coming to self from its ownmost capacity for Being, it is therefore from the future that the Being of

Dasein is referred back to its having-been. This having-been is the past in the existential sense. As for the present in the existential sense, it does not consist in the fact of being currently given, that is, in *Vorhandenheit*, but in being-attentive-to, in being-close-to. Inasmuch as it is determined by this ad-vent, this return and this access-to, in a three-dimensional conjunction of these terms, temporality extends outside of itself. In other words, it is ec-static, and each of these determinations forms an ecstasis of primordial temporality. It belongs to the essence of those ecstases—each one temporalizing only in conjunction with the other two—to be open, tensed outward—or ec-static. That to which the ec-static extending is open forms the horizon of the ecstasis. Each ecstasis has a specific horizon which it keeps open, and temporality as the unity of the three ecstases is ecstatic-horizonal. It is ultimately in the ecstatic-horizonal character of temporality that intentionality finds its condition of possibility: "Being-there is intentional only because it is in its essence determined by temporality" (379). And it is also from the ecstatic-horizonal character of this existential time that the characteristics of time as it usually finds expression (significance, datability, etc.) are derived.

Yet, in order to characterize primordial temporality more closely, it is necessary to exhibit its purest, i.e., ownmost, existentiality. If the structural characteristics of the now, the later-on, the no-longer (significance, datability, etc.) and a fortiori their foundation in the ecstatic-horizonal character of temporality went unrecognized in the tradition and remained hidden in the ordinary conception of time, this covering-up (*Verdeckung*), whose result is the concept of time as an infinite sequence of nows, could not originate anywhere else but in Dasein itself. This origin is the phenomenon of *Verfallen*, of falling, which consists for Dasein in the fact that "it determines its own being by means of the mode of being of the extant (*vorhanden*)" (271–72; 384). Falling as a mode of being of Dasein founds the traditional and common concept of time as the extant sequence of nows, whether this be given "in nature," "in the subject," or in both. By comparison with primordial time, the sequential form of time is not time, but only something intratemporal. But because falling is the inauthentic counterpart of authentic and ownmost being, only by detaching oneself from the inauthentic element, will it be possible to grasp—at the core of existentiality—the most primordial temporality.

In order to move one step closer to primordial temporality, we must consider understanding more closely. We saw that perception can only relate itself to uncovered *vorhanden* beings insofar as they are uncovered as such in the light of an understanding of the Being of those beings. In order to penetrate to the founding ground of that understanding of Being, we must first specify the nature of such understanding. Understanding is a primordial determination of the existence of Dasein. Its primordial existential concept is *"to understand oneself in the being of one's most peculiar ability-to-be"* (276; 391). Generally speaking, this understanding consists in *projecting itself upon* a possibility, in holding oneself within a project by means of which alone possibility is revealed; but what is at stake in that project is the one projecting itself: in the project, Dasein makes itself manifest to its own seeing, acquires a self-understanding. In this understanding, which manifests itself as project, there is constantly projected, at the same time as a *world,* "*a particular possible being with the others* and a *particular possible being toward intraworldly beings*" (278; 393–94). This project is completely *free,* but precisely because it is so, "factical Dasein can understand itself primarily via intraworldly beings which it encounters. It can let its existence be determined primarily not by itself but by things and circumstances and by others. It is this understanding that we call *inauthentic understanding"* (279 modified; 395).

Before investigating the foundations of the distinction between authentic and inauthentic understanding, we must grant that all understanding consists in projecting (or understanding) beings upon Being, for example the being called Dasein upon the Being of Dasein, i.e., existence, or the being called *vorhanden* upon its Being, i.e., *Vorhandensein,* presence-at-hand. We must also grant that such a projection implies an understanding of Being, which in turn—since all understanding is a projection—implies that Being must be projected upon something. That upon which a being is projected is Being, but that upon which Being is projected is time. It is time that must be deployed, *epekeina tes ousias,* as the condition of possibility for the understanding of Being.

In order to do this, we must show how temporality is the condition of possibility of understanding in general, at various levels: *existentiell* understanding, the relationship of understanding to *Vorhandene* (and *Zuhandene*), and the understanding of Being inherent in both. It is at the first level of *existentiell* understanding, if it be determined in what is ownmost as opposed to what is inauthentic, that temporality will be revealed in its originary and proper character.

The ownmost *existentiell* understanding is the understanding inherent in authentic existence, in which "Dasein is itself in and from its own peculiar possibility, a possibility that has been seized on and chosen by the Dasein itself" (287; 406). Such an understanding, such an existing is what Heidegger calls *Entschlossenheit,* resoluteness. Primordial temporality is the temporality of resoluteness. In resoluteness, Dasein understands itself and exists in its ownmost capacity-for-Being. This understanding is directed toward the future in the sense that it arrives at its self from its ownmost capacity-for-Being. But we must add that its ownmost possibility is death, which is unexchangeable and not to be outstripped. The specific mode of this future, is anticipation (*Vorlaufen*) of its own death. In coming to its self from this most peculiar possibility, Dasein has already taken upon itself the being which it already was. Coming to its self is reappropriating this self in everything that it once was, and as such. The specific mode of the existentiell past is thus a re-casting (*Wiederholung*) or repetition.

"In the ecstatic unity of *repetitive self-precedence,* in this past and future, there lies a specific present": this is the *Augenblick,* the moment of vision or blink of an eye. This specific mode of the present, a mode which is an ecstatic-horizonal phenomenon, is defined as an

> enpresenting of something present which, as belonging to resolve, discloses the situation upon which resoluteness had resolved. In the instant as an ecstasis the existent Dasein is carried away, as resolved, into the current factically determined possibilities, circumstances, contingencies of the situation of its action. The instant (the *Augenblick,* the twinkling of an eye) is that which, arising from resoluteness, has an eye first of all and solely for what constitutes the situation of action. It is the mode of resolute existence in which the Dasein, as being-in-the-world, holds and keeps its world in view. (287; 407–08)

The instant is the phenomenon Aristotle had isolated under the name of *kairos* in the *Nicomachean Ethics,* and Kierkegaard properly understood in its tenor; yet neither of them ever managed to explain its specific temporality because both identified it with the 'now' of time as it is commonly understood, thus without grasping that primordial temporality is the original phenomenon from which the 'now' in its common understanding is derived.

But, "the present belonging to Dasein does not constantly have the character of the instant." Far from existing always as resolute, Being-there "proximally and for the most part" exists in an irresolute manner in which its ownmost capacity-for-Being is closed to itself. This means that "the temporality of Dasein is not always temporalized from its authentic coming-to-self" and that therefore it is "variable concerning its distinct ecstases, particularly concerning that of the future." Unlike authentic existence, the existence prevailing "proximally and for the most part," the existence of everydayness, is inauthentic and irresolute. Its mode of enpresenting is not that of the instant, but "for the most part and chiefly, dwells with things, gets entangled in its own self, lets itself be drawn along by things so as to be merged with what it is enpresenting . . . runs away from itself, loses itself within itself, so that the past becomes a forgetting and the future an expecting of what is just coming on'' (287; 407).

This everyday, inauthentic, and irresolute way of existing characterizes the comportment related to beings given proximally, i.e., to disposable and extant things. In other words, in the improper way of existing and in its derivative temporality are inscribed both the circumspective foresight directed on equipment in the most general sense and the perception of extant things. These comportments, as every comportment of existing Dasein, are permeated with understanding, but the understanding specific to them is always a self-understanding that at the same time understands something else, and is therefore an improper understanding (since authentic understanding is not a projection of oneself upon possibilities, but upon the ownmost possibility, see 289; 409).

When the issue for Heidegger is to ''turn his exploratory regard solely to understanding comportment toward things handy and things extant,'' he describes this relationship as a distraction from oneself. Understanding things is to understand oneself improperly; for Dasein, it amounts to understanding itself

> from the ability to be that is determined by the success and failure, the feasibility and infeasibility of its commerce with things. The Dasein thus comes toward itself from out of the things. . . . It is as though the Dasein's can-be were projected by the things, by the Dasein's commerce with them, and not primarily by the Dasein itself from its own most peculiar self. (289; 410)

The capacity-for-Being is thus distracted from its own specificity by things, and the future specific and proper to that capacity is modified into a future that is no longer proper: The self-precedence of one's most peculiar can-be is transformed into the expectation (*Gewärtigen*) of ''the can-be of a being which relies on what things give or what they refuse''(289; 410). Unlike self-precedence, this expectation is not linked to the repetition of what Dasein was, but rather to the *forgetfulness* by Dasein of its ownmost having-been and facticity. This self-forgetfulness (*Sichvergessen*) can be described as the primordial form of forgetfulness. It is the derivative conservation (or memory of what was expected as possible) as well as a corresponding derivative forgetfulness. Thus determined by an improper future, the present of this improper understanding no longer has the character of the instant.

It is in relation to this modified and derived temporality that we can clarify the understanding of Being inherent in circumspective foresight or perception. In the everyday commerce of Dasein with intraworldly beings that proximally offer themselves to it as handy, an understanding of the

Being of those beings (*zuhanden*) takes place, which is based on a specific—and derivative—temporality of Being-in-the-world. For a piece of equipment to offer itself to us as the available being that it is, for us to give ourselves over to its use, for a hammer to appear to us as bound to hammering, there has to be a prior understanding of destination itself, of relationships of destination, and of the totality of destinations. This understanding is temporal (see 291; 412, ff.). It consists in the expectation of an "in-order-to" regulating the support or conservation of a "by-means-of," and it is on the basis of this expectation and support that the tool is present as tool. In this understanding, a going-beyond the *zuhanden* toward a goal is operative. This going-beyond is a form of transcendence, and transcendence as such is constitutive of Dasein. More profoundly, transcendence coincides with primordial temporality, in such a fashion that the transcendence of any *zuhanden* toward its goal is derived from the transcendence of Dasein toward its own can-be. In the last analysis, the "in-order-to," in relation to which anything *zuhanden* is encountered as tool, presupposes the "for-the-sake-of-the-ownmost-capacity-for-being." It is in this "for-the-sake-of-itself" that every "in-order-to" is rooted and the latter is nothing but a modification and derivation of the former. But in this modification what is at stake is a fall of authentic temporality into the intraworldly and this falling modifies the connection of the ecstases. Even though all three continue to function together, the ecstasis of the present now rules over that of the future. And the ruling function of the present is even more accentuated when we cease dealing with the tool and move to the pure perception of the extant thing.

After this long exploration of foundations or conditions of possibility, we may now return to Kant's thesis on Being, which guides the Heideggerian phenomenology of perception. It is now possible to say that the thesis lends itself to a retrieval, which can be formulated as follows:

> "When Kant says that Being equals perception, then in view of the ambiguity of perception, this cannot mean that Being equals perceiving; nor can it mean that Being equals the perceived, the entity itself. But also it cannot mean that Being perceivedness equals positedness. For perceivedness already presupposes an understanding of the *Being* of the perceived entities" (314; 447).

This perceivedness is a mode of uncoveredness, i.e., of truth, or of the unveiled character of the perceived as an extant being. This uncoveredness, or truth, of the extant being is strictly correlated with the uncovering, unveiling or truth-bearing character of perceiving Dasein, and this uncovering character of perception as an act of Dasein, in turn, presupposes an understanding of the Being of the extant being. This understanding, and along with it perception in its entirety (i.e., considered in the totality of its intentional structure linking the perceiving, the perceived, and the perceivedness) "is grounded in the ecstatic-horizonal constitution of temporality" (315; 447), that is to say in the foundational transcendence characteristic of Dasein. Perception is a specific mode of the enpresenting of something. The ecstasis of the present is the basis of this specific intentional transcendence. And to each ecstasis belongs a horizon, more precisely a horizonal schema. Presence is the horizon, or the schema of the enpresenting of the perceived. "Being equals perception" therefore means: Being equals presence, the presence of a present.

Thus far we have been dealing with the set of presuppositions that, according to Heidegger, ground perceiving comportment. It will be an entirely different task to tackle now the set of presuppositions involved in his phenomenology of perception. How can we address this issue? It is impossible even to outline this inquiry without animating it more or less obliquely with a variety of reflections taken from Heidegger's later itinerary. However I propose to delay for a while the consideration of that itinerary and for the time being to concentrate on the specific theoretical constellation exhibited in the text of the *Basic Problems.* In that constellation, perception is considered as a thoroughly derived comportment. Taken in the strict and narrow sense as contemplating an extant being, perception is a comportment derived from the more primordial comportment of circumspection and foresight of surroundings. This comportment of circumspection is a seeing, which in turn is derived from a still more properly primordial and original sight, the *Augenblick,* the instantaneous blink of an eye. The first mode of seeing has to do with *things* pure and simple, i.e., with extant entities, the second with *equipment,* i.e., with *zuhanden,* ready-to-hand entities, and the third one with a *situation* in that it reveals to Dasein what is at issue concerning its ownmost can-be. At the foundational level, the passage from the mode of seeing given in the instant, or the moment of vision, to the strictly perceiving mode of seeing, involves a derivation or a modification of primordial temporality in which the ecstasis of the future is replaced by that of the present.

One should inquire into this notion of derivation. Obviously, one can bestow a derivative status on perception only because one takes it to be affected with a limitation. Perception is supposedly limited to apprehending an extant being and the subsisting properties of such an entity. Its intentional correlate is the thing, limited to the status of a bearer of properties. Perception is strictly oriented toward extant things taken as bearers of characteristics. Judging from the internal economy of the texts dating from the

Marburg period, these propositions are taken for granted by Heidegger. Moreover he never questions their self-evidence. In spite of the admirable rigor of the transcendental foundation of perceiving intentionality, everything happens as if, from the outset, Heidegger imposed on perception a concept uncritically inherited from the tradition. He thoroughly examines everything in Kant's thesis on Being and perception, except the idea that perception is an immediate contact with something purely and simply present-at-hand. As we have seen, he inspects and rejects many aspects of Husserl's theses on intentionality, but never questions the idea expressed in the *Logical Investigations* that perception is the intuitive "enpresenting" of something given. Like Husserl, Heidegger never meditates upon the *Leibhaftigkeit*—which he also attributes to the perceived. He never wonders whether the fleshy characteristic of perceived things is entirely and adequately expressed in the notion of *Vorhandenheit*. The fact that the perceived has a flesh means—without any further qualification—that it is before-the-hand.

But there is another aspect of the inherited concept that Heidegger does not question either: the idea that perception, thus understood, is incipient science. Indeed everything happens as if the project (to be sure a very innovative one) of an existential genesis of science had two simultaneous and contradictory effects. On the one hand, the project calls into question the primordial status of knowledge and the privileged character of intuition which had ruled over "all interpretation of knowledge" from the time of Greek ontology until Kant and Husserl inclusively (see Section 69 in *Sein und Zeit*). But on the other hand, this idea seems to have no bearing on the profoundly traditional connection between perception and science, since both deal with a "pure consideration" of something presently given, taken as the extant bearer of a certain number of characteristics.

It is perhaps no exaggeration to say that this uncritical repetition of the concept of perception, inherited from the tradition, prevents Heidegger from asking whether perceiving—even in the modality of pure contemplation—might not consist in something other than the apprehension of a subsisting support of a certain number of properties. At Marburg, he never raised this question, or the related question: "What is a Thing?"

The difficulty with this phenomenology of perception consists in the fact that its deconstruction or its de-struction of the traditional theses reinforces them at the very moment when it might seem that it was shaking their foundations. The proposition that perception has a derivative status does not unsettle, but rather confirms, the status that had been assigned to it in the tradition.

But there is more: the internal structure of this phenomenology entails no fewer difficulties than the tradition whose legacy it surreptitiously reinforces. Let us attempt to inscribe within the theoretical constellation of the *Basic Problems* a particular case of perception. Take an example as simple as the sight of a tree, of a cloud, of a flight of birds. We would have to say that because nature in these perceptions is either the as yet unshaped antecedent phenomenon against which the producing comportment is held in check, or what appears by virtue of a shrinking and narrowing of the circumspective foresight originally concerned with equipment, our sight of a tree, of a cloud, etc. either deals with what production has not yet carried out in its movement, or manifests a sort of abstraction and suspension from the utilitarian, tool-related, circumspection. One might object perhaps that, if the Being of nature is irreducible to intraworldliness, then nature presents itself as being in excess of productive comportment, circumspective foresight and purely perceptual consideration. Yet, all things considered, this objection does not stand. For, at this time (in Marburg), nature is not taken by Heidegger as being in excess of production and perception; instead, as soon as it manifests itself, nature shows itself as exclusively intraworldly. And if the Being of nature escapes reduction to intraworldliness, it is, according to Heidegger, only because we are not capable of proving the necessity of the existence of a Dasein. Nature's escape from intraworldliness is in no way exhibited in the ways in which nature appears. It is inferred only *a posteriori* from the facticity and contingency of the existence of Dasein. In manifesting itself, nature does not exceed the world, it is inscribed within the world. And because nature is inscribed therein, it cannot be taken as manifesting any excess with regard to worldly entities. If we sought to inscribe the "pure consideration" of a pictorial work of art in the theoretical context of this phenomenology, the result would be just as surprising. The work of art would be immediately caught in the alternative of making it either a tool deprived of its usefulness, or an as yet unshaped purely extant entity. In both cases, no "charge" of nature, in the sense of an excess vis-à-vis the worldly or the intraworldly could be detected in the work of art. At the very most, it might manifest a "charge" of world.

But even this is not clear, as shown by Heidegger's long quotation from Rilke. It deserves careful attention because the commentary which accompanies it reintroduces the difficulty. The passage cited by Heidegger is as follows:

> "This is what I have seen. Seen. [Significantly enough, Heidegger's quotation begins after these words]. Will anyone believe that there are such houses? No, they will say I'm falsifying. But this time it's the truth, nothing left out and naturally also nothing added. Where should I get it from? It's well known that I'm poor. Everyone knows. Houses? But, to be precise, they were

houses that no longer existed. Houses that were torn down from top to bottom. What was there was the other houses, the ones that had stood alongside them, tall neighboring houses. They were obviously in danger of collapsing after everything next to them had been removed, for a long framework of long tarred poles was rammed aslant between the ground of the rubble-strewn lot and the exposed wall. I don't know whether I have already said that I mean this wall. But it was, so to speak, not the first wall of the present houses (which nevertheless had to be assumed) but the last one of the earlier ones. You could see their inner side. You could see the walls of the rooms on the different storeys, to which the wallpaper was still attached, and here and there the place of the floor or ceiling began. Along the whole wall, next to the walls of the rooms, there still remained a dirty-white area, and the open rust-stained furrow of the toilet pipe crept through it in unspeakable nauseating movements, soft, like those of a digesting worm. Of the paths taken by the illuminating gas, gray dusty traces were left at the edges of the ceilings, and here and there, quite unexpectedly they bent round about and came running into the colored wall and into a black hole that had been ruthlessly ripped out. But most unforgettable were the walls themselves. The tenacious life of these rooms refused to let itself be trampled down. It was still there; it clung to the nails that had remained; it stood on the handsbreath remnant of the floor; it had crept together there among the onsets of the corners where there was still a tiny bit of interior space. You could see that it was in the paint, which had changed slowly year by year: from blue to an unpleasant green, from green to gray, and from yellow to an old decayed white that was now rotting away. But it was also in the fresher places that had been preserved behind the mirrors, pictures, cupboards; for it had drawn and redrawn their contours and had also been in these hidden places, with the spiders and the dust, which now lay bare. It was in every streak that had been trashed off; it was in the moist blisters at the lower edge of the wall-hangings; it tossed in the torn-off tatters, and it sweated out of all the ugly stains that had been made so long ago. And from these walls, once blue, green, and yellow, which were framed by the tracks of the fractures of the intervening walls that had been destroyed, the breath of this life stood out, the tough, sluggish, musty breath which no wind had yet dispersed. There stood the noondays and the illnesses, and the expirings and the smoke of years and the sweat that breaks out under the armpits and makes the clothes heavy, and the stale breath of mouths and the fusel-oil smell of fermenting feet. There stood the pungency of urine and the burning of soot and the gray reek of potatoes and the strong oily stench of decaying grease. The sweet lingering aroma of neglected suckling infants was there and the anguished odor of children going to school and the sultriness from beds of pubescent boys. And much had joined this company, coming from below, evaporating upward from the abyss of the streets, and much else had seeped down with the rain, unclean above the towns. And the domestic winds, weak and grown tame, which stay always in the same street, had brought much along with them, and there was much more too coming from no one knows where. But I have said, haven't I, that all the walls had been broken off, up to this last one? Well, I've been talking all along about this wall. You'll say that I stood in front of it for a long time, but I'll take an oath that I began to run as soon as I recognized the wall. For that's what's terrible—that I recognized it. I recognized all of it here, and that is why it goes right into me: it's at home in me.[6]

In the internal structure of the phenomenology of perception developed by the *Basic Problems,* this long passage at the same time confirms and unhinges the whole problematic of derivation. The wall in question was seen in Paris by Malte Laurids Brigge during one of his unchartered promenades along the Seine. It is quite different from the one Fichte asked his listeners to think about, before thinking about the Ego that thinks it. The Fichtean wall is, according to Heidegger, nothing but an abstraction extracted from the surrounding world. It is a tool that has become a pure thing, something purely extant resulting from the exclusion and concealment of its everyday functional context. The Fichtean wall presents itself to perception in the narrow sense: it is a *Vorhandenes.* The everyday wall is given to a broader sight, practical circumspection: it is a *Zuhandenes.*

Now what about Rilke's wall? It is clear that the Rilkean wall does not fit into the first category: it is not something extant, a *Vorhandenes.* But can it fit the second? When Malte writes, "This is what I have seen. Seen," it is overwhelmingly clear that these words are not a preliminary to the description of an extant being. Are they a preliminary to the description of a *Zuhandenes?* As soon as we address this question to Heidegger's text, we realize that the apparently clear-cut delineations in the articulation of his phenomenology now become fuzzy and unclear. Things *zuhanden* are that

6. Rainer Maria Rilke, *The Notebooks of Malte Laurids Brigge,* trans. M. D. Herter Norton (New York: Norton, 1949), quoted by Heidegger in *The Basic Problems of Phenomenology* (172–173; 244–246).

with which Dasein proximally and for the most part concerns itself in everydayness. A specific mode of seeing belongs to the everyday relationships of Dasein with ready-to-hand beings. This specific mode of seeing is *Umsicht*, circumspection, whose specific correlate is never an isolated tool, but the utilitarian contexture of the surrounding world. The strictly perceptive mode of seeing is blind to this contexture. But the broader and more concrete *Umsicht* is also affected with a certain blindness. Its specific mode of seeing always presupposes the world as an *existentiale* belonging to the constitution of Being of Dasein as Being-in-the-world. But it is precisely what it presupposes that never appears to it. While the latter mode of seeing grasps what is *zuhanden* within the *Umwelt* which itself is visible, it does not see the world though the world has always already been unveiled to it. It sees the intraworldly but not the world. Precisely because it is concerned with intraworldly things, it never perceives the world in a proper mode, but in an improper mode, that is, understood in terms of intraworldly things. Therefore, to the circumspective sight and foresight of everydayness, the intraworldly cannot possibly be expected to exhibit the property of being "laden, charged as it were, with world" (171; 244). Yet it is such a world-charge that is exhibited for Rilke on that wall in Paris, now exposed to the elements, and which formerly was one of the inside walls of an inhabited building. Let us recall Heidegger's words of introduction to his quotation of *The Notebooks of Malte Laurids Brigge*:

> What is important is only whether the existent Dasein, in conformity with its existential possibility, is original enough still to *see* expressly the world that is always already unveiled with its existence, to verbalize it, and thereby to make it expressly visible for others. Poetry, creative literature, is nothing but the elementary emergence into words, the becoming uncovered, of existence as being-in-the-world. For the others who before it were blind, the world first becomes visible by what is thus spoken. (171–72; 244)

It is as though the mode of seeing invoked here is devoid of any theoretical status in the framework of the Marburg phenomenology. Rilke's seeing is irreducible to perception in the strict and narrow sense, but also it is not reducible to circumspective foresight because the latter remains essentially blind to the world that it presupposes. Shall we say that Rilke's seeing is to be put on a par with the primordial and authentic vision that Heidegger had assigned to the *Augenblick*, the moment of vision? The answer to this question is negative because Heidegger stresses that any self-understanding taking its departure from things can only reveal an inauthentic and improper self. Moreover, after the quotation, Heidegger insists that in Rilke's pages, "the world leaps toward us from the things," that it does nothing but depict "what is 'actually' in the wall which leaps forth from it in our *natural comportmental* relationship to it" (173; 246). Finally he makes reference to the same pages much later (289; 410) as an illustration of "inauthentic self-understanding," i.e., starting from things. We get the impression that the theoretical context of his phenomenology forced Heidegger to minimize the import of these pages, in which nevertheless he acknowledges a "proper" seeing of the world within the seeing of a thing. This contradiction may be explained by two facts: On the one hand, the "natural or everyday relationship to things" cannot extend beyond the self-understanding which is improper and inauthentic; on the other hand, the authentic seeing of the world as existential (that is, the moment of vision) is, so to speak, purified of any relationship to things. The moment of vision is attained by Dasein in the self-precedence of its ownmost capacity for Being, that is, in its anticipation of death and a call for its ownmost resoluteness, such that the authentic sight of the *Augenblick* pays no attention to things. Thus it can be said that "in a way almost reminiscent of Gnosticism, the Instant of authentic temporality remains without a world and is only characterized negatively."[7]

These are the difficulties brought into this phenomenology of perception by the unquestioned repetition of an inherited concept and by its own internal articulation, particularly the distinction between ownmost authenticity and fallen inauthenticity. In addition to the difficulties just mentioned, there are also some specific to the style of Heidegger's own debate with the tradition. Because his phenomenology, or phenomenological ontology, has as its "center" the temporality of Dasein (327; 465) and because the neglected Being which it investigates can indeed be brought to reminiscence [*remémorée*] in the light of temporality (which is the true transcendental condition on the foundation of which philosophy will finally become scientific), this phenomenology does not allow itself to be challenged by conceptual formations belonging to other epochs of philosophy. Instead, it translates them immediately into its own theoretical constellation and interprets them as expressions of certain comportments of Dasein, that is, as modifications of the temporality that ontologically constitutes Dasein. A "History of Being," in the sense of the various epochs of its forgetfulness, is not thinkable within this framework. Furthermore, if Greek thought is granted an undeniable privilege therein, it is definitely not at all because its most evocative words (*phusis, aletheia, logos*) might indicate a secret of Being. In the framework of fundamental ontology, Greek thought is mentioned only because, without any discontinuity from Parmenides and Hera-

---

7. O. Pöggeler and F. Hogemann, "Martin Heidegger: Zeit und Sein," in *Grundprobleme der grossen Philosophen*, Hrsgg. von J. Speck, *Philosophie der Gegenwart V*, p. 67.

clitus to Plato and Aristotle, it elaborated a "naive ontology," that is, an ontology based on the field of everydayness, or *praktische Umsicht*. An undeniable advantage of this Greek ontology is that it naively showed the derivative status of *Vorhandenheit* from *Zuhandenheit* and thus proved to be less artificial than subsequent ontologies which had only one concept of Being, *Vorhandenheit*. Another advantage lies in the fact that, in spite of its naivete or rather because of it, Greek ontology already attempted to grasp the Being of beings "by having regard to the Dasein (*psuche, nous, logos*)" (110; 155), that is, by virtue of a discovery of the *a priori*, of a transcendental approach, for which the Platonic recollection from forgetfulness served as an early model. This Marburg phenomenology shows no desire to meditate on the unthought of Greek thought; instead, its goal is to overcome the naivete of their transcendental approach. Heidegger writes peremptorily: "We not only wish, but we must, understand the Greeks better than they understood themselves. Only thus shall we be in possession of our heritage" (111; 157).

III

There is no need to establish the fact that, within a few decisive years, Heidegger profoundly altered the theoretical constellation that had governed the Marburg phenomenology. It would be impossible here to spell out the stages of this transformation and to discuss the extent to which it affected the concept of perception. Taking a clue from a text whose importance for his evolution Heidegger later acknowledged, let us limit ourselves to a consideration of how perception is approached once the change was completed.

Whereas the *De-struktion* practiced during the Marburg years remained under the influence of the tradition, the thought that governs the later transformation was on the contrary a movement of setting oneself free from it, while nonetheless using the most ancient texts of the Western philosophical legacy. By virtue of this disowning of the tradition, the center of thought is displaced: it is no longer Dasein and the transcendental understanding of Being founded in the temporality of existence, but the very unveiling of Being, the enigmatic interplay of reserve and unconcealing, which is supposed to be more primordial and more *a priori* than anything transcendental. If *aletheia* is one of the names of Being, then the uncovering role of Dasein can no longer grant any special privilege, or any constitutive power, to Dasein itself. If *phusis* is also one of the names of Being, a name designating a process of unveiling which is always reserved in what it brings to display, then one should find totally unwarranted the concept of nature as derived from a process that cancels the worldly character of the world and thus reduces nature to the totality of the intraworldly present-at-hand. If the reserve of *phusis* is at the very core of its unconcealment, one should also find unwarranted the dissociation between the Being of nature which does not appear and the intraworldly appearing of nature, an appearing supposedly connected to nature only in an accidental manner. But if *phusis* is such, the things which emerge from it to display themselves, cannot legitimately be reduced to the status of the derivative Being of *Vorhandenheit*. But then what is a thing? If this question now comes to the forefront as a result of the new center of thinking (*aletheia, phusis*), the question itself must be put into an historical perspective beginning with what is suggested by the most evocative words of the very first thinkers of the tradition. In any case, because the question "What is a Thing?" is historical in its conception, it cannot leave untouched the claim (central in the Marburg years) that there was a continuity in the privilege bestowed upon *Vorhandenheit* from Parmenides to Kant and Husserl, nor can it leave untouched the notion of a continuity from Parmenides to Plato, nor the conception that there was a global "naivete" of "Greek ontology" originating in its attempt to find a basis in everydayness. Indeed, what kind of "everydayness" can possibly be involved in the verses of the Tragic poets, which in more ways than one are so close to the Saying of the first thinkers of the Greek world? Instead, if it is true that the most insistent and recurring themes and concepts of those thinkers and poets still continue to awaken our thought, then should not the relationship of Dasein to the "simple things" be revised in the light of the upheaval imposed upon the transcendental privilege of Dasein? Furthermore, do not the recentering and upheaval require that we rethink the connection between foreseeing/productive comportment and instrumentality? Does not this inevitably involve a questioning of the pivotal function which this connection had in the years of the Marburg phenomenology? And if the ontological constitution of Dasein ceases to be at the center of the thought of Being, then should not the very distinction between the authentic and the inauthentic, relative to the foundational character of that constitution, also be called into question?

It is impossible to follow up each of these questions, which we formulate here in too simple a way: for they emerged at the same time as many other questions, and are entailed by the new approach to perception that we find in the essay on *The Origin of the Work of Art,* where they vibrate in unison. In conclusion, let us now consider this text.

We have seen that in the Marburg phenomenology, perception, in the strict and narrow sense, is related to things, that is, to extant bearers of properties. We found that this strict and narrow sense was taken for granted in that phenomenology. But this evidence is unsettled by *The Origin of the*

Work of Art. Indeed this essay shows that the pair substance-accident, whose status had become self-evident in the wake of a long tradition, refers back, as soon as one meditates on its Greek origins, to the enigmatic and secretive character of the unconcealment of *phusis.* Furthermore the essay insists that "even before all reflection, attentive dwelling within the sphere of things already tells us that this thing-concept does not hit upon the thingly element of the thing, its spontaneous independence (*Eigen-wüchsiges*) and its self-contained character" (*The Origin of the Work of Art,* pp. 24–25, translation modified).[8] Now, what could this spontaneous independence and immanence refer to except *phusis* at the core of the thing, and how could this dwelling be attentive if it were not perceiving? There is therefore a "consideration" of things, familiar to each one of us, which, far from being a "*divertissement*" in Pascal's sense (i.e., far from leading us into the fallenness of the inauthentic), relates us to what is most worthy of being thought and invites us to a thought that is more meditative than any foundational rationality. Later, the essay makes the following assessment of the transformation accomplished since the time of the Marburg phenomenology:

> What seems easier than to let a being be just the being that it is? Or does this turn out to be the most difficult of tasks, particularly if such an intention—to let a being be as it is—represents the opposite of the indifference that simply turns its back upon the being itself in favor of an unexamined concept of being? We ought to turn toward the being, think about it in regard to its being, but by means of this thinking at the same time let it rest upon itself in its very own being.
>
> This exertion of thought seems to meet with its greatest resistance in defining the thingness of the thing. . . . The unpretentious thing evades thought most stubbornly. Or can it be that this self-refusal of the mere thing, this self-contained independence, belongs precisely to the nature of the thing? Must not this strange and uncommunicative feature of the nature of the thing become intimately familiar to thought that tries to think the thing? If so, then we should not force our way to its thingly character. (31–32)

The thing has therefore lost the intuitive evidence of something present-at-hand. From now on, it is its strangeness that calls as much for perception as for thought.

---

8. *The Origin of the Work of Art in Poetry, Language, Thought,* trans. Albert Hofstadter (New York: Harper and Row, 1971).

We have seen that the Marburg phenomenology credited the "naive ontology" of the Greeks, because it remained close to everydayness, with subordinating perception, in the narrow sense, to foreseeing and productive comportment. It was in light of this comportment that Heidegger then interpreted the fundamental concepts of Greek thought. From the very moment thought is centered on the *aletheia* of *phusis*, it is no longer foreseeing and productive comportment, but rather this new center that becomes the focal point for the interpretation of these concepts. I am not attempting here to investigate this new interpretation. I would only like to point out, concerning two important concepts (*hule* and *morphe*) how it allows Heidegger to question his former determination of the relationship of the tool to the thing pure and simple. Let me recall the sentence from the Marburg period quoted earlier: "The understanding of being in production is so far from merely understanding beings as produced that it rather opens up precisely the understanding of the being of that which is already simply extant" (*The Basic Problems of Phenomenology*, 116; 163–64). According to this interpretation, the thing (because it was indeed the thing that was defined as "simply extant" in Marburg) was nothing more than a prior matter not yet shaped or what remains after a subtraction of utility. But Heidegger now takes a stand against this approach, stressing that the pair—matter and form—has its origin in Being-instrumental, and not in the Being of the thing:

> The situation stands revealed as soon as we speak of things in the strict sense as mere things. The 'mere,' after all, means the removal of the character of usefulness and of being made. The mere thing is a sort of equipment, albeit equipment denuded of its equipmental being. Thing-being consists in what is then left over. But this remnant is not actually defined in its ontological character. It remains doubtful whether the thingly character comes to view at all in the process of stripping off everything equipmental. (*The Origin of the Work of Art*, 30)

These lines do not mean at all that the relationship between thing and instrument has been inverted nor that the former now holds a privilege over the latter. What is meant rather is that each of them is what it is only in its connectedness to the *aletheia* of *phusis*. The self-containment, the compactness, the self-enclosure of the thing point in the direction of the secret of *phusis*. And the essence of instrumentality now points in the same direction. It resides in what is deeper than usefulness, in reliability (*Verlässlichkeit*), i.e., in the enigmatic bond between the world and what is secretly folded in it, i.e., *phusis*, to which the essay gives the name "earth." When we trust in instrumentality, we entrust ourselves to a world and this world entrusts us to an ungraspable and intractable background interwoven within it. We no longer hear the mention of anything inauthentic or of fallenness into the inauthentic in the description of our everyday intercourse with instrumentality, which the Marburg phenomenology had called "circumspective foresight." To be sure, it is a work of art, the famous painting of "peasant shoes" by Van Gogh, that is invoked to provide the first manifestation of this new essence of instrumentality, at a level deeper than *Zuhandenheit*. Heigegger writes that "it is only in the picture that we notice all this [i.e., the mutual belonging of world and earth at the core of the tool] about the shoes. The peasant woman, on the other hand, simply wears them". But he adds immediately, as if to stress that everyday intercourse with instrumentality is endowed with no less a mode of seeing than that of the artist:

> If only this simple wearing were so simple. When she takes off her shoes late in the evening, in deep but healthy fatigue, and reaches out for them again in the still dim dawn, or passes them by on the day of rest, she knows all this without noticing or reflecting. . . . By virtue of this reliability the peasant woman is made privy to the silent call of the earth; by virtue of the reliability of the equipment she is sure of her world. World and earth exist for her, and for those who are with her in her mode of being, only thus—in the equipment. We say "only" and therewith fall into error; for the reliability of the equipment first gives to the simple world its security and assures to the earth the freedom of its steady thrust. (34)

It is obvious in the above lines that not only the attentive dwelling near simple things, but the everyday relation to instrumentality are no longer affected with a restriction. There is no longer question of antagonism between the authentic and the inauthentic, between the world and the intraworldly. In the everyday relationship to instrumentality, the world which is presupposed by this relationship is no longer covered up: the tool itself is what exhibits the world as well as the natural ground with which it now communicates and which no longer is in any way intraworldly because "the earth is that into which the work sets itself back and that which causes it to come forth from this setting back of itself" (46 modified).

It is obvious that these two modes of seeing have been profoundly transformed. But what about the mode of seeing of the artist? Let us recall Heidegger's hesitation about Rilke's pages which left us an indecision as to whether, by bringing existence as Being-in-the-world to speech, *Dichtung* revealed 'world' in its authenticity, or in its improper sense as weighed down by things and tools. There is, of course, no such indecision in the essay on the work of art. Whereas the Marburg phenomenology character ized the uncovering performed by the work of art as "elementary," this essay now characterizes it as "foundational." It would be perhaps no exaggeration to say that the former uncovering owed its elementary character to its link to things and instrumentality, and that the latter now owes a foundational character to the same link. This indicates how deep the transformation was. The uncovering no longer exclusively focuses on Being-in-the-world, but involves instead the mutual belonging of an intimacy and of a struggle between the world and *phusis*. From now on, to let things be themselves or to restore them to their thingliness—color to coloration, light to its luminosity, the stone to its heaviness, and tools to their Being-instrumental (*Verlässlichkeit*)—in no way constitutes an impediment to authentic uncovering.

There remains the fourth mode of seeing, that of the *Augenblick*, which the Marburg phenomenology located at the intersection of the ecstatic unity of the anticipation of death and of self-retrieval, that is, in the midst of authentic existence and understanding which define resoluteness, *Entschlossenheit*. This notion of resoluteness is evoked in the essay on *The Origin of the Work of Art* when Heidegger says that the work is a call for guardians capable of dwelling in the unveiling that takes place in the work and of keeping it safe. This safekeeping, Heidegger says, is a knowledge that has nothing to do with representation, it is a will which consists neither in applying a knowledge nor in deciding prior to knowing. At this juncture he evokes the analytic of *Sein und Zeit*:

> Knowing that remains a willing, and willing that remains a knowing, is the existing human being's entrance into and compliance with the unconcealedness of Being. The resoluteness (*Entschlossenheit*) intended in *Sein und Zeit* is not the deliberate action of a subject, but the opening up of human being, out of its capacity in that which is, to the openness of Being. However, in existence, man does not proceed from some inside to some outside; rather, the nature of *Existenz* is out-standing standing-within the essential sundering of the clearing of beings. Neither in the creation mentioned before nor in the willing mentioned now do we think of the performance or act of a subject striving toward himself as his self-set-goal.
>
> Willing is the sober dis-closing resolution (*Entschlossenheit*) of that existential self-transcendence which exposes itself to the openness of beings as it is set into the work. In this way, standing-within is brought under law. Preserving the work, as knowing, is a sober standing-within the extraordinary awesomeness of the truth that is happening in the work. (67–68)

If it were possible to compare individually the themes that now characterize the notion of *Entschlossenheit* (knowing, willing, ecstasis, truth, transcendence) with the same themes, as they determined the notion of *Entschlossenheit* in *Sein und Zeit*, we would realize the scope of the metamorphosis contained in the very claim of a continuity between *Sein und Zeit* and the essay on *The Origin of the Work of Art*. It should be enough for us to recall that in *Sein und Zeit*, knowing, which is a willing, defines the state of openness (*Erschlossenheit*) of Dasein, as it is revealed in Dasein by *Gewissen*, conscience, more precisely by *Gewissen-haben-wollen*, the will-to-have-a-conscience. Such a will-to-know was then characterized as "self-understanding in one's own can-be". And the state of openness inherent in the self-understanding of this will-to-know was revealed as constituted by the effective situation of anxiety, by the understanding as self-projection upon one's ownmost guilt, and by silent discourse. It is at this juncture that *Entschlossenheit* appeared. The text of *Sein und Zeit* reads:

> This distinctive and authentic disclosedness, which is attested in Dasein itself by its conscience—*this reticent self-projection upon one's ownmost Being-guilty, in which one is ready for anxiety*—we call *"resoluteness," Entschlossenheit*.

> Resoluteness is a distinctive mode of Dasein's disclosedness. In an earlier passage, however, we have interpreted disclosedness existentially as the *primordial truth*. . . . Truth must be conceived as the fundamental *existentiale*. . . . In resoluteness we have now arrived at that truth of Dasein which is most primordial because it is authentic. (*Being and Time*, Section 60, 343; 296–97)

Now we would only have to compare this passage to that of the essay to realize that resoluteness has undergone a drastic change of meaning. It was then characterized as self-project, it is now characterized as an enduring effort to withstand exposure to an enigmatic outside (see the last pages of this book's *Epilogue*). Between the first text and the second, the meditation on the *aletheia* of *phusis* has shifted the site of truth: it is no longer authentic existence as Dasein's coming to self concerning its ownmost possibility, but the unconcealment of Being, inasmuch as it provides clearing and lighting to beings while excepting itself from them. In this transformation, there is, in addition to many other things, a metamorphosis of perception. Formerly "improper and inauthentic" because it distracted Dasein from its ownmost can-be, perception is now rehabilitated because it is linked to the possibility of dwelling in the exposure to the enigma of Being.

As Being-towards-death, the Dasein of the Marburg period meant resolute existence without dwelling in the proximity of things. From now on, it is when Dasein dwells in their proximity, i.e., in the exposure to their secret, that its existence and resoluteness are as those of a mortal being.

3

The Reappropriation of the Nicomachean Ethics: *Poiesis* and *Praxis* in the Articulation of Fundamental Ontology[1]

I would like to affix as an exergue to this essay the words of Aristotle from the beginning of the *Politics*:

ho de bios praxis ou poiesis estin[2]

These words deal with life, not in the sense of *zoe*, but in the sense of the mode of being (or existing) specific to humans. Translated: The mode of being of humans does not consist in producing, but in acting. In Greek, the verb *poiein* and the substantive *poiesis* designate an activity involving things rather than people, whereas the verb *prattein* and the substantive *praxis* designate an activity concerned first and foremost with the agents themselves.

Certainly, the distinction between these two activities played a decisive role in the way the Greeks of the *polis* viewed the excellence of their mode of living as compared to that of the barbarians. To the Greeks, the barbarians were conspicuous in their patent deficiency regarding *praxis*. The barbarians—in the least favorable case—could spend their entire existence immersed within the eternal cycle of life and under the yoke of its necessities. Or—in the most favorable case—they could reach high achievements in the activity of making or producing all sorts of artifacts not found in nature and in the know-how necessary for such a production. Yet, for the Greeks of the city, the barbarians could never attain the excellence of

---

1. This text combines two papers, the first presented in English at the University of Essex, England, for a colloquium on Reading Heidegger (May 1986) and the second in French at L'Université catholique de Louvain-la-neuve for a colloquium on *Heidegger et l'idée de la phénomenologie* (September 1986), published in *Phaenomenologica* 108 (1988).

2. *Politics*, 1254 a.

praxis: eu prattein (acting well). For the Greeks of the city, such an excellence, such an *eu prattein* resided in the very activity of the citizen, in *politeuein*. This political *praxis* is neither an activity by which a living being relates to the eternal cycle of life, nor one by which the craftsman relates to the demands of his work. It is the activity by which individuals relate to others in their sharing of words and deeds; in such a sharing, what is at issue is their being-together and the exercise of all the virtues that this sharing presupposes: temperance, courage, justice, and prudence (*phronesis*).

Praxis, equated with the very exercise of citizenship, is tightly connected to speech, to *lexis,* and to the individuals' assertions and discussions on what, to them, appears true and essential. Naturally, this exercise occurs through the renewed efforts required for the preservation of their precious common world, a safekeeping which they express and carry out from various and opposed perspectives. Thus understood in terms of the *polis, praxis* cannot possibly be separated from a plurality of actors and speakers, a plurality whose vitality depends upon the fact that they are all peers sharing a bond of friendship and challenge (*philia* and *eris* are both indispensable). For the city, *praxis* entails a close proximity between the expressions *zoon politikon* and *zoon logon echon*. Because *praxis* is tightly bound with the discussion of issues from various and changing perspectives, it requires the strict condition of parity and equality of participants, for those who take part in it. For the same reason, during the period of *isonomia* (equality before the law), it entails a permanent distrust for those who boast of a superior expertise, thereby threatening the continued exercise of the other citizens' rights to pass judgment on issues and to speak their minds. But also more importantly, these people threatened to shape all human affairs according to their own plans (since they passed themselves off as experts in things public) and to subordinate *praxis* to a form of *poiesis*: The success of this process would have reduced the Greek world to the level of the barbarians.

Meditating on the fundamental role of the distinction between *praxis* and *poiesis* in the Greek city, Hannah Arendt produced analyses that decisively identify some of the essential features by which *praxis* is differentiated from *poiesis*. A short review of her teaching will help introduce my point.[3]

---

3. See in particular *The Human Condition* (Chicago: University of Chicago Press, 1958). For a confrontation of Heidegger's thought by Arendt's, see our paper "Arendt, disciple de Heidegger?" in *Etudes Phénoménologiques* 2 (1985), and "Heidegger et Arendt, lecteurs d'Aristote" in *Cahiers de Philosophie* (Lille) 4 (1987): 41–52.

Whereas *poiesis,* or the productive activity, is characterized by the univocity of its model, of its means and of its goal, the activity of *praxis* is thoroughly ambiguous because it connects one or several individuals to others. In effect, the productive activity is defined by its characteristics: (a) its beginning, the plan elaborated by the producer, (b) its goal, the completion of the product, (c) the means available for its implementation, (d) the capacities required of the producer, and beyond itself (e) by a specific use of the product.

In *praxis,* such univocal characteristics cannot be found. Taken at the most elementary level (the very life of somebody in relation to and among others), every *praxis* is indeed inscribed within a preexisting network of relationships and of verbal exchanges which create multiple and constant factors of ambiguity. Since this preexisting network is constantly renewed as newcomers arrive, the action or *praxis* constitutive of somebody's life is such that he is thrown into the roles of both passive recipient and actor. And the effects of such acting are almost infinite and unpredictable. In contrast to the unpredictability of *praxis,* the productive activity, or *poiesis,* is ruled by predictability as a result of its very univocity. Moreover, *poiesis* is reversible whereas *praxis* is irreversible. Lastly, the agent of the productive activity is not required to reveal himself in his most singular aspects, but only as exhibiting general skills. Therefore he is someone, but someone that anyone else might be, someone not unique. He is one exemplar of a kind that can be repeated. Anonymity and neutrality are the burdens carried by every agent. In short, *poiesis* prevents individualization. In contrast, the activity of *praxis* fundamentally promotes individualizing, by providing a plurality which allows individuals to differ from one another while at the same time maintaining similarities. Because of all these characteristics (ambiguity, unpredictability, irreversibility and individuation within plurality), *praxis* is threatened with extreme frailty. Arendt is justified in thinking that the Greek invention of the *bios politikos* (and specifically of the system of *isonomia*) was not destined to abolish such frailty, but instead to acknowledge and establish it in its own right. However, we can also wonder with her whether this very frailty was not precisely targeted by the efforts of those who wished to replace the excellence of *bios politikos* with the excellence of quite another kind of *praxis*: that of *bios theoretikos.*

Deploring the characteristics of equivocation, inconsistency and ambiguity in human affairs, Plato more or less suggests that the distinction between *poiesis* and *praxis* (as it was understood by the city until then) should be abolished. In his Ideal city, human affairs must be organized on the model of *poiesis.* In it, everyone would fulfill a well-defined and controllable activity. Everyone would be a good craftsman in the workshop and conform to the principle "one man, one job," to borrow the phrase from Leo

Strauss. The univocity of *poiesis* would therefore replace the ambiguity of *praxis*. This ideal of univocity in human affairs is no doubt regulated by an ideal of univocity pertaining to the type of activity (i.e., of *praxis* or *bios*) which for Plato is the noblest of all: *bios theoretikos*. Such *bios* aspires to envision ideas devoid of ambiguity; its ideal is *theoria* whose correlative object is not prone to birth, change or decay. Comparable to the activity of the craftsman, the goal of *theoria* is univocity. This theoretical *bios* is, therefore, radically opposed to *doxa* and to the intrinsically ambiguous way in which human beings consider, judge, and discuss their affairs—an ambiguity that permeates these affairs as long as they are not organized as the work of the craftsman.

It is beyond dispute that Aristotle, without ever questioning the eminent dignity of *bios theoretikos*, disagrees with Plato's way of considering the actions performed by human beings. On this point, as on scores of others, Aristotle's desire to be faithful to the phenomena allows him to rehabilitate *praxis* as the city understood it. Ambiguity and mobility are viewed by him as phenomenal features characteristic of human affairs such that one could not attempt to do away with the former without causing some injurious effect to the latter. The acceptance of the features of ambiguity and mobility is not inherent in the know-how of the craftsman, nor in the *episteme* of the philosopher. For this acceptance entails a rehabilitation of *doxa*: only a properly considered opinion can correspond to the phenomenal features of human affairs. *Phronesis* is the aptitude of reaching this right opinion.

This short presentation of the terms and themes essential to Arendt is internally connected to the topic of my investigation. For the distinction between *poiesis* and *praxis*, which Arendt brought to the forefront of her meditation on Aristotle and which she took beyond his immediate teachings, had for the first time been brought to her attention in a 1924 lecture course given by Heidegger on Plato's *Sophist* in Marburg. This lecture course started with a long discussion on the sixth book of the *Nicomachean Ethics*, in which the distinction in question plays a central role. In 1924 Heidegger mastered the articulation of the project of fundamental ontology. Just a year later, the 1925 lecture course on the *Prolegomena to the History of the Concept of Time* introduced the essential teachings of *Sein und Zeit*.

I would like to outline how fundamental ontology, in its very structure, involves a specific reappropriation of the Greek distinction between *poiesis* and *praxis*. I will also raise questions concerning this reappropriation.

Let us begin with a few words on the context of this reappropriation and the very project of fundamental ontology. Fundamental ontology poses the question of the meaning of Being, or, more precisely of the unity of the manifold meanings of Being.[4] If, as common language suggests, there are different meanings to Being (life, existence, persistence, subsistence, actuality, presence, etc.), is there, then, a focus of intelligibility which illuminates these various meanings? More essentially, if (as the founders of metaphysics and in particular as Aristotle thought), it is true that the Being of beings can be expressed in several ways (as *ousia,* as potentiality and actuality, as truth, or according to the categories), is there a common source for all these various ways of predicating Being and where are we to look for it? As early as *Sein und Zeit,* Heidegger indicates that he is indebted to Husserl for conquering the ground (*Boden*) on which this common origin could be sought. In the last years of his life, Heidegger added that he conquered that ground thanks to a meditation on the theory of categorial intuition in the sixth *Logical Investigation.* If we pay close attention to the sixth *Investigation,* we learn that the most elementary intentionality (which for Husserl is perception) is not at all limited to the reception of sensory data: it also involves a complex set of *a priori* elements, among which Being is to be included. Perception is animated not only by the prior and *a priori* understanding (thanks to ideations and categorial intuitions) of what is the reality or thing-ness (*Realität*) of the perceived entity, but also by the prior understanding of the Being of this being. Thus Husserl, repeating Kant's ''Being is not a real predicate'' and correcting him at the same time (because for Kant we cannot have an intuition of a category), invited Heidegger to conceive of Being as beyond beings, yet manifesting itself in an understanding of Being which permeates all our comportments. Hence the ground on the basis of which the common source of the various meanings of Being will be investigated is the being that we are, inasmuch as we are animated by an understanding of Being. It is this being, Dasein, that is taken as the ontical foundation of fundamental ontology. It is by analyzing this entity with regard to the structure of its Being and by conceptually determining what is most radical in the understanding of Being articulated within Dasein, that we will be able to reveal the unique horizon from which the manifold meanings of Being can be clarified. This horizon will turn out to be the ec-static and finite temporality of Dasein itself.

The project of fundamental ontology requires two stages: first, an ontological analysis of Dasein, and then, on the basis of what the analytic reveals (temporality), an elucidation of the various meanings of Being. The first stage is linked to the second and temporality provides the transition:

---

4. See our essay ''Heidegger and Husserl's Logical Investigations: In Remembrance of Heidegger's Last Seminar'' (Zähringen, 1973) in *Dialectic and Difference,* (Atlantic Highlands, N.J.: Humanities Press, 1985, trans. and ed. Robert Crease and James T. Decker).

temporality is at the same time the primordial constitution of Dasein and the horizon for the intelligibility of the meanings of Being. Both stages are furthermore accompanied by a third: the deconstruction of the history of ontology in light of both the analytic of Dasein and the ontological problems systematically raised regarding temporality. We will focus on the first stage, yet without neglecting some indispensable references to the deconstruction characterizing the third.

This first stage is structurally ruled by the difference between *Eigentlichkeit* and *Uneigentlichkeit*. I would like to show that this difference came to Heidegger from the Greek distinction between *poiesis* and *praxis*, more precisely from the distinction investigated by Aristotle in Book Theta of the *Metaphysics* and in Book VI of the *Nicomachean Ethics*. In this attempt, I will do nothing but use—at my own risk—an indication made discreetly by Heidegger himself in his letter-preface to Richardson's book.

In this letter, Heidegger evokes the genesis of the project of fundamental ontology, and stresses the important benefit he derived from "the dialogues with Husserl [which] provided the immediate experience of the phenomenological method." But he immediately adds that, on the basis of this experience,

> a renewed study of the Aristotelian treatises (especially Book IX of the *Metaphysics,* or Theta, and Book VI of the *Nicomachean Ethics*) resulted in the insight into aletheia as a process of revealment, and in the characterization of truth as non-concealment, to which all self-manifestation of beings pertains.[5]

Since truth is expressly thematized only in Chapter 10 of Book Theta of the Metaphysics, one might be justified in presuming that Heidegger aims at the whole development taking place in these two books. In these two books the difference between two types of action—*poiesis* and *praxis*—plays a central role. One can therefore surmise that the discovery or rediscovery of truth as unconcealment is connected to the discovery or rediscovery of the specific *aletheic* function pertaining to each of these activities. For it is significant that the sentence just quoted should evoke first *aletheuein,* i.e., an uncovering activity. Finally, I must say that I am less interested in tracing the influence of Aristotle upon Heidegger than in calling in question the peculiar style of the reappropriation that took place.

---

5. William J. Richardson, *Heidegger: Through Phenomenology to Thought,* (The Hague: Martinus Nijhoff, 1967), pp. x–xiii.

II

Let us consider *poiesis* first. We know that the analytic of Dasein progresses toward what Dasein is in its ownmost by distancing Dasein from everydayness, i.e., a mode of being in which it is not properly itself. In the everyday mode of being (characterized by preoccupation), Dasein is absorbed in its *Umwelt* or immersed in an environment which thoroughly involves it. Thus absorbed, Dasein constantly encounters something which is intrinsically (but nonthematically) referred to (in the sense of being used for, relevant to, etc.) something else; each time the entities encountered are inscribed in a referential contexture: this contexture forms a closed totality and is already familiar and common to many individuals. The first version of the existential analytic, which we find in the lecture course *The History of the Concept of Time,* refers to the everyday world, to the common world of the environment (which is the specific correlate of preoccupation) as the world of work, more precisely the world of work-making, *Werkwelt.* *Werken* was *poiein* in Greek. The world of everydayness is the world of *poiesis.* The fact that in such a world, Dasein never exists in any way revealing its ownmost, means that what preoccupies it is never itself, but always beings handy (*zuhanden*) for this or that end. Thus their capacity for useful manipulation presupposes that beings stand by themselves before a hand actually takes hold of them, i.e., that they be *vorhanden,* present-at-hand. The absorption of Dasein in that world is such that Dasein can grasp its own Being only in an improper mode (foreclosing the ownmost self) by way of a sort of optical reflection: it sees itself in light of the mode of being of those beings with which it is involved, and therefore is led to conceiving itself as something belonging to the realm of things *vorhanden.* Finally, this means that to the question "Who is the Dasein of everydayness?" the answer cannot be individuated: it is anybody, it is everybody and nobody, it is the "they." The world which fosters the preoccupation of everydayness is defined as *Werkwelt.* This world of *poiesis* is such that this failure of individuation in the public leveling of Dasein obliterates its ownmost Being and the prestige of *Vorhandenheit* veils the openness of Dasein to its ownmost possibility of Being, to its *Zu-Sein.* In other words, the work-world of everydayness covers up existence.

We are not saying at all that everyday *poiesis* is blind, whatever it does [*quelle qu'en soit la teneur*]:

> working on something with something, producing something, cultivating and caring for something, putting something to use, employing something for something, holding something in trust,

giving up, letting something get lost, interrogating, discussing, accomplishing, exploring, considering, determining something (*History of the Concept of Time,* 159; 213–14).

Far from being blind, *poiesis* is entirely open to and preoccupied with the significance of its surroundings and is empowered by *praktische Umsicht,* a circumspection which projects light on these surroundings and is adjusted to the very environment with which Dasein is in daily intercourse (*Umgang*). But precisely because circumspection gives itself over to the surroundings and to the specific poietic possibilities looming within them at every moment, it is never projected anywhere but on the surroundings of Dasein and is oblivious to what constitutes Dasein in its ownmost (that is, oblivious to the care of Being specific to its finite temporality). In a word, it is oblivious to what individualizes Dasein radically and without substitution.

Let us postpone for a while the question of the link between this selfhood, this ownmost Being, and *praxis.* For now let us limit ourselves to *poiesis.* What the analytic unveils regarding *poiesis* is corroborated by the deconstruction of the history of ontology. Heidegger says and repeats at Marburg that the history of ontology gives an unwarranted privilege to only one concept of Being: *Vorhandenheit.* The word *Vorhandene* is a colloquial term in German. To the phenomenologist the term has a double advantage. By its root, *Hand-,* the term immediately relates Being to the active comportment of someone. Moreover, it happens to be the exact linguistic equivalent to the Greek word *procheiron* which Aristotle uses in the first book of the *Metaphysics* (A 2, 982 b 13), where he says that the first objects of the philosophical *thaumazein* are *procheira,* before-the-hand.

Indeed, the deconstruction of the history of ontology, a history in which *Vorhandenheit* is an ever-present yardstick, requires a genealogy of this notion. The method of fundamental ontology is phenomenology. This means, as Heidegger explains in *The Basic Problems of Phenomenology,*[6] that it is a method which combines reduction, construction, and deconstruction. Reduction takes the phenomenological seeing back from the attention paid to beings and directs it toward the understanding of the Being of these beings, an understanding which resides in Dasein. [Reduction means "leading phenomenological vision back from the apprehension of a being, whatever might be the character of that apprehension, to the understanding of the Being of this being (projecting upon the way it is uncon-

---

6. *The Basic Problems of Phenomenology,* trans. Albert Hofstadter (Bloomington: Indiana University Press, 1982).

cealed)" (21; 29).][7] Construction consists of the bringing into sight of the ontological structures of beings, in a "free projection" enacted by the one who thinks. [But this construction itself, which requires a conceptualization adjusted to the illumination of ontological structures, is not separable from a specific debate with the tradition.] Deconstruction, thus, consists in critically (that is to say with all the discernment possible) exposing the phenomenal origin of the ontological concepts—which have now become traditional, self-evident, and standard.

In the deconstruction of *Vorhandenheit, poiesis* plays a decisive role. This deconstruction shows that the activity of making or producing (*Herstellen*) is the comportment within which the Greek philosophers understood the Being of beings and imposed upon the tradition of metaphysics the notion of Being as *Vorhandenheit* (along with some other fundamental ontological concepts). *The Basic Problems of Phenomenology* unravels this genealogy within the framework of a critical and phenomenological discussion of the medieval thesis on Being according to which both essence and existence are necessary to the ontological constitution of every being. I shall only stress a few points of this genealogy. In the scholastic sense existence is *actualitas,* from which the modern words *Wirklichkeit* and "actuality" are derived. But *actualitas* is the Latin translation of the Aristotelian *energeia.* According to Heidegger, the verb *energein* from which the substantive is derived, suggests that the ontological concept of *energeia* "refers back to an acting on the part of some indefinite subject or, if we start from our own terminology, that the extant [*das Vorhandene*] is somehow referred by its sense to something for which, as it were, *it comes to be before the hand* (*vor die Hand*), at hand, to be handled" (101; 143). *Actualitas* and *energeia* both denote "a relationship to our Dasein, as an acting Dasein or, to speak more precisely, as a creative, *productive* Dasein" (101; 143). Similar remarks could be made concerning the Greek ontological notions which served to characterize essence in the medieval sense. Heidegger maintains that these notions (*eidos, morphe, to ti èn einai, genos, teleion, phusis,* etc.) all refer to productive activity. *Eidos* is the prototype which the producer takes into consideration; *morphe* is the distinctive shape given to the product; *teleion* is its completion or "finishedness," and so forth. The Greek notion of *ousia*—the medieval translation of which is *essentia*—displays unambiguously, or univocally, its specific relationship to the productive activity: initially the word meant assets, goods, patrimony, or estate, or what is "at hand disposable" (*vorhandenes Verfügbares*). Concerning this point, Heidegger writes:

---

7. This sentence and the next one in brackets were added by the author for the English text.

The basic concept of ousia . . . lays more stress on the produced-
ness of the produced in the sense of things disposably present at
hand (verfugbaren Vorhandenen). What is meant here primarily is
what is present at hand, house and yard, the Anwesen, as the German has it—property as the present premises—the extant as what
is present in that way. (109; 153)

And Heidegger further claims that

the verb einai, esse, existere must be interpreted by way of the
meaning of ousia as the disposably present-at-hand and that which
is present in that way [as property and premises are present]. Being, being-actual or existing, in the traditional sense, means
presence-at-hand, Vorhandenheit. (109; 153)

This historical genealogy is supported by the phenomenological analysis of
the specific intentionality of productive comportment. To be sure, the orientation specific to this comportment and its manner of apprehending that
to which it is related, entails a specific understanding of the Being of beings
intended by this comportment as product, as producible, or as a being that
does not have to be produced. This orientation consists of more than using
items to create products, shaping products, and using products. It consists
also of *liberating, freeing, and delivering* these products from their link to
the producer. Heidegger writes: "Not only is [the product], as finished,
factually no longer bound to the productive relation, but also even as something still to be produced, it is understood beforehand as intended to be
released from this relation" (113; 160). Hence we find that a specific understanding of Being permeates this type of comportment. The productive
comportment understands the Being of the beings (to which it is related) as
standing-by itself (Ansichsein), and independent (Eigenständiges). Indeed,
Heidegger agrees that "the very being which the Greeks especially made
the starting point of their ontological investigations, that which is as nature
and as cosmos, is surely not produced by Dasein as the producer" (115;
163). But this admission, correct though it is, should not be held as an
objection. Nature, ever-present and in no need of being produced,

can really be understood and discovered only within the understanding of Being that goes with production. In other words, it is
first of all in the understanding of what does not need to be produced that there can grow the understanding of a being which is
extant (vorhanden) in itself *before* all production and for all further
production. (116; 163)

Heidegger concedes indeed that such a being (Nature) which is present before anything else, has a mode of being "standing-by-itself," which the

Greeks turned into the correlate of an activity that is no longer productive at all; this no-longer-productive activity is the contemplative apprehension, a pure *theorein*, either in the form of *noesis* or of *aisthesis*. Correct though this remark may be, it too should not be held as an objection against the primordial character of productive comportment in the ontological understanding of the Greeks. From the fact that the Greeks claimed the rank of pure *theoria* for their ontology, one cannot conclude that this ontology is completely unrelated to the productive activity of *poiesis*. Precisely because the Being to which this *theoria* is related is understood as *Vorhandenheit* and because the understanding of Being as *Vorhandenheit* is specific to productive comportment, we are instead invited to think that *theoria*, purely intuitive though it may be, "is only a modification of seeing in the sense of circumspection, of productive behavior" (110; 154). All this, then, invites us to consider that as early as Parmenides, *noein*—to which *einai* was related—was nothing but a modification of *poiesis*.

Fundamental ontology in no way aims at discarding the understanding or seeing of Being as *Vorhandenheit*, inherent in *poiesis*, but at reappropriating it (or at assigning it a proper place by preventing it from completely expanding throughout the entire field of the understanding of Being). Such a reappropriation presupposes that we overcome the naivete of Greek ontology. The Greeks were correct in thinking that the elucidation of the Being of beings must take place on no other ground than the being that we are, a ground which Parmenides characterized as *noein*. Plato characterized it as the soul (*psyche*) which is involved in a dialogue with itself, and Aristotle in terms of the apophantic *logos* of the *nous*. They were right in thinking that the *einai* of the beings that we are not is *Vorhandenheit*. Heidegger at Marburg maintained that *Vorhandenheit* is the mode of being of things, or—as he often says—of nature, of *phusis* in the broad sense. Moreover the Greeks were also right (as we have seen) in inscribing the mode of being of the beings that we are not within the horizon of productive comportment, or *poiesis*. But they were naive in their belief (or in making it possible for others to believe) that all seeing (or *theorein*) of Being is a simple modification of the seeing inherent in *poiesis*. In other words, they were naive in believing (or at least in making it possible for the tradition to believe) that the mode of being of the being that we are can be determined by a reflection—in the optical sense of the word—by which the mode of being of the beings that we are not (products, tools, materials) is projected upon ourselves. More precisely, their naivete consisted not in failing to acknowledge the necessity of ontology to return to "the Dasein's comportments," but in limiting this necessary return from considering anything but the comportments pervasive in "Dasein's everyday and natural self-understanding" (110; 156). Exposing and discarding their naivete is tantamount to overcoming this limitation. Overcoming this limitation requires that we understand that the mode of seeing inherent in *poiesis*—whether this be practical circumspection or intuitive (noetic or aesthetic) apprehension, the second being a modification of the first—does not exhaust the understanding of Being. More profoundly, it requires that we understand that the mode of seeing inherent in *poiesis* is only the decline, or the fall of a higher mode of seeing, adequately adjusted to the ownmost mode of being of Dasein. More precisely, this higher seeing is inherent in the acting and in the comportment that are Dasein's ownmost. This seeing is what, at its sharpest point, Heidegger characterizes as the *augenblickliches Sichselbstverstehen,* "instantaneous self-understanding."[8]

Parodoxically, in order to discard the naivete which he imputed to Greek ontology and, consequently, to the tradition founded on the Greeks, Heidegger still seeks his inspiration from Greek philosophical texts. In order to overcome the limitation and obscuring brought in the wake of *poiesis,* Heidegger relies on the Greek analysis of another activity, *praxis,* which Aristotle explored in the previously mentioned texts.

III

Let us then consider *praxis*. The two major Aristotelian texts on *praxis* are Book Theta of the *Metaphysics* and Book VI of the *Nicomachean Ethics*. During the period of fundamental ontology when Heidegger analyzes Book Theta of the *Metaphysics,* his approach alternatively deals with the first three chapters and with the tenth chapter. In his reading of the first three chapters, Heidegger considers the topic of *poiesis*. In his reading of Chapter 10, he credits Aristotle with conceiving truth as the characteristic beings have of standing unveiled. Aristotle is also credited with having closely linked this unveiling to the uncovering comportment of the being that we are. However no lecture course has been published to date [May 1986] that expressly deals with the Aristotelian confrontation between *poiesis* and *praxis,* which nevertheless is a major theme in *Metaphysics,* Book Theta. Perhaps the publication of the lecture course on the *Sophist* will fill this lacuna.[9] Whatever the case, it seems appropriate to recall the features by which Aristotle characterizes *praxis* in Book Theta.

First, *praxis* is an activity which, instead of being related to an end external to it, includes the end within itself. Because of the inclusion of the

---

8. *Metaphysische Anfangsgründe der Logik,* p. 9.
9. See the appendix to this chapter, pp. 139–43.

end within the activity, *praxis* relates to time in a way much different than *poiesis*. In the activity of *praxis*, at each time we are the one who presently is and the one who has been. For example, each time we are involved in the activity of understanding, we are the one who understands and who has previously understood. Seeing, too, is a *praxis*: in it, there is no opposition between the fact of seeing now and the fact of having already seen. And, similarly, between thinking and the fact of having already previously thought, between living now and the fact of having previously lived. In contradistinction, *poiesis* is an activity characterized by the fact that we are not, for example, at the same time the one in the process of building and the one who has already built; or the one in the process of learning and the one who has already learned. Consequently, *energeia* and *dunamis*, actuality and potentiality, do not function identically in the case of *praxis* as in *poiesis*.

In the case of *poiesis*, it is within the *ergon* (the product) that *energeia* (i.e., effectiveness) is implemented. In the case of *praxis*, *energeia* is contained within the activity, more precisely within the agent himself, who, as an agent, always has the potential of acting or not acting. Consequently in the case of *poiesis*, *dunamis* is external to *energeia*, whereas in the case of *praxis*, *dunamis* is internal to *energeia*. In both cases however, *dunamis* is a fallible and perishable capacity; it can fail to actualize itself, it is a power of being and of not-being. ["Everything which is capable may fail to be actualized. Therefore that which is capable of being may both be and not be. Therefore the same is capable both of being and of not-being (*Metaphysics*, Theta, 1050b, 10)."][10]

Concerning Book VI of the *Nicomachean Ethics*, I shall only present Aristotle's views on *phronesis*, that is, the disposition of the soul (*hexis*) which has as its function the disclosure of matters of *praxis*. Aristotle distinguishes *phronesis* from *techne* (a know-how adjusted to *poiesis*) and from *episteme* (the knowledge of what is eternal and necessary). Like products of fabrication, human deeds are variable and contingent. But because acting is not geared toward producing anything, the disclosing (or *aletheic*) disposition adjusted to action should in no way be confused with the one presiding over production, that is, *techne*. *Techne* aims at a goal, a product, that is external to the *technites*. *Phronesis* aims at a goal that intimately concerns the *phronimos*: the goal of acting well, *eupraxia*. The theme of time resurfaces here. *Phronesis* is self-referential inasmuch as it is related to the future of the *phronimos*, a future which might or might not come to pass. Since *phronesis* concerns neither products (as *techne* does) nor imperishable

---

10. Quotation added in the English text.

beings (as *episteme* does), it is not concerned with anything universal, but with what pertains to the individual, *ta ekasta,* and the proper time, *to kairos.* Hence, it only concerns human affairs, *ta anthropina,* which are changing and diverse, apprehended not through *episteme,* but through *doxa.* "*Doxa* applies to what can vary, and so does *phronesis*" (1140b, 25). *Phronesis* is a doxastic (deliberative) virtue. But because there is no *doxa* without a debate between varying and opposing views, *phronesis* is not limited to what matters to the *phronimos* alone. One could not possibly be *phronimos* by being involved exclusively with oneself. This is why *phronesis* is identical to political wisdom.

There are reasons to believe that this Aristotelian meditation on what is specific to *praxis* and what differentiates it from *poiesis* is reappropriated by Heidegger (with the significant omission of the doxastic component connected to a plural and political dimension, a point to which we shall come back later) in his fundamental ontology and that this reappropriation provides the project with its articulation.

Fundamental ontology is regulated by the basic distinction between *Uneigentlichkeit* and *Eigentlichkeit,* the former characterizing everyday preoccupation and concern (*Besorgnis*), the latter care (*Sorge*). Such a distinction contains a hierarchy in that both preoccupation and concern are forms of fallen care. This distinction reappropriates the Aristotelian distinction between *poiesis* and *praxis. Praxis* in the Aristotelian sense rules over *poiesis.* It owes this ruling status to its self-referential character. "In *poiesis,*" Aristotle argues, "the thing done (*to poieton*) is not an end in itself, it is only for something or somebody else (*pros ti kai tinos*). The opposite should be said about what is achieved in and by *praxis,* since *eupraxia* is the end and this is what desire aims at" (1139a 35–b 4). This contrast between *pros ti* and *hou heneka* (between *Wozu* and *Worumwillen*) and the hierarchical superiority of the latter over the former are features which, in my view, are reappropriated by Heidegger when he opposes preoccupation (a comportment always delivered over to what is foreign) to care (a comportment which delivers Dasein over to its ownmost). From this, it becomes increasingly clear that Heidegger's famous sentence about Dasein: "*Das Dasein existiert umwillen seiner*" (Dasein exists for the sake of itself) can be considered a transposition of the Aristotelian theory of *praxis.*

Likewise, the Heideggerian phenomenology of truth in fundamental ontology—which contrasts the aletheic function of practical circumspection with the aletheic function of Dasein's resoluteness—can be interpreted as the radicalization of Aristotle's theory of the different levels of intellectual excellence. Aristotle makes clear that *praxis* can understand *poiesis,* but that the latter is not able to understand the former precisely because the unveiling character of *phronesis* is higher in rank than the unveiling character of poietic know-how, or *techne*. At least four fundamental features determine the Aristotelian notion of *phronesis*: a specific seeing oriented towards a specific future (*eupraxia*), a sense of the right moment, a deliberate choice with awareness of a possible failure, and a prior disposition (*hexis*). All these features contribute to the Heideggerian notion of *Entschlossenheit*. Likewise, the Heideggerian critique of the traditional concept of knowledge as pure intuitive seeing—free-floating and without anchors in Being-in-the-world—can also be interpreted as the result of a reappropriation of Aristotle. Indeed, seeing as well as knowing and understanding are examples of *praxis* given by Aristotle.

And finally, there is reason to suspect that the Heideggerian notion of authentic time, the intrinsically finite and ec-static temporality of Dasein, such as it is revealed to resoluteness (*Entschlossenheit*), radicalizes a suggestion made by Aristotle himself. To be sure, there is no specific thematization of a time proper to *praxis* in Aristotle. The only explicit theory of time is formulated by Aristotle in the *Physics* and we can concede to Heidegger that the time of Aristotelian physics is only adjusted to extantness, *Vorhandenheit*, that is, to beings understood in poietic or productive comportment. However, a close examination of some suggestions made by Aristotle with regard to time in his analysis of *praxis* shows that he does not account for the time of *praxis* in terms of the mere number of movement according to the 'earlier' and the 'later.' Indeed, Book Theta of the *Metaphysics* stresses (1048 b, ff.) that *praxis*, as an activity which includes its own end, does not fall under the category of movement, *kinesis*, in the manner in which this category applies to *poiesis*. Movement in connection with *poiesis* is a means to an end at which it terminates, so that we may not say that being-in-motion is already containing the end brought about by the process. Because its goal is external to it, this movement is *ateles*, or incomplete. In contrast, *praxis* includes its own goal, and, as such, is *teleia*, or complete. It means that at each moment, *praxis* unifies what it previously was and what it will be, its past and its future, whereas the *kinesis* of which *poiesis* is a species, leaves its past and future unrelated to one another.

It is therefore now plain to see that the analyses by which Aristotle shows the specificity of *praxis* and distinguishes it from *poiesis* confirm that Heidegger articulated his fundamental ontology thanks to a reappropriation of the distinction between these two notions. Yet, I would not claim that any direct allusion to the Greek distinction between *poiesis* and *praxis* is made by Heidegger in the text. I will refrain from elaborating on his silence [*discrétion*]. To a large extent, it can be explained by the simple fact that the reappropriation attempted to be a radicalization. Furthermore, with the exception of the yet unpublished lecture course on the *Sophist*,[11] there is at least one lecture course from the Marburg period in which Heidegger expressly acknowledges this reappropriation (albeit in the form of a remark that sounds like an allusion), the last course offered in the summer of 1928 at Marburg published as *The Metaphysical Foundations of Logic*. In a section on the phenomenon of world and on the way in which the Greeks understood it, we read the following assessment:

> The phenomenon of the world gets approached [namely in Greek philosophy] ontically and gets diverted into an extant (*vorhandene*) realm of ideas accessible to a mere looking. Among other reasons, this is because transcendence, from early on, was taken primarily in the sense of *theorein*, which means that transcendence was not sought in its primordial rootedness in the real being of Dasein. *Nevertheless, Dasein was known to antiquity also as authentic (eigentlitche) action, as praxis* [my emphasis]. (183 modified; 236)[12]

The use of *eigentlich* to characterize Greek *praxis* is in itself extremely significant. It amounts to acknowledging that Heidegger's own concept of *Eigentlichkeit* owes something important to a meditation on the Greek concept of *praxis*. In other words, in spite of the privilege bestowed upon *poiesis* and *Vorhandenheit* by their ontology, the Greeks were aware of the proper mode of being of Dasein, i.e. , transcendence. Then, the text of the lecture adds:

> Though in Plato transcendence was not investigated down to its authentic roots, the inescapable pressure of the phenomenon nevertheless brought to light the connection between the transcendent intended by the idea and *the root of transcendence, praxis* [my emphasis]. The idea is the correlate of intuition, but there is a passage in Plato according to which the idea of the Good, the *idea tou agathou* still lies beyond beings and *ousia,* beyond the ideas, *epekeina tes ousias.* Here a transcendence emerges that one must consider the most primordial, insofar as the ideas are themselves already transcendent with regard to the beings that change. . . . What we must learn to see in the *idea tou agathou* is the characteristic described by Plato and *particularly Aristotle* [my emphasis]

---

11. See the appendix to this chapter, pp. 139–43.
12. *The Metaphysical Foundations of Logic*, trans. Michael Heim (Bloomington: Indiana University Press, 1984).

as the *hou heneka,* the for-the-sake-of-which, that on account of which something is or is not, is in this way or that. The idea *tou agathou,* which is even beyond beings and the realm of ideas is the for-the-sake-of-which. . . . If we thus keep in mind the *hou heneka* characteristic of the highest idea, the connection between the doctrine of ideas and the concept of world begins to emerge: the basic characteristic of the world whereby wholeness attains its specifically transcendental form of organization is the for-the-sake-of-which. (184; 236–37)

If the *hou heneka* of *praxis* has to be viewed as the *Worumwillen* of Dasein, or as that towards which Dasein transcends (i.e., the world), then the phrase "we must learn to see" comes very close to an admission on Heidegger's part that he saw or discovered the transcendence inherent to being-in-the-world in Aristotle's theory of *praxis.*

Let me add a few concluding remarks. I have already said that it is paradoxical (a) to pretend that the Greeks displayed a form of naivete by founding their ontological notions within the horizon of intelligibility of the activity of *poiesis,* and (b) to discard such naivete by basing the new [*non-naïve*] ontology on the horizon of intelligibility of the activity of *praxis* as the Greeks understood it. In a first approximation, we can say that the paradox consists of this: On the one hand, Heidegger stresses that the Greeks were naive (they determined the mode of being of Dasein by optical reflection from the mode of Being of the beings that we are not, but to which *poiesis* is related and which Dasein understands). On the other hand, he suggests that the Greeks were not so naive after all: their analysis of *praxis* proves that they properly understood the ownmost way of Being of Dasein, and it is their analysis that is radicalized in fundamental ontology. It is difficult to believe that Heidegger was not aware of such a paradox. It would explain his remarkable silence [*discrétion*] regarding the Greek analysis of *praxis.* This discretion notwithstanding, we can surmise that it was in an effort to confront this paradox that Heidegger attempted the subsequent transformation [*métamorphose*] of the notions previously determining the entire field of *Uneigentlichkeit* in fundamental ontology. If the Greeks were not at all naive concerning *praxis,* perhaps they also were not naive with regard to *poiesis.* Perhaps then, the naivete which Heidegger first imputed to them was more the result of distinctions and constraints in the framework of his reappropriation than inherent in what they were trying to think.

For, *if poiesis* (as it is reappropriated in light of the approach combining reduction, deconstruction, and construction) is the equivalent of a fallen modification of *praxis* (i.e., of existence), and *if poiesis* is identified with preoccupation as the comportment in which the Being of existence is not authentically addressed, but in which we correctly understand *Vorhandenheit* as the Being of the beings that we are not, *then* a question such as "What is a thing?" does not deserve much attention. For in the framework of fundamental ontology, it is by a sort of distraction, or *"divertissement"* (in Pascal's sense of the word) and by way of falling out of our ownmost possibility, that we care for things. Neither is a question such as "What is dwelling?" worth raising. It is obvious that in the framework of fundamental ontology a house is not a home, but a dwelling tool, a *"machine à habiter"* to use Le Corbusier's expression. Going on a pilgrimage to the cabin in Todtnauberg is a pointless journey because the fundamental ontologist who wrote *Sein und Zeit* could not without contradiction have conceived his cabin as a home for thinking Being. The fundamental ontologist never dwelled in the cabin except by *"divertissement."* According to fundamental ontology, we dwell in an *Umwelt* (a fallen modification of the world), but we do not dwell in a world. For with regard to the world in its proper sense, Dasein is without dwelling, and *Un-heimlichkeit* is the element in which thinking is engaged. The cabin, therefore, was nothing more than a Platonic cave. In addition, a theme like nature is not worthy of much attention in fundamental ontology. *Phusis* therein is simply conceived as the correlate of *poiesis*. It is nothing more than something extant, available for manipulations; its Being is that of simple extantness or *Vorhandenheit*. No polemical tension is to be found in it. It is not the earth in conflicting relationship with the world, because the world according to fundamental ontology is not built upon *phusis*. At this point in Heidegger's itinerary, *phusis* is not at all an enigmatic source regulated by the tension of unconcealment and reserve. Instead, as soon as it appears, nature is *innerweltlich*, intraworldly.

In short, the previous remarks aim at suggesting that Heidegger's later essays, which deal with these questions, might be considered as subsequent corrections of fundamental ontology. It is a fact that the very questions that fundamental ontology deemed answerable immediately—because of their connection to everyday fallenness and their standing opposition to Dasein's ownmost—suddenly imposed themselves as most worthy of investigation for thought at its ownmost (that is, in its care of Being). These questions were raised at a cost: in the wake of a new reading of Greek philosophy, Heidegger abandoned his previous relegation of *poiesis* as inauthentic and sought to perform a true ontological rehabilitation of it. At this juncture, notions such as *setting-into-work* (*energeia*) came to the forefront as related to the truth of Being, that is, to the polemical struggle of unconcealment and reserve. In the process of this rehabilitation, *phusis* is no longer equated with *Vorhandenheit*, but instead with truth in what is most primordial. Thus the disclosing activity of Dasein is no longer granted the unique privilege of unveiling truth; instead *phusis* is the ambiguous and most initial manifestation of Being itself unveiled, to which Dasein is called to respond, rather than over which it rules. Also in this rehabilitation, fabrication and the use of tools, far from being absorbed in the *Umwelt* (the fallen figure of the world in its ownmost), are related to this ambiguous manifestation. Hence the knowledge specific to *poiesis*, i.e., *techne*, is no longer limited to an intercourse with the *Umwelt*. Thus, in *The Origin of the Work of Art*, the peasant woman when using reliable tools gleans the secret fold of the earth within the world and entrusts world and earth to each other. In this new context, modern *techne* (technology) alone receives the status of fallenness, inasmuch as its generalized mechanization is based upon the obliteration of the ontological *polemos*. The rehabilitation of *poiesis* is so radical as to be accompanied by the claim that the thinker himself is a sort of craftsman (*Letter on Humanism*).[13]

Our goal is not to trace the manifold transformation of *poiesis*. Unquestionably these changes erupted in *The Origin of the Work of Art* all at once, in spite of some hesitations and Hegelian resurgences also found in this essay.[14] It remains to be seen whether these transformations were accompanied by a parallel metamorphosis of Heidegger's notion of *praxis*. Here the paradox mentioned earlier is reactivated.

For is it not paradoxical that fundamental ontology should claim to establish the new universal science of the meanings of Being on the basis of the activity of *praxis* which in Aristotle was linked to human plurality and, as such, was incompatible with the universality pursued by *prima philosophia*? Is it not paradoxical that the Heideggerian reappropriation should search for the universal horizon of intelligibility of the meanings of Being within a transcendence which in the terms of the existential analytic is radically individuated, nonsubstitutable, and, most of all, non-relational (*unbezuglich*)?

Obviously, because in its very structure, fundamental ontology is decisively supported by a reappropriation of *phronesis*, Aristotle plays in it a more significant role than Plato. Yet, Heidegger's selection of what had to be reappropriated in the Aristotelian doctrine of *praxis* and *poiesis* seems to indicate a Platonic bias. Indeed, is it not surprising that Heidegger neglected in this doctrine the *doxastic* (pertaining to opinion) and the plural (and political) dimensions? Is it not surprising that neither of these dimen-

---

13. In *Martin Heidegger, Basic Writings,* ed. David F. Krell (New York: Harper and Row, 1977).

14. See our essay "Le dépassement heideggérien de l'esthétique et l'héritage de Hegel" in *Recoupements* (Brussels: Editions Ousia, 1982).

sions belongs to his concept of *Entschlossenheit* if we grant that it is indeed this term that radicalizes the Aristotelian notion of *phronesis*? In its essence, *Entschlossenheit* is linked to what Heidegger calls *"existential solipsism"* (*Being and Time*, 233; 188). *Doxa*, the relationship to others, and the plural debate are excluded from the radicalized *phronesis* and relegated to the sphere of concern, i.e., to the inauthentic comportment of Dasein. Consequently, the very distinction between inauthenticity and authenticity seems to coincide with the distinction between public and private. We have reason to suspect that this distinction echoes Plato's disdain for human affairs. As a matter of fact, this disdain appears as early as the introduction to *Sein und Zeit* where Heidegger contrasts Thucydides' accounts with the "unprecedented character of the formulations" of Plato's *Parmenides* and Aristotle's *Metaphysics* (*Being and Time*, 63; 39). To be sure, his very description of everydayness as subjected to the weight of productive mentality and to equivocation in opinions is easily in accord with Plato's description and depreciation of human affairs, which in Plato are conducted with a view toward justifying as supreme the *bios theoretikos*, i.e., the solitary activity in which the soul is in dialogue with itself. The insistence on the dominance of the "they" in the public character of everydayness echoes Plato's disdain for *hoi polloi* in the Republic. And the very reappropriation of the notion of *doxa* as characteristic of the inauthentic understanding and speech supposedly prevalent in everydayness is certainly more inspired from Plato's critique of sophistry than from Aristotle's justification of *doxa* concerning matters of *phronesis*. In fundamental ontology there is no room for what Aristotle calls "right opinion." Instead there are many echoes of the Platonic distinction between *sophia* and sophistry, and between science and rhetoric.

This Platonic bias, which Hannah Arendt noticed and stressed, deserves more attention than it usually receives and raises a question: Is *praxis*, as reappropriated by Heidegger, described for its own sake—or only in order to provide a nonambiguous basis for the ultimate science of the meaning of Being, that is, for the completion of metaphysics? In other words, is the Heideggerian reappropriation a radicalization of Aristotle's teaching—or is it a combination of radicalization and obliteration? To be sure, Aristotle agreed with Plato in ranking *bios theoretikos* as the highest form of *praxis*. But there is no doubt that Aristotle at the same time rejected Plato's ambition to submit the entire field of *praxis* to the ruling of *bios theoretikos*. The *Nicomachean Ethics* precisely shows his disagreement with Plato on this point. After indicating at the beginning of the work that his inquiry "is in a way the study of politics," Aristotle stresses in contrast to Plato that his own treatment of political science will be adjusted to its subject which contains "much difference of opinion and uncertainty" and which, for this very reason, is not required to show the total precision and exactness "one must expect in other disciplines of philosophy." Consequently for him,

It is the mark of an educated mind to expect that degree of precision in each kind of study which the nature of the subject at hand admits: it is obviously just as foolish to accept arguments of probability from a mathematician as to demand strict demonstrations from an orator. (1094 b)

In these words we hear the echo of the spirit of the city that we recalled earlier: difference of opinion and uncertainty are inherent in *praxis,* and the philosopher's objective should be to accommodate them rather than to discard them. Although the political philosopher in the Aristotelian sense is not a rhetorician, he is, in contrast to Plato, closer to the orator than to the mathematician. And the reason for his proximity is connected to Aristotle's sense of the essential link between *praxis* and plurality, that is, of the fact that humans are at the same time all alike and all different. By reason of human plurality, or the Aristotelian *plethos* found in the *Politics* (which stands opposed to Plato's monist and unanimous aspirations), *praxis* is an essentially ambiguous reality. It cannot therefore be the object and the ground of a science devoid of ambiguity. But are not this essential plurality and its resulting ambiguity precisely obliterated by the attempt to found fundamental ontology on the basis of *praxis,* conceived as the free transcendence of Dasein that understands Being inasmuch as it exists resolutely in the care of itself alone?

In fundamental ontology, the concept of transcendence is totally dominated by the resistance of the ownmost to inauthenticity, or in Platonic terms, by the resistance of the One to the Many. This is why in fundamental ontology transcendence prevents us from conceiving *praxis* in connection with a common realm of shared deeds and words, as did the Greek city and its Aristotelian account. Taken in its purity, the Heideggerian concept of world present in fundamental ontology, i.e., *hou heneka* metamorphosed into *Worumwillen,* is a self-referential focus empty not only of things, but also of people. It is not a dwelling or a common realm, but the pure and clear nothingness grasped in the moment of vision (*Augenblick*) by a Dasein resolutely confronting—in separate individuation—the absence of dwelling, which brings about the *Grundstimmung* of anxiety. To be sure, Being-with-others and speech are essential characteristics of Dasein, i.e., *existentialia.* But, if we ask what authentic *Mit-Sein* amounts to, we soon realize that this *existentiale* taken in its purity is strictly monadic. Heidegger underlines the fact that in everydayness, our relationships with others and our solicitude for them are inauthentic. Proximally and for the

most part, he says, *Mit-Sein* is discovered in the context of worldly usefulness: we discover others "at work," caught as they are in productive preoccupation, in *poiesis*. Because preoccupation is in a position of fallenness
with regard to care, authentic *Mit-sein* cannot possibly consist in sharing
the preoccupations of others. It is therefore only at the level of *praxis* that
such authenticity is possible. Authentic solicitude for somebody else can
only consist of helping him take upon himself his care in the ownmost. But
if this care (which the other individual *is* for himself) also entails in the end
his resolute confrontation of mortal selfhood, which, in his radical separa-
tion and finitude, is non-relational (*unbezüglich*) and without a dwelling,
then authentic solicitude is a paradoxical relation in that, while seemingly
uniting people, it refers them to their radical unrelatedness. Similar remarks
can be made for speech. Taken in its purity as a specific *existentiale,* speech
is as monadic as solicitude, and not at all aimed at communication. Speech
reaches its essence in the retreat into the internal forum of conscience, in
Gewissen—or to use Platonic terminology, in the solitary dialogue of the
soul with itself.

Hence the deliberate orientation of the Heideggerian reappropriation of
praxis in the direction of a solitary understanding of Being bears witness to
the abandonment of the Aristotelian resistance to Plato. In fundamental ontology, *bios theoretikos* apparently consumes and absorbs [*dévorait*] the entire domain of *praxis* over which it rules. Everything happens as if this
bios, which ultimately is solitary, were the only authentic form of individuation. In the 1928 lecture course on Leibniz (*The Metaphysical Foundations of Logic*) we read: "Philosophy is the central and total concretization
of the metaphysical essence of existence" (158; 202).

The famous *Rectoral Address on the Self-Assertion of German
University*[15] can be viewed as a confirmation of such a Platonic bias. Its
theme is the normative position of metaphysics as the queen of the sciences, and its very framework is taken from Plato's *Republic.*[16] In response
to the question of what *theoria* was for the Greeks, Heidegger writes:

---

15. *Die Selbstbehauptung der deutschen Universität. Das Rektorat 1933/34*
(Frankfurt am Main: Klostermann, 1983).

16. To get rid of the painful inadequacies, ambiguities, and multiple tensions
inherent in *praxis* in the isonomic city, Plato proposed to get rid of *praxis,* for the
benefit of *poiesis.* He thus transformed the city into a vast workshop in which everybody was to have a well-defined function within a well-defined organ of the body
politic. To this view corresponds—and this is not without some Hegelian resurgences—the Heideggerian image of a corporate state, in which each of the *corpora,*
the *Stände,* fulfills a specific task: the various forms of labor, the service of defense,
the service of knowledge ranking highest.

Some people define it as the pure consideration which remains linked exclusively to the matters in their full disclosure and conforming to their requirements. It is by an appeal to the Greeks that this contemplative comportment is supposed to emerge for its own sake. But this appeal is erroneous. On the one hand, *theoria* does not emerge for its own sake, but only as part of the passion to remain close to beings as such and under their constraints. Furthermore, the Greeks fought precisely in order to understand and accomplish such a contemplative interrogation as the highest manner of Being, or even as the supreme modality of *energeia*, of the "being-at-work" of man. Their intention was not to equate *praxis* with *theoria*, but on the contrary, to understand *theoria* itself as the highest implementation of true *praxis*. For the Greeks, science is not "a cultural good," but the very medium that determines, in its ownmost Being, the Dasein of a people and of the State. Neither was science for them a simple means to make conscious the unconscious; instead, it was the power that sharpens and encircles the totality of Dasein. (*Die Selbstbehauptung*, 11–12)

No specific analysis of this text is needed to highlight the repetition and accentuation of what we have stressed. In being applied to an entire people organized in a state, the concept of Dasein loses none of the features it had in *Sein und Zeit*. It maintains them because the Dasein of the people-State is a *praxis*, and the highest actualization of *praxis* is the articulated understanding of beings as they are, or is the science of the Being of beings as such, i.e., metaphysics. In addition, this passage also accentuates these features in the application of the concept of Dasein to an entire people-State, which is equivalent to intensifying the monadic (solipsistic) features pointed out above, equivalent also to turning the State and its Chief, not the citizens, into the real individual. To posit the people-State as Dasein amounts to the negation of plurality, the cancelation of the pluralistic sharing of deeds and words, and to the replacement of the pluralistic debate regarding what appears to each and every one (*dokei moi*) with a unanimous passion for the Being of all beings. In these lines Platonism is blatant and in strict conformity with the disdain for Thucydides stated in *Sein und Zeit*. It seems as though after claiming allegiance to the Greeks all along, Heidegger did not even take the trouble of questioning the fact that Plato and the birth of the science of the Being of beings, not only did not occur at the height of Pericles' Athens, but came in the wake of its decadence. It is as if Heidegger wanted to believe that the Greeks invented the *polis* for speculative reasons. For he does not seem to suspect that the Greeks of the city, at the time of its shining glory, considered *nomos* and the legal organization of the debate about the plurality of *doxai*—and not at all the science attained by sages and experts—to be pivotal conditions for their being-together (*isonomia*). Heidegger's concept of *polis* here turns out to be aligned with Hegel in the preface to the *Philosophy of Right,* a text which also interprets the Greek city in light of Plato's *Republic.* Like Hegel, Heidegger takes it for granted that Plato's image of *politeia* adequately reflects the essence of the *polis.* It seems as though when he hears the word "*Kampf*" a term so dreadfully loaded with Hitler's Germany, Heidegger translates it without flinching as the "*gigantomachia peri tès ousias*" (a struggle of giants for the sake of Being) mentioned by Plato in the *Sophist.* There is indeed no doubt that the *Rectoral Address* is in close agreement with Plato's concept of the philosopher-king. And it is not questionable that such an agreement is opposed to the spirit of pluralism characteristic of the city and of Aristotle's concept of *praxis* (as opposed to Plato's).

We find no indication at all that this speculative and Platonic bias, with its blindness to human affairs, their plurality and their ambiguity, ever disappeared from Heidegger's subsequent itinerary. Ten years after the *Rectoral Address,* in a 1942–43 seminar on Parmenides where Heidegger copiously draws from the *Republic,* we find the following definition of the Greek city:

> What is the *polis*? The word itself directs us toward the answer, provided we commit ourselves to acquiring an essential understanding of the Greek experience of Being and truth. *Polis* is the *polos,* the pivot, the place around which gravitates, in its specific manner, everything that for the Greeks is disclosed amidst beings. As this location, the pivot lets beings appear in their Being subject to the totality of their involvement. The pivot neither makes nor creates beings in their Being, but as the pivot, it is the site of the unconcealedness of beings as the whole. The *polis* is the essence of a location, so we speak of the regional location of the historical dwelling of Greek humanity. Because the *polis,* in one way or another, always lets the totality of beings come forth in the unconcealedness of their involvement, it is essentially related to the Being of beings. Between *polis* and Being, a relation of same origin rules.[17]

It seems to me that this passage on the concept of city is in strict continuity with the *Rectoral Address.* As in the 1933 text, Heidegger in 1942–

---

17. *Gesamtausgabe* 54: 132–133. (The translation given here corresponds to the translation of the French text—Trans.).

43 considers the city as the location for the unconcealment of beings in their totality and in their Being. By the same token, he still implies that the essence and the ground of the political realm are speculative in nature. Consequently the lines quoted from the seminar on Parmenides suggest that the individuals who spend their lives inquiring into the Being of beings are most qualified to rule human affairs, or at least to be counsellors of the prince. These lines are in conformity with Plato's views in the *Republic* and also betray some Hegelian resurgences. I find it very significant with regard to this point that after claiming in the same seminar that (inasmuch as they are not "close to the usual business of life, or *lebensnah*") the thinkers represented for the Greeks the highest necessity "of the essential needs of men," Heidegger should add: "The Germans would not be the People (*Volk*) of thinkers if their thinkers had not also thought likewise: In the Foreword of the first edition of his *Logic*, in 1812, Hegel says that 'an educated people without a metaphysics is like a richly decorated temple without a holy of holies.' " In the same seminar, we read an equally significant passage on *phronesis*. In the *Republic* Plato says: "Those who are not saved by *phronesis* drink beyond all measure" (*Gesamtausgabe*, 54, p. 178), which Heidegger interprets in the following manner: "*Phronesis* here means philosophy, and the word says: to have an eye for the essential." Although these words may correctly interpret the Platonic concept of *phronesis*, we can suspect them of greatly diverging from the Aristotelian understanding of the term in light of the essential distinction made in the sixth book of the *Ethics* between *phronesis* and *sophia*. In addition, we can suspect that the Hegelian concept of "an educated people" with which Heidegger agrees, greatly differs from the Aristotelian notion of "education" concerning human affairs.[18]

We find no overwhelming evidence that this Platonic bias disappeared from Heidegger's thought when the meditation on the history of Being finally replaced the project of fundamental ontology. Recall the beginning of the *Letter on Humanism*, which was the first text published after the war. In it, Heidegger forsakes all desire to complete metaphysics as the science of Being. We read: "We are still far from pondering the essence of action decisively enough. We view action only as causing an effect. The actuality of the effect is valued according to its utility. But the essence of action is accomplishment" (*Letter on Humanism*, 193). [At issue in these elliptical sentences is still the distinction between *poiesis* and *praxis*. *Handlung*, i.e., action, (*praxis* in Greek) should not, Heidegger says, be confused with *Bewirken*, that is, the production of effects (*poiesis* in Greek). The confusion

---

18. See above remarks on the "educated mind" according to Aristotle, p. 131.

gets worse if the actuality (*energeia* in Greek) of the effect is measured by utilitarian standards.][19] It is easy to recognize in these lines the echo of Aristotle's teaching: *poiesis* aims at effects that lie beyond it, whereas *praxis* aims at its own accomplishment (*Vollbringen*). But our puzzlement returns when the next sentences define accomplishment: "To accomplish means to unfold something into the fullness of its essence, to lead it forth into this fullness—producere. Therefore only what already is can be accomplished. But what "is" above all is Being. Thinking accomplishes the relation of Being to the essence of man." (ibid.).

Here the Platonic bias resurfaces: the highest possibility and achievement of action is nothing other than thinking, [which is something that Heidegger repeats in 1950 in a lecture on the *Kehre*: "Thinking is acting at its ownmost."] Naturally, this thinking no longer aims at the science of Being and is no longer metaphysical. But we might consider it a sign of Platonism that Heidegger's treatment of "action" (commitment or "*engagement*," to use Beaufret's term) never gives the slightest consideration to its inclusion within a human plurality as the word implies. We can take it as an additional sign of Platonism that Heidegger's answer to Beaufret's question about "*engagement*" turns in favor of a modality of *bios theoretikos*. Even if—on the one hand—this modality of thinking is meticulously involved in distinguishing the thinking meditation on Being from the knowledge of Being (a confusion still permeating fundamental ontology), [and even if—on the other hand—he now takes great care to dissociate thinking from willing, essentially from willing-to-know,] we could not say that he also distinguishes with extreme care the thinking meditation on Being from the judgment relative to human affairs. The entire issue of *praxis* for the Greeks of the isonomic city was the pursuit of a form of excellence strictly conditioned upon the free expression of individuals, upon their sharing a public realm through words and deeds, upon a common world whose uniqueness is not to be divorced from the pluralistic perspectives inscribed therein. This pluralistic and ambiguous manifestation is what Aristotle in his *Ethics* attempts to preserve (against Plato) by his refusal to absorb *phronesis* in *sophia*. *Phronesis* in his sense must be recognized as the general aptitude of each and every one—something not limited to the professionals of thinking—to pass judgment in public matters as in private ones. But, if the only appearance or expression to which *praxis* is related when it is understood as thought, turns out to be the unconcealment of Being, then, in spite of its ambiguity, this unconcealment displaces the pluralistic traits of human affairs toward marginal insignificance. Their pluralistic mode of

---

19. This and the next three bracketed clauses or sentences before the end of the chapter were added by the author in the English text.

appearing, then, deserves no more attention than Plato gives it: it is the futile agitation of the surface, the bubbles and the foam, the agitation of the "they," the *hoi polloi*. And these allegedly cover up the essential, which only very few elect ones (the thinkers and the poets) can heed.

Appendix to Chapter 3

Since the previous pages on Aristotle were written, I have been able to consult transcripts made by a student of Heidegger of the Introduction to the lecture course on *The Sophist* and on *Philebus* (winter semester 1924–25), and of the entire course on *The Basic Concepts of Ancient Philosophy* (summer semester 1926). It seems to me that these transcripts confirm my interpretation on several points.

1. In the introductory section to the course on *The Sophist* we can see expressed, with regard to Plato, what *Sein und Zeit* soon thereafter will call "Dasein's ontico-ontological priority" for fundamental ontology, and, more precisely, the idea that "the roots of the existential analytic are . . . *existentiell,* that is, *ontical"* (*Being and Time,* 34; 13). In other words, Heidegger articulates the notion that the inquiry into Being is a form of existence, even the highest one. In *The Sophist,* according to Heidegger, "Plato considers human existence (Dasein) in one of its most extreme possibilities, viz. the philosophic existence." Plato explains such a possibility indirectly in terms of what it is not, i.e., sophistry. To *doxa* where the latter is confined, Plato opposes truth. But the Greek expression for truth, *aletheia,* which is negative and privative, shows that the Greeks understood that the "uncoveredness" (*Unverdecktsein*) of the world needs to be "conquered" (*errungen*) and that truth is not available from the outset. It is only by means of a struggle against the absence of truth—i.e., against opinion and idle talk which incessantly cover up what was once seen—that *aletheia* can be conquered. Truth as a characteristic of beings, or the unveiled state of beings, requires therefore a "seeing" (*Hinsehen*), an "uncovering" (*Aufdecken*) and an "opening" (*Erschliessen*) which correspond to the uncoveredness of these beings. Such an uncovering is a comportment characterizing the mode of being of "human existence" (*des menschlichen Daseins*).

Truth is indeed a characteristic of beings as they confront us, but in its ownmost sense, it is nevertheless a determination of the Being of human Dasein itself, which Aristotle expresses in the *Nicomachean Ethics* by the words: "*aletheuei he psuche*" (113ab, 5). Inasmuch as *psuche* constitutes the ownmost Being of man, Being-in-truth is a determination of the Being of Dasein.[1]

Because the *Nicomachean Ethics* conducts a thematic inquiry into the various ways of Being-in-truth available to man and ranks *theoria* highest (as the philosophic existence entirely devoted to inquiring into the Being of beings), Heidegger calls the *Ethics* an "ontology of Dasein" whose study, retrospectively, sheds light on the Platonic conquest of the philosophic existence. From the outset therefore, the *Nicomachean Ethics* is considered in an ontological perspective with an obvious Platonic bias.

2. Thus oriented toward the superiority of the philosophic existence, the Heideggerian reading of the *Nicomachean Ethics* examines in detail the various possibilities of *aletheuein* in Aristotle. It considers these possibilities according to their rank and the comportments, or ways of being, to which they are related. These modalities of *aletheuein* are: *techne, phronesis, episteme, sophia, nous.*

Concerning the first two, let us only stress the points relevant to our interpretation. Heidegger insists on the fact that the two modalities of *aletheuein*—or of *Erschlossenheit,* as he says—are not of the same rank. In *techne,* the principle (*arche*) of the beings to be produced is within the producer, because he grasps the *eidos* of the product. It is not in the product because the product does not appear by an intrinsic spontaneity of its nature [*spontanément*]. Conversely the goal, the end or object, of *techne* is in the product, because it is the product that the producer strives to produce. But the product, that is, the work (*ergon*), is a *telos* only so long as the activity of *poiesis* is in operation. Once the product has reached a separate existence, the *telos* is released from the productive activity and the product then stands ready to serve other ends, for the benefit of one person or another. It results from this phenomenon that the product lies outside, besides (*para*) the activity that brings it into existence, and that the object of *techne* is not intrinsically related to the *technites.* For these various reasons, the ontological status of *techne* is marked by a flaw. It is not an excellent disposition of

---

1. All passages quoted in this section that are not otherwise identified are quoted by the author from the manuscripts of Heidegger's lecture courses, which the author consulted. Hence no page reference is given for them. (Trans.)

psuche (a *beltiste hexis*). The fact that this reading of Aristotle's doctrine of *techne* and *poiesis* inspires the analysis of everydayness in fundamental ontology, is in no way publicly acknowledged by Heidegger. Yet this inspiration is suggested to us with enough clarity, first by the emphatic ontological depreciation of *techne* (a depreciation which is not a matter of course in Aristotle), and secondly by the German terms used to express the meaning of *techne*. *Techne*, he says, involves "knowing how to go about an occupation" (*Sich auskennen in einer Hantierung*). Now, *Hantierung* is synonymous with what *Sein und Zeit* soon thereafter will call *Besorgnis*, preoccupation or concern.

As for *phronesis*, the uncovering comportment specific to *praxis*, Heidegger stresses that its subject matter is "the ownmost Being of Dasein" (*das eigentümliche Sein des Daseins*). Consequently both its *arche* and its *telos* overcome the ontological deficiency characterizing the principle and the goal of *techne*. Whereas the *telos* of *techne* and *poiesis* is a being outside Dasein and indifferent to it, the goal of *phronesis* is man himself, more precisely his action, and its principle is the *hou heneka*, the "for-the-sake-of" for which the actor has already made his choice (*proairesis*). Again, Heidegger does not publicly acknowledge the fact that this reading of the Aristotelian doctrine of *phronesis* and *praxis* inspires the analysis of care in the existential analytic. But the constellation of the German notions by means of which the structure of *phronesis* is clarified, turns out to be parallel to the analysis of care and the specific mode of seeing of care, i.e. , resoluteness. Heidegger says that: "*phronesis* is *Gewissen* set in motion which makes an action transparent (*durchsichtig*)" (commenting on 1140b, 28). Also regarding 1141a, 31 ff., he stresses that *phronesis* is properly what it is in its ownmost, as *euboulia* only, i.e., what he calls *Entschlossen-sein*, resoluteness. Finally, concerning 1143b, 1 ff., he emphasizes that *phronesis* contains a *noein*, a perception (*aisthesis*) of an *eschaton*, or a mode of seeing which concerns the present and is the moment of vision, *der Blick des Auges, der Augenblick*.

3. Because this reading centers on the pre-eminence of *sophia* as "Dasein's highest possibility," it is, so to speak, a form of hyper-Platonism. Far from looking for signs of a resistance of Aristotle to Plato, Heidegger's interpretation seeks in Aristotle the signs of "a positive elaboration on a direction opened by Plato." For Heidegger, Aristotle does not stand in a position antithetical to Plato's, but rather radicalizes Plato's position by showing that "*sophia* not only *can* be man's highest way of being, but also *must* be so." Hence, no matter how extraordinarily encompassing, enlightening, and deep the Heideggerian reading of the *Nicomachean Ethics*

is, we have to admit that it pays no attention whatsoever to those features within the Aristotelian analysis of *praxis* that concern human plurality and political life. It makes not a single reference to Pericles, to *sunesis* (the understanding of another human being), to *suggnome* (clemency and tolerance for him), or to the ironic allusion to Thales and Anaxagoras by which Aristotle reminds us that one can be *sophos,* without ever being *phronimos.* The fact that the *Nicomachean Ethics* also turns out to be an inquiry into politics and that *phronesis* is the capacity of judgment in political matters completely fails to attract Heidegger's attention.

4. According to the Heideggerian reading at Marburg, philosophic research is animated by one single question, that of the Being of beings, in which Being must not be confused with any being. Aristotle, according to Heidegger, only treats physical topics in order to discover motion as the departure point for this ontological problematic. He only treats life in order to establish an ontology of life. He only treats *logos* and concept formation to consider modalities according to which Being is unveiled and expressed in speech. Finally, he only treats ethics to present "an ontology of Dasein."

Heidegger, nevertheless, says that Aristotle's ontological researches suffered from two flaws: equivocation and indeterminacy. Equivocation, because the question of Being as such tends to be confused with the question of which being is being the most; therefore ontology is confused with theology, the science of the most eminent being which, for Aristotle, is the prime mover of all moving entities of *phusis.* Indeterminacy, because while he says that the Being of beings is expressed in many ways, Aristotle never raises the question of what confers a unity upon this multiplicity. He does not, therefore, pose the question of the meaning of Being.

Heidegger thus combines his praise of Aristotle's ontological authority with caution concerning two flaws that he intends to correct: the ontotheological equivocation and the indeterminacy of the meaning of Being. Aristotle himself prepares the foundation for Heidegger to remedy the flaw of indeterminacy. By not expressly asking what unifies the four ways in which Being is expressed (the categories, substance and accidents, truth, *potentia* and *actualitas*), Aristotle implicitly answers the question with a term: *ousia.* This word is translated by Heidegger as the *Vorhandenheit* of *vorhanden,* or the *Anwesenheit* der *Gegenwart,* the presence of the present. The meaning of Being for Aristotle is therefore a mode of time: present time. The course on *The Basic Concepts of Greek Philosophy* ends with the following assessment:

> Greek ontology is an ontology of the world in the sense of *phusis*;
> Being is interpreted as presence and constancy (*Beständigkeit*). Be-

ing is understood from what is present, naively from the phenomenon of time within which present time (*Gegenwart*) is but one modality. The question must be raised: How does the present acquire such a privilege? Why could not the past or the future claim the same right? Should we not understand Being in the light of the whole of temporality?

To overcome the indeterminacy of the meaning of Being amounts therefore to understanding Being in light of the global temporality within which future and past count as much as present and together even supersede it. Such temporality is brought to the forefront as foundational in the ontology of Dasein conducted in *Sein und Zeit*.

It seems to me that the Marburg lecture courses mentioned indicate that the new ontology of Dasein is attempted in a global transformation of the "ontology of Dasein" which Heidegger had detected in the *Nicomachean Ethics*; in other words, he sought to reappropriate not only the Aristotelian notions of *poiesis* and *praxis*, but also Aristotle's notion of *theoria*. The introduction to the course on *The Sophist* stresses that with relation to time, the *Nicomachean Ethics* establishes a hierarchy of two types of dianoetical virtues: one type is called "logistical" or "deliberative" and the other "epistemic" or "scientific." The first type is linked to what is born, becomes, and perishes; the second is linked to what is not born, does not undergo becoming, and does not perish. The supreme deliberative excellence, *phronesis*, is always concerned with *aion*, the finite time of mortal existence. The supreme epistemic excellence, *sophia*—a mode of seeing entangled in the onto-theological equivocation—concerns the "always being" (*das Immer-seiend*), and the everlasting and motionless prime mover or principle of all motions in *phusis*. *Sophia* in the Aristotelian sense is the highest mode of being to which man can attain because contemplation (*theoria*) of the everlasting absorbs man in what always is. In contrast to *sophia* which accompanies the apprehension of the purely present, *phronesis* concerns the becoming of *praxis* and is in a position of fallenness. To overcome the onto-theological equivocation and ambiguity requires that we abandon the Greek distinction between the divine *aei* and the mortal *aion* by showing that the so-called eternity of the former hypostasizes only one temporal mode of the mortal *aion*: the present. This amounts, therefore, to an inversion of the Aristotelian hierarchy. It views any consideration of the present as a fall from the time of *praxis* into the inferior time of *poiesis*. But because Heidegger subscribes without reservation to the ontological privilege of *bios theoretikos*, meaning the philosophic existence dedicated to grasping the sight of Being, the only task remaining for an inquiry into Being is to reflect upon the finite time of *praxis*.

4

From One Fundamental Ontology to the Other: The Double Reading of Hegel[1]

At the time when Heidegger focused upon the project of a *fundamental ontology*, only two books (the masterwork, *Sein und Zeit*, and *Kant and the Problem of Metaphysics*) and two essays (*What is Metaphysics?* and *The Essence of Reasons*) had disclosed to the public the stakes of the enterprise and its unique style. In all of these works, with the exception of the last, Hegel is mentioned, quoted, or analyzed to some greater or lesser extent. A meticulous inspection of these references, quotations and analyses, is beyond the objective of this essay. Although I will not attempt such an inventory, I believe that it would ultimately indicate that the elaboration of Heidegger's fundamental ontology owes very little to a meditation on Hegel's thought. In other words, to express my point more cautiously and more precisely: on the basis of what those works expressly say about Hegel, nothing authorizes us to maintain that fundamental ontology was supported, at the core of its elaboration, by some sort of a reappropriation or retrieval (*Wiederholung*) of Hegel. A review of some broad textual points should suffice to prove this claim.

Concerning *Sein und Zeit*, it is easy to notice that the most explicit pages on Hegel aim only at opposing some Hegelian theories to certain analyses required by fundamental ontology. These pages can be found in the sixth chapter of the second part. The title alone of the section in which we find them all (Section 82) is meaningful: *"Die Abhebung des existenzial-ontologischen Zusammenhangs von Zeitlichkeit, Dasein und Weltzeit gegen Hegels Auffassung der Beziehung zwischen Zeit und Geist"*.[2] And indeed,

---

1. This text was presented as a paper at the *Stuttgarter Hegelkongress 1987.*
2. Literally, the title means *"The demarcation* of Existential-ontological Connection of Temporality, Dasein, and World-Time, *as opposed to [as against]* Hegel's View of the Relation between Time and Spirit" (my emphasis).

the entire paragraph stresses the opposition between the two approaches. To be sure, Heidegger does not arbitrarily stress this opposition. Rather, if the difference between the two approaches deserves attention, it is because, at its most salient point, the existential analytic of Dasein seems to display a sort of accord and concordance with Hegel. But it is precisely in order to show clearly that such an accord is merely superficial, that *Sein und Zeit,* in the last chapter, confronts the Hegelian conceptions. Consider how, although there seems to be such a concordance, Section 82 declares that it lies only on the surface. Heidegger's words at the beginning of Chapter 6 enable us to understand the terms of this concordance. The last chapter of *Sein und Zeit* aims at showing that the ordinary concept of time as the world-time (*Weltzeit*) *in which* beings appear and events occur, is formed within the horizon of everyday concern by leveling-off the primordial temporality constitutive of the Being of Dasein. Showing this amounts to establishing the genealogy of the common concept of time (the one conceptualized by Aristotle in the *Physics*) on the basis of the ec-static temporality constituting the Being of Dasein, that is, on the basis of care, which everyday concern at the same time presupposes and obliterates. In order to clear up any suspicion that such a genealogy is arbitrary, Heidegger must show that the traditional theories of time, which were all satisfied with an ordinary and everyday concept of time, nevertheless testify to a link between time and the comportment of Dasein. Heidegger formulates this connection as follows:

> In the development of this ordinary conception, there is a remarkable vacillation as to whether the character to be attributed to time is 'subjective' or 'objective'. Where time is taken as being in itself, it gets allotted pre-eminently to the 'soul' notwithstanding. And where it has the kind of character which belongs to 'consciousness', it still functions 'objectively.' (*Being and Time,* 457; 405)

At this juncture of the last chapter of *Sein und Zeit,* Hegel is mentioned. Heidegger writes: "In Hegel's interpretation of time both possibilities are brought to the point where, in a certain manner, they are brought to an *Aufhebung*" (405). In other words, Hegel does not vacillate between "objectivity" and "subjectivity": he takes both upon himself [he embraces both]. Indeed he tries to determine the cohesion (*Zusammenhang*) between "time" and "spirit" in order to explain why Spirit, as history, "falls into time." And insofar as Hegel determines the existence of a connection between time and Spirit, it might appear that he illustrates some sort of concordance with the analytic of Dasein. Let us clarify this point. The analytic, in its final step, attempts to show that time in the commonly accepted "objective" characterization is something measured and viewed as the medium in which events occur and intratemporal beings come to pass, but that such world-time (*Weltzeit*) in the last analysis derives from the primordial temporality constitutive of the Being of Dasein. We can formulate, in terms of a "result," what the analytic of Dasein shows: world-time as an intratemporal medium for beings and events results from a leveling-off of primordial temporality. And such a result seems to be in line with Hegel's thesis: Spirit falls into time. This thesis means that world-time as the intratemporal medium is that *into which* the primordial, the Spirit, falls.

But it is precisely this concordance that Section 82 of *Sein und Zeit* claims to be a mere semblance. This claim is justified by Heidegger in section 78:

> We seem to be in accord with Hegel in the results of the interpretation we have given for Dasein's temporality and for the way world-time belongs to it. But . . . our analysis differs in principle from his in its approach, and . . . its orientation is precisely the *opposite* of his in that it aims at fundamental ontology. . . . "
> (p. 405)

One could not have stressed more clearly that fundamental ontology is extraneous to Hegel's position and that a Hegelian inspiration or repetition cannot be claimed in the elaboration of fundamental ontology. Consequently, the analysis of the Hegelian theses conducted in Section 82 does not intend to reveal a closeness, or a difference within a proximity. Rather it intends to highlight an opposition which, as such, can "serve" (*dienen*) to "indirectly bring light" (*indirekt zu verdeutlichen*) upon the existential and ontological interpretation of the temporality of Dasein (405). Hence, Heidegger has no intention at all of crossing paths with the Hegelian itinerary and following it for a short while. On the contrary, in order to discard any semblance of a proximity, Heidegger finally accedes to the expected presentation of Hegel's views in order to show better the sharp contrast between their two approaches.

Let me now briefly present the main symptoms of the contrast (*Abhebung*). For Heidegger, it is within an ontology of nature and never within a framework remotely anticipating the ontology of Dasein, that Hegel, in strict conformity with the tradition leading back to Aristotle, thematizes time. Like Aristotle, Hegel does nothing more than conceptualize the ordinary understanding of time on the basis of the "now." By characterizing time as "intuited becoming," [Hegel] reveals that he also interprets it on the basis of a "now" as an entity delivered to a pure and simple intuition, and that, for him, the ontological status of this present "now" is presence-at-hand, or *Vorhandenheit*. This status obliterates and levels off the ec-static dimension of the existential present. Furthermore, far from questioning the traditional and common conceptions, Hegel reinforces them inexorably by formalizing them to an extreme and by deliberately making them more abstract. It is precisely by means of formalizing abstraction (an abstraction which is obvious in the characterization of time as *negation of negation*) that Hegel can intimately connect time and Spirit. Spirit in Hegel is understood as Concept, i.e., apprehension of the self in the apprehension of the non-self. The Hegelian Concept is essentially characterized by an "apophantic formal determination" which again is the negation of negation, or absolute negativity. Because such a negativity induces unrest throughout the development in which the Spirit comes to its Concept, "the only outcome is that, as [Spirit] conquers effectiveness, it will 'fall into time,' as the immediate negation of negation." Heidegger continues with a quotation from the end of the *Phenomenology of Spirit*:

> Thus time appears as the very fate and necessity which spirit has when it is not in itself complete: the necessity of its giving self-consciousness a richer share in consciousness, of its setting in motion the *immediacy* of the *"in-itself"* (the form in which substance is in consciousness), or, conversely, of its realizing and making manifest the *"in-itself"* taken as the *inward* (and this is what first is inward)—that is, of vindicating it for its certainty of itself. (*Being and Time*, 486; 435)

Heidegger summarizes his analysis of the Hegelian theses by the assessment: "Spirit and time get disposed of, with the very emptiest of formal-ontological and formal-apophantical abstractions, and this makes it possible to produce a kinship between them" (*Being and Time*, 485; 435). As opposed to this emptiness, this abstraction and this formalism, Heidegger argues that his fundamental ontology displays concreteness in the sense of the concretion of the analyses exploring the existential and ontological articulation of temporality. The aspects Hegel leaves in the dark—the ontological meaning of a "fall" of the Spirit, the ontological meaning of an "effectiveness" of Spirit in time when such time is external to it, and the origin of leveled-off temporality based on the "now"—are exactly brought to light by fundamental ontology.

> 'Spirit' does not first fall into time, but it *exists as* the primordial temporalizing of temporality. Temporality temporalizes world-time within the horizon of which 'history' can 'appear' as historizing within-time. 'Spirit' does not fall *into* time; but factical existence 'falls' as falling *from* primordial, authentic temporality. This 'falling' (*Fallen*), however, has itself its existential possibility in a

mode of its temporalizing—a mode which belongs to temporality. (486; 435–36))

By closely examining the allusions to Hegel in *Kant and the Problem of Metaphysics*, we would no doubt hit upon a contrast similar to the one just outlined. These can be found in the last section of the book. The whole book has already shown that the *Critique of Pure Reason* is not a theory of knowledge, but a questioning concerning the intrinsic possibility of ontology, that is, the intrinsic possibility of discovering the ontological constitution of beings. Heidegger showed that this questioning is conducted by Kant transcendentally because he does not examine beings, but the possibility that we, as humans, prior to any experience of beings, have of understanding their Being. He also showed that this questioning is tantamount to a questioning regarding the essence of transcendence, i.e., the essence of an extending-toward by virtue of which the being that we are is opened *a priori* to Being, over and beyond beings. According to Heidegger, this questioning concerning the essence of transcendence led Kant to the discovery of transcendental imagination as the medium (*Mitte*) in which ontological knowledge is formed. Finally, for Heidegger, Kant's discovery of the fundamental ontological function of imagination is tantamount to having discovered that the source of imagination is time, and that the Kantian foundation of metaphysics consists in discovering time as the root of transcendence, and consequently of our understanding of Being.

The last section of the book outlines, in questions raised and left open by Heidegger, the critical axes for a recasting or repetition of the Kantian foundation of metaphysics. That foundation culminates in the question left open by Kant: What is man? Kant indicates that the essence of man is intrinsically finite, given that the three fundamental interests of human reason (our capacity for knowledge, our duty, and our hope) are the evidence of a fundamental finitude and that "the innermost interest of reason is focused on that very finitude" (*Kant und das Problem der Metaphysik*, 195).[3] What is unique in the Heideggerian reappropriation is that it takes this finitude upon itself as a question. Heidegger writes: "We attempted the present interpretation of the *Critique of Pure Reason* in order to highlight, regarding the foundation of metaphysics, the fundamental problem concerning the necessity of a questioning of finitude in man" (*Kant und das Problem der Metaphysik*, 197–98).

---

3. *Kant und das Problem der Metaphysik* (Frankfurt am Main: Klostermann, 1951). This quotation and the next are translated from the German original by the author; we translate them here into English from the French text. (Trans.)

This problem can only be solved by the primordial elaboration of the question of Being attempted in fundamental ontology, which with the title "Being and Time" indicates an intimate link between the unveiling of the meaning of Being and the intrinsically finite mode of being of Dasein (the only being which understands Being and can do so only by spontaneouly projecting Being upon a radically finite temporality). Heidegger claims that he sees this very problematic emerge and take shape in Kant. The last section of his book therefore bears the title "The Idea of Fundamental Ontology and the Critique of Pure Reason." The words beginning the section are:

> Kant's laying of the foundation of metaphysics, which for the first time subjects the internal possibility of the overtness of the Being of the essent to a decisive examination, must necessarily encounter time as the basic determination of finite transcendence if, indeed, it is true that the understanding of Being in Dasein spontaneously projects Being on time. But at the same time this laying of the foundation must go beyond the ordinary conception of time to the transcendental understanding of it as pure self-affection (*Kant and the Problem of Metaphysics,* 251–52 modified; 219).[4]

Hence time acquires a central metaphysical function in the *Critique of Pure Reason,* and "it acquires this function because, by virtue of the finitude of the Dasein in man, the understanding of Being must be projected upon time" (*Kant and the Problem of Metaphysics,* 252 modified; 219). Heidegger concludes: "*The Critique of Pure Reason* thus threatens the supremacy of reason and of the understanding. 'Logic' is deprived of its traditional primacy relative to metaphysics. Its basic idea is brought into question" (252; 219). It is at this juncture that the contrast between Hegel and Kant is introduced:

> If the essence of transcendence is based on pure imagination, i.e., originally on time, then the idea of a "transcendental logic" becomes non-sensical especially if, contrary to Kant's original intention, it is treated as an autonomous and absolute discipline. . . . And yet, in the second edition of the *Critique* did not Kant reestablish the supremacy of the understanding? And as a result of this did not metaphysics, with Hegel, come to be identified with

---

4. *Kant and the Problem of Metaphysics,* trans. Churchill (Bloomington: Indiana University Press, 1962). The first page number refers to the English translation, the second to the German text.

"logic" more radically than ever before? What is the significance of the struggle initiated in German idealism against the "thing in itself" except a growing forgetfulness of what Kant had won, namely, the knowledge that the intrinsic possibility and necessity of metaphysics, i.e., its essence, are, at bottom, sustained and maintained by the original development and searching study of the problem of finitude? What is the outcome of Kant's effort if Hegel defines metaphysics in these terms: "Logic is consequently to be understood as the system of Pure Reason, as the Realm of Pure Thought. This realm is the Truth as it is, without husk in and for itself—one may therefore express it thus: that this content shows forth God as He is in His eternal essence before the creation of Nature and of a finite Spirit?" (252–53; 219–20)

This contrast between Kant's efforts (albeit hesitant and soon relaxed) and the forgetfulness to which Hegel falls prey, very clearly suggests that the project of fundamental ontology was almost anticipated by Kant on one side, but not at all by Hegel on the other side. It also suggests that the phenomenon called "transcendence" in fundamental ontology is not to be found in Hegel.

An inspection of the essays would very likely lead us to similar conclusions. Since Hegel is not mentioned in *Vom Wesen des Grundes* (*The Essence of Reasons*), let us limit ourselves to *Was ist Metaphysik?* (*What is Metaphysics?*)[5] Indeed, this text seems to state an agreement with Hegel on two points.

First, by his decision not to talk about metaphysics but to assume the responsibility of a properly metaphysical question, Heidegger announces at the outset that he is in accord with Hegel's comment that "from the point of view of sound common sense, philosophy is the 'inverted world' " (*What is Metaphysics?* 95). The question treated in the lecture unfolds in the first part of the text. Its formulation suffices to justify this first accord with Hegel and, by the same token, to make it formal: metaphysics questions nothingness, with which neither science nor common sense wants to bother.

In order to answer the question, we must provide a proper elaboration, which cannot come from the understanding because the understanding cannot make sense of nothingness. But answering it becomes possible if there is a fundamental experience of nothingness (*Grunderfahrung des Nichts*). Anxiety is the very experience in which nothingness manifests itself. It is

5. *Martin Heidegger, Basic Writings,* ed. David F. Krell (New York: Harper and Row, 1977), pp. 97–112.

on the basis of this experience that Heidegger reveals a second point of accord with Hegel.

Secondly, anxiety reveals that Dasein holds itself out into nothingness. It is by virtue of holding itself out into nothingness that a Dasein experiencing anxiety transcendentally exceeds the totality of beings. Anxiety manifests the transcendence of Dasein. The answer to the initial question is: "For human existence the nothing makes possible the openedness of beings as such. The nothing does not merely serve as the counterconcept of beings; rather it originally belongs to their essential unfolding as such. In the Being of beings the nihilation of the nothing occurs" (*Basic Writings*, 106). This very answer gives Heidegger the opportunity to quote Hegel:

> '*Das reine Sein und das reine Nichts ist also dasselbe*'. *Dieser Satz Hegels (W.d.L. I Buch, WW III, S. 74) besteht zu Recht. Sein und Nichts gehören zusamen* . . . (*Wegmarken*, 17) 'Pure Being and pure Nothing are therefore the same' This proposition of Hegel's (*Science of Logic*, vol. I, Werke III, 74) is correct. Being and the nothing do belong together. (*Basic Writings*, 110)

Yet, this second point of agreement is no less formal than the first one, since Heidegger immediately adds:

> not because both—from the point of view of the Hegelian concept of thought—agree in their indeterminateness and immediacy, but rather because Being itself is essentially finite and reveals itself only in the transcendence of Dasein which is held out into the nothing. (*Basic Writings*, 110)

Hence, as in *Sein und Zeit* and in *Kant and the Problem of Metaphysics*, Heidegger's reference to Hegel ends up insisting on a fundamental divergence in spite of a formal convergence. Nothing in these references indicates that Hegel should be credited with approaching the problematic of fundamental ontology, much less with gaining access to its core, that is, to transcendence.

As it happens, the lecture courses given by Heidegger during the same period present a picture that is markedly different from the one emerging in the publications just mentioned. Such is indeed the case with the 1927 course on *The Basic Problems of Phenomenology*. In this lecture course we find two references to Hegel that have no equivalent either in *Sein und Zeit*, published the same year, or in *Kant and the Problem of Metaphysics* (which at that time was on his table and already announced in *Sein und Zeit*).

The first reference is found in Chapter IV of the first part of the lecture course. The topic investigated is the thesis regarding Being contained in logic as a discipline, and according to which "every being, regardless of its particular way of being can be addressed and talked about by means of the 'is'."[6] In other words, the topic is the being of the copula. Because logic developed into a separate discipline within philosophy and detached itself from fundamental philosophical problems, this thesis is blind to the connection between the "is" expressed by the copula and the fundamental ontological problems. What we must understand—and this is what Chapter IV shows—is that the thesis found in logic reduces Being to a propositional state of affairs. It removes Being and truth from the space where Being primordially discloses itself: the Dasein who can discover beings to the extent that it understands Being.

It is at the beginning of this chapter, in a sort of foreword announcing the ontological reappropriation of logic, that Hegel is mentioned in the following terms:

> It was Kant who first gave logic a central philosophical function again, though in part at the cost of ontology and above all without trying to rescue so-called academic logic from its philosophically alienated superficiality and vacuity. Even Hegel's more advanced attempt to conceive of logic as philosophy once again was more an elaboration of the traditional problems and stock of knowledge than a radical formulation of the problem of logic as such. The nineteenth century is not at all able to maintain itself at the level of Hegel's approach to the question but relapses into academic logic. (*The Basic Problems of Phenomenology,* p. 177)

If we contrast the words quoted from this lecture course with the published works, we are bound to surprised. Whereas *Kant and the Problem of Metaphysics* credits Kant with having deprived logic of its traditional philosophical supremacy and with undermining the Idea of a metaphysical logic, the 1927 course on *The Basic Problems,* in contradistinction, credits him with having reassigned a central philosophical function to logic. Whereas *Kant and the Problem of Metaphysics* detects in Hegel the forgetfulness of what had been conquered by Kant, the 1927 course on *The Basic Problems,* in contrast, gives no evidence that Hegel represents a step backward from Kant, but rather a step forward beyond him. Such a position suggests at the very least that Hegel deserves a reappropriation as well. And it is indeed in this direction that the text continues to unfold. It calls philosophy to rise

---

6. *The Basic Problems of Phenomenology,* trans. Albert Hofstadter (Blomington: Indiana University Press, 1982), p. 177.

again to the level of Hegel by overcoming the decline precipitated by the positivism and the Neo-Kantianism of the nineteenth century. Asking that the problem of the copula be once again linked to the problems of philosophy as the science of Being, Heidegger writes:

> The problem will make no further progress as long as logic itself has not been taken back into ontology, as long as Hegel—who, in contrast, dissolved ontology into logic—is not comprehended. And this means always that Hegel must be overcome by radicalizing the way in which the problem is put; and at the same time, he must be appropriated. This overcoming of Hegel is the intrinsically necessary step in the development of Western philosophy which must be made for it at all to remain alive. (178; 254)

To be sure, this language, like that found in *Sein und Zeit* and in *Kant and the Problem of Metaphysics* previously analyzed, underscores a contrast between fundamental ontology and the Hegelian problematic, but, unlike those published works, the lectures on *The Basic Problems of Phenomenology* closely associate the contrast to a proximity. It is no longer the case that Heidegger accedes to a presentation expected of him regarding Hegel's views so as to "indirectly cast light" on fundamental ontology by virtue of a contrast alone, but now the objective is to allow the contrast to spring forth from a true recasting or repetition of Hegel. Although the word *Wiederholung* is not used in this text, it fundamentally represents what is at stake in overcoming and reappropriating Hegel in a way that would also radicalize him. More importantly, this recasting should not be viewed as gratuitous if it is decisive for the pursuit of philosophy.

In the same lecture course, we read another meaningful reference to Hegel confirming this point. We find it in Section 20—in the second part of the course—which in reference to the fundamental question of ontology on the meaning of Being, leads Heidegger to the problem of the ontological difference. According to Heidegger, the fact of posing the question of the meaning of Being anew implies that we understand that from Plato onward, philosophy had no other aspiration but "to come to itself." Heidegger adds:

> In Hegel, philosophy—that is, ancient philosophy—is in a certain sense thought through to its end. He was completely in the right when he himself expressed this consciousness. But there exists just as much the legitimate demand to start anew, to understand the finiteness of the Hegelian system and to see that Hegel himself has come to an end with philosophy because he moves in the circle of

philosophical problems. This circling in the circle forbids him to move back to the center of the circle and to revise it from the ground up. It is not necessary to seek another circle beyond the circle. Hegel saw everything that is possible. But the question is whether he saw it from the radical center of philosophy, whether he exhausted all the possibilities of the beginning so as to say that he is at the end. (282; 400)

Coming from a phenomenologist, such words are far-reaching. His words *"Hegel hat alles gesehen, was möglich ist"* (Hegel saw everything that is possible) now mean that Hegel is no longer accused of formalism and abstraction. Instead he is treated as if he were a phenomenologist. By the same token, this treatment suggests that fundamental ontology, i.e., the basic phenomenological investigation as Heidegger understood it at the time, crosses the Hegelian path.

Such an overlapping of the two paths is at the core of the winter semester lecture course of 1930–31, which is an interpretation of *Hegel's Phenomenology of Spirit.* My remarks shall close with a consideration of this course.

Let us highlight the major characteristics of this interpretation before attempting to determine the location of its center of gravity. By major characteristics, we mean both the way in which Heidegger proposes to describe the *Phenomenology of Spirit* and the specific manner of his interpretation. Relying on the initial complete title of the 1807 work (System of Science, First Part, Science of the Experience of Consciousness, Science of the *Phenomenology of Spirit*) and on various information pertaining to Hegel's systematic projects at the time, Heidegger characterizes the Phenomenology of Spirit as the Hegelian foundation of metaphysics, that is, as the *Grundlegung* or the preparation of the ground (*Boden*) upon which metaphysics stands. This metaphysics founded on Phenomenology is divided by Hegel into two parts: 1. Logic; and, 2. *Realphilosophie,* which itself is divided into a philosophy of nature and a philosophy of spirit. Because Hegel's logic, according to Heidegger, unifies ontology as the science of the Being of beings and theology as the science of *ens realissimum,* metaphysics in Hegel's sense encompasses what came to be called after Suarez, *Metaphysica generalis* and *Metaphysica specialis.* Indeed, another articulation was later found by Hegel: the encyclopedic articulation which seems to reduce Phenomenology to one internal component of the system. Such a reduction, for Heidegger, is only a half-truth because "the Phenomenology of Spirit remains the work and the way that not only once, but always, and in a definite and indispensable manner, prepares the ground—better: the space, the dimensionality, the realm of expansion—for the encyclopedia-system" (*Hegel's Phenomenology of Spirit*, 8; 12).[7]

The *Phenomenology of Spirit*, thus characterized as a "*Grundlegung der Metaphysik*" (a status which we recall was reserved in *Kant and the Problem of Metaphysics* exclusively for the *Critique of Pure Reason*) leads Heidegger in the lecture course to move no longer in the direction of a simple *Abhebung*, or demarcation, but in the direction of a debate, or *Auseinandersetzung*. The condition for that debate, Heidegger points out relying upon a famous passage from *The Difference between the Systems of Fichte and Schelling*, is our acceptance of a kinship with Hegel, provided we grant that the kinship between an interpreter and the interpretee is based on the fact that both are "dependent upon the first and last requirements involved in the philosophical inquiry arising from the things themselves (*die Sache*)" (*Hegel's Phenomenology*, 31 modified; 45). This debate, in the midst of a kinship of spirits, is what accounts for the specificity of the 1930–31 lecture course on Hegel.

This debate certainly does not exclude the highlighting of a major contrast between Heidegger's questioning and that conducted by Hegel. The contrast is presented in the introduction of the course. Heidegger repeats that the leading problem of Western philosophy is the question: "What is a being as far as it is?" and indicates that starting in ancient times, the question was intrinsically connected to *logos*. This means that "beings, as far as their Being is concerned, were understood from the *logos*, as *logos*." The ancient way of asking the question brought about the answer: the Being of beings is *logos*. Such an answer, Heidegger says, was "brought to completion in a radical way by Hegel" who "really carries through the answer and implements a thorough unfolding of it."

> Accordingly, a *being as such*, the actual in its genuine and whole reality, is the idea, or concept. The concept however, is the power of time, i.e., the pure concept annuls time. In other words, the problem of being is properly conceived only when time is made to disappear (12; 18) [i.e., when philosophy has become the science of absolute knowledge].

This Hegelian view could not be more opposed to *Sein und Zeit*, because by showing that the question of Being is only properly understood exclusively in connection with the horizon of temporality, the treatise asserts that "with regard to the actual content of philosophy, its guiding question can-

---

7. *Hegel's Phenomenology of Spirit*, trans. Parvis Emad and Kenneth Maly (Bloomington: Indiana University Press, 1988).

not be left in the form it had for the ancients, nor, consequently, can it be left to stand on the foundation provided by Hegel's problematic'' (12 modified; 18). This contrast is captured in two formulas given in the lecture course: on the one hand, the *Phenomenology of Spirit* is an onto-theo-egology, on the other hand fundamental ontology is an onto-chrony.[8]

But, unlike *Sein und Zeit,* the lecture course associates this contrast with a proximity which emerges with total clarity when we proceed to determine the axis and the center of gravity of the interpretation. The axis is mentioned in the preliminary considerations, before the interpretation proper. Concerning the stakes of the *Phenomenology of Spirit,* Heidegger writes:

> The issue is the problem of the Infinite. Now how can the infinite become a problem more radically without finitude becoming a problem—which means that the ''No'' and the ''Naught'' (*das Nichtige*) also become a problem, whereby the non-finite is nevertheless bound to come to truth. The inquiry into finitude is certainly that within which we attempt to meet Hegel in the acknowledgement of the first and last requirements of philosophy, i.e., its *Sache,* or subject-matter. This means, according to what we said earlier, that through a confrontation with Hegel's problematic of the infinite we shall try to create, on the basis of our own inquiry into finitude, *the* kinship needed in order to reveal the spirit of Hegel's philosophy. (38 modified; 55)

In other words, we gain nothing by simply opposing as fixed antithetical philosophies the philosophy of the absolute and the philosophy of finitude. Instead, it is at the core of the inquiry into the infinite—in positive terms, an inquiry into the absolute—that the phenomenological itinerary of Hegel is akin to that of Heidegger, the thinker of finitude. But if it is true that such a kinship concerns the central issue of philosophy, that is, the question of Being, then we can certainly expect that Hegel's itinerary will never cross paths with Heidegger's in those places where Hegel specifically treats Being (or time), but only at the center of gravity of his inquiry into the infinite.

This center of gravity lies for Heidegger in the transition from the section called ''Consciousness'' (*Bewusstsein*) to the section called ''Self-Consciousness'' (*Selbstbewusstsein*). We will not attempt to follow his reading. Rather, we only want to isolate the points which indicate an ac-

---

8. See *Hegel's Phenomenology:* concerning Hegel's *onto-theo-ego-logy* (126; 182–83) and concerning *Sein und Zeit* as *onto-chrony* (100; 144). (Trans.)

knowledgement of a kinship of spirits. There are three closely connected points. First, in the transition from Consciousness to Self-Consciousness, Hegel, according to Heidegger, attempts "nothing less than the unfolding of a new concept of Being," which is not caught in the traditional notion of *Vorhandenheit*, presence-at-hand. This new concept is 'life', not as an immediacy, but as self-sameness animated with differentiation, as rest-within-itself of an absolute unrest, or as return to itself through the quest for the Self (*Sucht des Selbts nach ihm selbst*) (*Gesamtausgabe*, Bd 32, p. 199). Such a mode of being differs radically from *Vorhandenheit* because it is concerned with the process through which the self comes to its own, with its *Zu-Sich*.

Secondly, Heidegger points out that this transition naturally presupposes the absolvent movement of absolute knowledge. This means the following decisive feature:

> With the speculative explication of consciousness in all its forms and with the interpretation of its transition to self-consciousness, consciousness is from the beginning posited and unfolded as *transcendental* (taken in its transcendence and only in it). In spite of all our fundamental critical reservations regarding the manner of the absolvent overcoming of the finitude of transcendence, we must consider in a positive sense and admire the unprecedented power, confidence and fullness with which philosophizing here moves in the very space of transcendence itself. (135 modified; 195)

Thirdly, we will not be surprised if Heidegger in this context came to view the *Phenomenology of Spirit* as the "fundamental ontology of absolute ontology" (141; 204), which is to say, as the fundamental ontology of onto-theo-ego-logy.

To conclude: what is said of Hegel in the lecture course on the *Phenomenology of Spirit* is, as it were, in a position of inverted symmetry with respect to what is said of him in the works published by Heidegger between 1927 and 1931. Those works in essence considered it possible to notice points of apparent convergence between Hegel and Heidegger, but these points should vanish completely when our attention focuses on a clear fundamental divergence: the divergence separating absolute knowledge and the thought of finitude. In contrast, the lecture course on *Hegel's Phenomenology* says that the distinction between the absolvent movement of the absolute and the finitude of Being-in-the-world is not the essential point, because both thoughts move within the space of transcendence. What matters is that they cross each other at a juncture (*Kreuzweg*), so that we must learn to recognize, in the Hegelian Absolute, finitude itself—but veiled or "in disguise" (65; 92). *Kant and the Problem of Metaphysics* said that, with Hegel, we witness the end of Kant's efforts to grasp transcendence. The lecture course on *Hegel's Phenomenology* says in opposition that it is because Hegel "pushed for the speculative absolute overcoming of the Kantian position," which rested on the primordial synthetic unity of transcendental apperception, that he was able to "take as his starting point consciousness and the I in its transcendence." (135 modified; 194).

Such a turnabout deserves consideration. The lecture course on *Hegel's Phenomenology* was given in 1930–31. This was a time when fundamental ontology, though it was to collapse later on, was firmly established. Its particulars had been explored. Is it possible that the course on Hegel gave Heidegger an opportunity to recognize himself in Hegel after the fact? Or on the other hand, must one see it as the belated acknowledgement of a closeness which Heidegger had known to exist for a long time? The second possibility deserves consideration. I find at least the incipient confirmation of this possibility in the words of the 1927 lecture course previously mentioned: "Hegel saw everything that is possible" (*The Basic Problems of Phenomenology,* 282; 400). This possibility allows us to conclude that it is by virtue of a *Wiederholung,* a metamorphosing recasting of the absolvent movement essential to the Hegelian Absolute and to the transition from consciousness to self-consciousness, that Heidegger discovered what is ownmost in finite transcendence (a discovery also contained in the experience of anxiety): the identity of the understanding of Being and the holding of oneself into nothingness. In other words, it could very well be that because of this *Wiederholung,* the existential analytic achieved not so much its articulation (I attempted to show in the previous chapter that this articulation results from the reappropriation of the Aristotelian distinction between *poiesis* and *praxis*), but the proper ontological weight [*la teneur proprement ontologique*] of that articulation. To wit, consider the fact that, in fundamental ontology, the various modalities of inauthentic comportment are also preontological, just as the various figures of natural knowledge in the Hegelian sense are already prefigurations of the absolute knowledge, notwithstanding the fact that they are not yet the knowledge of the Thing itself. In other words, finally, if the 1927 lecture course on *The Basic Problems* is correct in suggesting that the accuracy of Hegel's sight and insights is linked to the circular character of his path and that the new objective for Heidegger is not to shift to another circle but rather to discover the true center of the Hegelian circle, then it is conceivable that the hermeneutical circle is the result of a *Wiederholung* of the speculative circle. If such is the case, then it might be appropriate to reread *Sein und Zeit* and *Kant and the Problem of Metaphysics* as intrinsically post-Hegelian texts.

5

On a Double Reading of Descartes[1]

At first sight, it might not seem that Heidegger's reading of Descartes entails a very complex field of investigation. For if we look at the titles of the books and essays published by Heidegger during his lifetime, we quickly realize that Descartes' name is not mentioned in a single one—either book or essay. In addition to containing no mention of Descartes in their titles, none of these texts seems to address any notoriously Cartesian problem. Among the historical heroes of "thinking thought" (to speak like Hegel), these titles—whether they expressly name various thinkers or aim at them indirectly—seem to pay special attention to several ancients: Anaximander, Parmenides, Heraclitus, Plato, and Aristotle, as well as to several moderns: Leibniz, Kant, Hegel, Schelling, Nietzsche—but never to Descartes. Similar remarks can be made about the lecture courses given by Heidegger at Marburg and then at Freiburg (whose publication, started when Heidegger was still alive, will make up the largest part of the *Gesamtausgabe*). The names just mentioned can be found in those courses, along with those of Thomas Aquinas and Fichte, but again Descartes is notoriously absent.

This absence might be interpreted as meaningful and might even lead to the suspicion that there is no Cartesian legacy in Heidegger. More precisely, since Heidegger liked to say that his writings and his teaching did not have the status of works, but were paths or milestones along a journey, this omission might suggest to us that his thought at no time claimed any allegiance to Descartes. Concerning the thinkers just mentioned, we might say that, at some point or other of Heidegger's itinerary, even perhaps continuously, they were favorite interlocutors who deserved particular attention, that is, a sort of recasting or reappropriation concerning what is at

---

1. This essay was presented as a paper at the colloquium Journées Descartes in Luxembourg, November 1987.

stake in the activity of thinking, i.e., the question of Being. Recall the most obvious cases of reappropriation. At the time of the conception and articulation of fundamental ontology, that is, when Heidegger was looking for the unique horizon of intelligibility for the various meanings of Being (which he discovered in the primordial temporality specific to the being that we are), he was directly involved in a dialogue with two thinkers of the first order: Aristotle for the ancients, Kant for the moderns.

Aristotle was essential to him because the question of Being owes its original impetus to the famous *to on pollachos legetai*. Also it is thanks to a meditation on Aristotle that Heidegger realized that the essence of truth is not *adaequatio,* or adequation, but uncovering, and that the space for such an uncovering is not judgment alone as in the tradition of logic, but the entire comportment of the being that we are. Moreover, it is the Aristotelian distinction between the productive activity of *poiesis* and the activity of *praxis* that influenced the existential analytic of Dasein, particularly the distinction between inauthenticity (linked to the preoccupation of everydayness) and authentic existence (linked to the ownmost character of individuation unveiled by care). Concerning the ownmost individuation, the *hou heneka* of the *Nicomachean Ethics* anticipated the *Worumwillen* of *Sein und Zeit.*

On the modern side, Kant was also essential. If we consider that the *Critique of Pure Reason* aims not so much at building a theory of knowledge, but at founding metaphysics, then the very center of that foundation (the transcendental deduction) reveals, within the doctrine of the schematism of imagination, that time is at the core of our *a priori* understanding of the Being of beings.

To these two major reappropriations, one could also add others, which, though less noticeable, are nonetheless real: one involving Plato and another Hegel. The pages on the "they" in the analytic of Dasein are indebted to the Platonic disdain for the "*hoi polloi*" and the sophists. In addition, the notion of *epekeina tès ousias* is greeted in the Marburg lecture courses as the first anticipation of the transcendence of Dasein.

There is also a recasting of Leibniz to the extent that a deconstruction can exhibit in his philosophy an attempt to found the logic of identity upon the monadological metaphysics of substance and thus detect in the very notion of monad (which is the unity of *intuitus* and *appetitus*) the anticipation—albeit obscure and awkward—of the openness of Dasein to the world.

Finally, there is a retrieval of Hegel if it is true (as the 1930 lecture course on *Hegel's Phenomenology of Spirit* indicates) that the Hegelian description of the transition from consciousness to self-consciousness moves entirely within the space of transcendence, notwithstanding the fact that Hegel transfers to his Absolute all the essential features of Dasein's finitude.

But among all these retrievals, whether publicly recognized or carried out discreetly, in the effort to build a fundamental ontology, Descartes does not seem to have a place. We therefore get the impression that he was not a thinker worthy of being reappropriated. This impression is further reinforced when Heidegger abandoned the initial project of a science of Being and proceeded to meditate on the history of the Western world as the history of the withdrawal of Being. Such a meditation became possible in the wake of a long debate with Nietzsche; the attention now paid to the Pre-Socratic thinkers certainly did not prevent Heidegger from a continued dialogue with Plato and Aristotle, with Leibniz, Kant, and Hegel. But again in this meditation, Descartes is held at a distance. While the *nihil sine ratione* of Leibniz lends itself to hearing the vibrating echo of the withdrawal of Being, one would be hard pressed to find the later Heidegger ascribing to Descartes any view worthy of a similar treatment.

Yet, it is not the case that the writings centered on the history of Being and of its forgetfulness completely ignore Descartes. On the contrary, they name, they quote, they interpret him frequently, and do so as much as did the writings from the time of fundamental ontology. But in both cases, the treatment given to Descartes seems to be one of *demarcation,* and never one of *reappropriation.*

After sketching the outline of our topic, we need to point out the most insistent themes of this demarcation. I shall proceed retrospectively from the writings meditating on the history of Being. For the most part, it is in the 1940 lecture course on Nietzsche that these themes are expressed with the greatest clarity and cohesion. The very title of the course indicates clearly and without ambiguity what specific treatment is reserved to Descartes in its analyses. The title is: *"European Nihilism."* The formula is borrowed from Nietzsche whom Heidegger credits with seeing that nihilism constitutes the movement of the modern history of the Western World, an insight however which did not allow its author to understand the essence of nihilism. Nihilism, in the Nietzschean sense, is the devaluation of the highest values. It is precisely because he thinks nihilism only from the notion of value that Nietzsche, according to Heidegger, cannot grasp the essence of nihilism. And if Nietzsche makes this assessment, it is because, unbeknownst to him and in spite of his antimetaphysical declarations, he thinks metaphysically. This means that Nietzsche's single project constantly remains the task of thinking human beings in relation to beings in their totality, without addressing the question of Being and of man's relation to

Being, without therefore addressing the question of the ontological difference. Thus, in spite of his well-publicized anti-Platonism, Nietzsche remains a Platonist. He remains indebted to the attitude by which Plato flattened *einai* into *ousia*, Being into beingness (*Seiendheit*), that is, into *idea*. From the Platonic idea to the Nietzschean value, there is a continuity.

> Because Nietzsche's philosophy is metaphysics, and all metaphysics is Platonism, at the end of metaphysics, Being must be thought as value; that is, it must be reckoned as a merely conditioned conditioning of beings. The metaphysical interpretation of Being is prefigured in the beginning of metaphysics. For Plato conceives Being as *idea*. The highest of ideas, however—and that means *at the same time* the essence of all ideas—is the *agathon*. Thought in a Greek sense, *agathon* is what *makes suitable*, what befits a being and makes it possible for it to be a being. Being has the character of making possible, is the condition of possibility. To speak with Nietzsche, Being is a *value*. (*Nietzsche IV*, 165–66)[2]

What is the connection between this quotation and our topic? It lies in the fact that, in the progression from the Platonic idea to the Nietzschean will-to-power as a positioning of values and—beyond the will-to-power—to the contemporary reign of the calculating and technological manipulation of beings in their totality, Descartes is an essential milestone. This means that ultimately Nietzsche is no less the heir of Descartes (in spite of his anti-Cartesianism) than of Plato (in spite of his anti-Platonism). It means also that if Plato anticipates Nietzsche from the distant past, Descartes anticipates him from the recent one. The passage quoted just above continues as follows:

> Was Plato therefore the first to think in values? That would be a rash conclusion. The Platonic conception of *agathon* is as essentially different from Nietzsche's concept of value as the Greek conception of man is from the modern notion of essence of man as subject. (*Nietzsche IV*, 166)

It is with Descartes that the notion of man as subject comes to the forefront. Heidegger's interpretation of Descartes in relation to the history of Being is therefore conducted on two fronts. The first pays attention to what in Descartes' works, notwithstanding the continued presence of Platonism, manifests a divergence from the Hellenic conceptions. The other approach

---

2. *Nietzsche*, Volume 4. *European Nihilism*, trans. Franz Capuzzi (New York: Harper and Row, 1982).

deciphers in Descartes elements that "anticipate" the Nietzschean will-to-power as well as the will-to-willing inherent in the contemporary reign of technology. In Heidegger's view the reign of technology is the reign of nihilism because, under the sway of calculating machination, Being no longer matters and turns out to be a mere vapor.

Let us now consider the first approach. Heidegger intends to show the divergence that separates Cartesianism from the Hellenic conceptions, by analyzing the words of Protagoras, the Greek thinker who, it seems, is the most similar to Descartes. On first inspection, the *cogito ergo sum* and the statement of the sophist—man is the measure of all things—express the same thing: the priority of man. Yet Heidegger points out that "Protagoras's fragment says something very different from the import of Descartes' principle" (*Nietzsche IV*, 90). The guidelines (*Hinsichten*) allowing these differences to be brought to light fall under four headings. It is by virtue of these that "the essence of a fundamental metaphysics is determined (*durch die sich das Wesen einer metaphysischen Grundstellung sich bestimmt*)" (II, 137), namely:

1. by the way in which man as man is *himself* and thereby knows himself;
2. by the projection of beings on Being;
3. by circumscribing the essence of the truth of beings and;
4. by the way in which each respective man takes the "measure" and passes it off as the truth of beings (*Nietzsche IV*, 92).

In his analysis of Protagoras's statement from these four perspectives, Heidegger remarks that:

1. The "I" for Protagoras is determined by the always limited belonging to beings in the unconcealed. The being-oneself (*Selbstsein*) of man is grounded in the reliability (*Verlässlichkeit*) of the unconcealed being and its radius (*Umkreis*).
2. Being has the essential character of presence (*Anwesenheit*).
3. Truth is experienced as unconcealment (*Unverborgenheit*).
4. "Measure" has the sense of the measuredness of unconcealment (*Nietzsche IV*, 95).

In contrast, the same guidelines applied to the Cartesian *cogito ergo sum* yield a very different assessment for each of the four considerations.
1. From now on, man is defined in this way because he is the:

distinctive ground underlying every re-presenting (*Vor-stellen*) of beings and their truth, on which every representing *and* its represented (*Vor-gestelltes*) is based and must be based if it is to have status and stability. Man is *subjectum* in the distinctive sense. (*Nietzsche IV*, 118)

As such a *subjectum,* man becomes the only being to which the concept applies, so that every being other than he is an object for him, the only subject.

2. Being's essential character is no longer presence (*Anwesenheit*) but the characteristic of being represented (*Vorgestelltheit*) in relation to a subject who insures himself of this representedness:

Being is representedness secured in reckoning representation, through which man is universally guaranteed his manner of proceeding (*Vorgehen*) in the midst of beings, as well as the scrutiny, conquest, mastery and disposition of beings in such a way that man, himself, can be the master of his own surety and certitude on his own terms. (119–20)

3. Truth is no longer experienced as an unconcealment to which man is entrusted. From now on, "the true is merely secured, the certain. Truth is certitude, a certitude for which it is decisive that, in it, man as subject is continually certain and sure of himself. Therefore, a procedure, an advance assurance is necessary for the securing of truth as certitude in an essential sense." Descartes has stressed this in the fourth of the *Regulae*, which stipulates that method—in the sense of that advance assurance—*necessaria est ad rerum veritatem investigandam*. (120).

4. Finally, the notion of measure itself undergoes a radical mutation from the meaning it had in the Greeks. It has nothing to do with moderation, and the proper sense of the limits to be maintained while focussing on the unconcealed. Because man is the only subject, because Being is representedness and, because truth is methodical certitude, man is committed, in his dealing with beings, to "progressing toward a limitless representing and reckoning disclosure of beings." Thus turned into the center of beings in their totality, the *subjectum* in the modern sense aims at "the discovery and conquest of the world" (121).

This four-point assessment of what separates Descartes from Protagoras reveals the basic connection between Descartes and Nietzsche. For in spite of Nietzsche's professed anti-Cartesianism, which authorizes many historians of ideas to detect several signs of a historical difference (*historische Verschiedenheit*) between Descartes and Nietzsche, this difference itself is seen by the thinker meditating on the History of Being as "the keenest indication of sameness in what is essential" (*das schärfste Anzeichen für die Selbigkeit im Wesentlichen*) (103).

In Heidegger's eyes, the objections Nietzsche levels at Descartes are either empty, or the proof of a deep-seated agreement with him. When for example Nietzsche charges Descartes with having turned the *I am* into a syllogistic conclusion and with having consequently inferred his alleged first certitude from a certain number of unclear presuppositions on *cogitatio* and *existentia*, he fails to recognize that in the *Principia Philosophiae*, Descartes had defended himself in advance against that accusation. *"Ubi dixi hanc propositionem ego cogito, ergo sum, esse omnium primam et certissimam, . . . non ideo negavi quid ante ipsam scire oporteat, quid sit cogitatio, quid existentia, quid certitudo"* (Adam et Tannery, VIII, 8). ("And where I have said that this proposition *I think, therefore I am* is the first and most certain of all . . . I have not thereby denied that one must know in advance of this principle what 'thinking', 'existence', and 'certitude' are (*Nietzsche IV*, 125). Likewise, when Nietzsche assesses that Descartes' *cogito ergo sum* posits the "ego" and the "subject" as the condition of "thinking," but when, contrary to Descartes, he asserts that it is thinking that conditions the "subject," the "object," the "substance," and the categories in general, Heidegger charges that Nietzsche fails to recognize that his objection to Descartes, "namely that the 'categories' emerge from 'thinking,' is indeed the decisive principle for Descartes himself" (129). More profoundly, when Nietzsche is convinced of successfully criticizing Descartes by arguing against the idea that *ego cogito* is an immediate certainty and attempts to derive the *ego cogito* from a will for truth (that is, from an *ego volo*), Heidegger charges that Nietzsche fails to recognize that such *velle*, considered as will-to-power and as a fundamental characteristic of beings in their totality, "became possible only on the basis of Descartes' fundamental metaphysical position" (129). Therefore at the same time as he is certain of his stance against Descartes, Nietzsche "adopts Descartes' fundamental position completely" (132). "The adoption goes so far that Nietzsche, without asking for reasons to justify this, equates Being with representedness and the latter with truth" (131). For him as for Descartes, "truth and Being mean the same, specifically they mean what is established in representing and securing" (131). Does this amount to saying that Nietzsche repeated Descartes purely and simply and did not know it? Not at all.

For Descartes, man is subject in the sense of the ego-centeredness of the understanding that reflects upon itself, whereas for Nietzsche man is *subject* in the sense of being subjected to the impulses of his body.

For Descartes, Being is defined as *representedness*. This is also the case for Nietzsche, but, Being has no longer for him the meaning of something stable. Stability is nothing but a semblance arising from the midst of becoming, and becoming is essentially the increasing of the will-to-power.

For Descartes, truth is synonymous with the certitude belonging to an understanding that perceives with total clarity what it sets in order in front of itself. For Nietzsche, truth consists in organizing every kind of stability as a provisional stepping stone to provide power for oneself. What is willed by the will is true.

Finally for Descartes, within the limits of a possible certainty, man is the measure of beings in their totality. Taking his clue from the fourth *Meditation*, Heidegger insists that at the core of Cartesian representation there exists a possibility for error and erring which restrains the essence of the subject and turns man into a *medium quid inter Deum et nihil*. Human knowledge remains conditioned by absolute knowledge. In Nietzsche however, such a limitation is nowhere to be found. The will is no longer subjected to the possibilities for certainty produced within a finite understanding. The will has an absolute and unconditional power over the true and the false, to the extent that the very distinction between true and false becomes null and void and drifts into the movement of a subjectivity which "is not merely delimited from every limit [but which] itself now enjoins every kind of restriction (*Beschränkung*) and delimitation (*Entschränkung*)" (145).

Since subjectivity for Nietzsche becomes absolutely unconditioned, he does not simply repeat Descartes. But for the thinker of the history of Being, what is retained is that Descartes anticipated Nietzsche, and that the beginning of the historical process which erupted with the Cartesian *cogito* (whose successive phases can be traced in Leibniz, in Kant and then Hegel) is completed in the will-to-power.

The clarification of such a historical process does not involve any reappropriation of Descartes, a fact that we will easily confirm after calling attention to the fact that the only appropriation associated with this historical process (*Ereignis*) concerns the belonging of man to the secret of Being. It is an essential characteristic of metaphysics as such, and of the metaphysics of subjectivity in particular, that it is permanently unable to recognize such a secret.

If from these remarks we turn our attention back to Heidegger's treatment of Descartes in the writings prior to the meditation on the history of Being—that is, in the works and the lecture courses carrying out the project of fundamental ontology—we might first be tempted to think that these works too make no acknowledgement to Descartes. Did not Heidegger indicate at different times that the Cartesianism espoused by Husserl after *The Logical Investigations* was one of the major reasons for their disagreement on the task of phenomenology?

Moreover, if we look carefully at the references made to Descartes in *Sein und Zeit* or if we investigate the Heideggerian analyses of some Cartesian theses, it seems that they first manifest an act of distancing. When, for example, in the introduction of the book, Heidegger credits Kant with being the first and only philosopher to have linked, in the doctrine of schematism, the ontological problem to the problem of temporality, he immediately adds that two defects limit the Kantian discovery: the lack of inquiry into the meaning of Being and the absence of an ontology of Dasein. The first defect betrays the weight of the entire tradition since the ancients. The second is linked to the fact that Kant took over "Descartes' ontological position quite dogmatically" (*Being and Time*, 46; 24). This means that he was a prisoner of the Cartesian *cogito*.

Thus Kant's dogmatism on this point is reminiscent of Descartes' dogmatism. A little later, at the beginning of the analytic of Dasein, Heidegger reproaches the Cartesian *cogito sum* with leaving "the *sum* completely undiscussed, even though it is regarded as no less primordial than the *cogito*" (*Being and Time*, 71; 46). More precisely Descartes is reproached with not having given the *sum* any mode of being other than *Vorhandenheit*, that is, with having attributed to the being that we are the mode of being specific to natural beings (247; 203), and to things in general.

Finally, the only detailed analysis of the Cartesian position we find in *Sein und Zeit* concerns the Cartesian concept of *res extensa*. The very title under which that analysis is conducted expresses an opposition. The title is: "*Die Abhebung der Analyse der Weltlichkeit gegen die Interpretation der Welt bei Descartes* (The *Demarcation* of our Analysis of Worldhood, *as against* Descartes' Interpretation of the World) [my emphasis]." I shall briefly recall the ways in which the analysis carries out a demarcation, or *Abhebung*.

First, the distinction between the *ego cogito* and the *res corporea*, which turns out to be historically fundamental for the distinction at work throughout modern philosophy between nature and spirit, remains indeterminate in its ontological foundations because only one term is used by Descartes to define the Being of both types of beings: *substantia*. This word is indeterminate because at times it designates the Being of a being, its substantiality, and at others it designates beings themselves (122–23; 89–90) considered in their ontical properties, for example the modes of *extensio*: *divisio, figura, motus, capacitas mutationum*. Moreover, substantiality itself, granting that it is possible to consider it ontologically and not ontically, remains indeterminate: at times it means the ontological status of a being (*ens perfectissimun*) which is in need of no other being in order to exist, while at other times it means the ontological status of those beings which depend on this *ens perfectissimum* in order to exist. Therefore Being, as substantiality, has such an inflated meaning, that "its meaning embraces an 'infinite' difference" (125; 92), the one that separates the creator from his creature. The ontological question of substantiality was, therefore, suppressed as Descartes himself acknowledged in the *Principia*: "*nulla eius [substantiae] nominis significatio potest distincte intelligi, quae Deo et creaturis sit communis''* (No signification of this name [substance] which would be common to God and his creation can be distinctly understood 126; 93). This means, Heidegger says, that for Descartes the Being of beings cannot be apprehended (*"per se non afficit,"* in itself it does not affect us) let alone become the subject of an inquiry.

Finally, as the result of its previous indeterminacies, Heidegger charges that the Cartesian ontology of the world is not really an ontology. It does not pay enough attention to what intraworldly (*innerweltlich*) beings are, such that the phenomenon of the world is announced in them.

The intraworldly entities upon which Descartes relies in order to show their worldliness, defined by him in terms of *extensio,* are beings which from the outset have been deprived of any properly worldly, that is, existential, import. They are beings which from the outset have been torn apart from the relations that we develop in the everyday preoccupation with our environment. Such beings are devoid of any pragmatic usefulness, they have lost their character of Being-ready-to-hand and, with them, we have no other relation than pure *mathematical intellection.* This intellection is primordial for Descartes, for it allows him to gain an ontological access to the world (in his sense of this term). Heidegger, on the other hand, wants to show that the status of intellection is in no way primordial, but derivative, as is always the case for every contemplation, whether sensible or intellectual. Intellection derives—after a loss—from the pragmatic view which constantly projects us upon usable beings, on the backdrop of various referential contextures. Because Descartes recognizes no other access to these intraworldly beings and to the world itself than intuitive contemplation, he is satisfied in granting them the only ontological status of *constant persistence,* a status Heidegger calls presence-at-hand (a mode of being which is in no way that of the world—since the world is an *existentiale*—but that of nature).

Because of this way of proceeding, Descartes is viewed by Heidegger as much less original than he otherwise appears and claims to be. For all his critique of sensory perception and emphasis on intellection, he continues to define intellection as *perception,* that is, *noein.* By virtue of this *noein,* Descartes finds himself in accord with the entire tradition since Parmenides, with whom *in finis* he agrees in thinking that there is no other meaning to Being than presence-at-hand.

Thus it seems that Heidegger's relation to Descartes is characterized by a demarcation, or *Abhebung,* with respect to both fundamental ontology and the meditation on the history of Being. Yet we should not stop at this point for it is now that our topic recoils and immediately reverts itself: a confrontation of these two demarcations gives food for thought.

Fundamental ontology charges Descartes in the end with having remained prisoner of the Greeks, that is, of the unquestioned privilege given to *noein* and to an unquestioned concept of Being, *Vorhandenheit* (presence-at-hand).

In contradistinction, the meditation on the history of Being stresses the magnitude of the distance between the Greeks and Descartes—as well as what anticipates the contemporary theme of the will-to-power.

Such a disparity between the two demarcations evokes a suspicion. It invites us to wonder whether the insistence with which Heidegger was led, at a certain point, to distance Descartes from the ancients, is not somehow connected to the insistence with which he had first brought Descartes within close proximity of the ancients. Hence this very disparity should invite the reader to wonder whether, in spite of the criticisms addressed at Descartes in *Sein und Zeit*, fundamental ontology is not more Cartesian than it claims to be. This suspicion is confirmed by pointing out some indications of proximity.

Consider for example the following sequence, which at the time of fundamental ontology was typical of Heidegger's relation to the history of metaphysics. What is at stake in the sequence is the link between the question of Being and the question of man, or Dasein.

> For Parmenides the clarification of Being takes place by way of a reflection on 'thinking,' *noein*, knowing what is (*einai*), knowledge of beings. Plato's discovery of the 'ideas,' which are determinations of being, is oriented to the conversation the soul has with itself (*psuche-logos*). Guided by the question about *ousia*, Aristotle obtains the categories by reference to reason's predicative knowing (*logos-nous*). In the search for *substantia*, Descartes founds "first philosophy" (*prima philosophia*) explicitly on the *res cogitans*, the *animus* [mind]. Kant's transcendental, i.e., ontological, problematic directed toward Being (the question of the possibility of experience) moves in the dimension of consciousness, of the freely acting subject (the spontaneity of the ego). For Hegel, substance is defined from the subject. The struggle over Being shifts to the field of thinking, of making statements, of the soul, of subjectivity. Human Dasein moves to the center. (*The Metaphysical Foundations of Logic*, 15; 18–19)[3]

---

3. *The Metaphysical Foundations of Logic*, trans. Michael Heim (Bloomington: Indiana University Press, 1984).

This sequence indicates not only that there is no radical discontinuity between the ancients and the moderns, but also that the history of metaphysics must be viewed as the progressive maturation of fundamental ontology, a maturation whose penultimate phase is the modern supremacy of subjectivity in the sense of *cogito*.

Indeed, on closer inspection, the early critique leveled at Descartes consists in showing that he remains caught in the initially Parmenidean correlation between *noein* and presence-at-hand. This critique does not aim at discarding the Cartesian *cogito sum*, but at radically reappropriating it. The nonradical element remaining in the Cartesian *sum* is the fact that the character of "mineness" of the *sum*, its *Jemeinigkeit*, is somehow neutralized. This neutralization happens because Descartes assigns to the "ego" a mode of being no different than that of the beings of nature and therefore projects upon it, by reflection in the optical sense, an ontological status originating from the things. At the outset Descartes therefore fails to recognize that it belongs to the existence of Dasein each time to be strictly mine, to be *jemeinig*. Thus the nonradical element remaining in the Cartesian *cogito* is its neutralization. The clarity enjoyed by the *clara et distincta perceptio* is the free-floating and uprooted characteristic of a pure *intellectio* severed from the openness of the disclosure (*Erschlossenheit*) inherent in existing for the sake of (*umwillen seiner*) and in the care of oneself. In other words, the nonradical remainder in the Cartesian *cogito* (which justifies the preference that Heidegger gives to Leibniz over Descartes) consists in the fact that the *intellectio* characteristic of the Cartesian *cogito* is detached from the *appetitus* inherent in the *Jemeinigkeit* of existing. Put in another way, the Cartesian *cogito* is nonradical because it is insufficiently monadic, i.e., unitary, inasmuch as the monad welds together what Descartes had dissociated: intelligence and will.

But in this case, if the *Abhebung* with regard to Descartes is less a rejection than an effort of radicalization, there is indeed a Cartesian legacy at the core of fundamental ontology. For it is hard to conceive how fundamental ontology could have centered on the character of "mineness" of Dasein without being in any way tributary to the Cartesian irruption of the *ego sum*. Of the fact that there is a legacy, three additional signs can be found, which we shall briefly present before concluding.

First indication: We alluded earlier to the relationship between Heidegger and Husserl and to the reproach addressed to Husserl after the *Logical Investigations* of deliberately recasting Cartesianism. This reproach is astonishing. First of all, in order to be valid, it would presuppose that the *Logical Investigations* manifest no Cartesian legacy of any sort, an assessment which seems quite exaggerated. Furthermore, the reproach is all the more surprising because when Heidegger recast what was in his own eyes the most important part of the *Logical Investigations*—that is, the doctrine of the categorial intuition of Being in which Being is not a real predicate— and metamorphosed it within the *a priori* understanding of Being by Dasein, he associated it very closely to a *sich selbst verstehen,* that is, to a theme of Cartesian origin.

Second indication: We know that the nonpublished part of *Sein und Zeit* was to be devoted to the deconstruction (*Destruktion*) of the history of ontology. Such a *Destruktion* was to bear on three essential thinkers. Two of these became the objects of a Heideggerian reappropriation: Kant and Aristotle. The third was to be Descartes. It is hard to conceive how Heidegger who understood this *Destruktion* as deconstruction and reappropriation in the case of the first two, could have contemplated a demolition pure and simple in the case of the third.

Finally, the third indication: When fundamental ontology established the genealogy of the notion of presence-at-hand (*Vorhandenheit*), that is, the mode of being of nature, it referred this concept of Being, which is the only one inherited from the tradition, to a comportment of Dasein (the productive comportment characteristic of everydayness). It is because the Greeks considered Being only in the light of this productive comportment that they supposedly imposed on the tradition the concept of Being as presence-at-hand.

> The sense of direction and apprehension peculiar to productive comportment toward something involves taking that to which the productive activity relates as something which, in and through the producing, is supposed to be extant[4] as finished in its own self. (*The Basic Problems of Phenomenology,* 113; 159)

Such a genealogy is obviously not to be found in the texts of Descartes. But with Descartes, this genealogy shares the idea that nature has no other mode of being than the subsistence or constant persistence of presence-at-hand. We can wonder moreover whether it does not consist in retrospectively projecting upon the Greek world a technical, and properly Cartesian, apprehension of *phusis,* i.e., the idea that nature in its essence offers itself to the mastery and ownership of man. Consequently, it is possible to reassess the meditation on the history of Being and view it now as a self-critique of fundamental ontology, that is to say specifically a critique of the way in which Heidegger had initially reappropriated Descartes.

Of course, it is nowhere asserted in the lecture course on Nietzsche that the meditation on the history of Being should be taken as of a self-

---

4. Note that "extant" is Hofstadter's translation of *Vorhanden,* translated by Macquarrie and Robinson as "present-at-hand" in *Being and Time.* (Trans.)

critique. Yet the point is suggested with enough clarity. For we deem it significant that in the course on "European Nihilism" the section that immediately follows the highlighting of the internal cohesion of the fundamental positions of Descartes and Nietzsche should contain a page-long assessment on the outcome of the project of *Sein und Zeit*, the master work of fundamental ontology. On the one hand, the passage in question deplores that the book was greeted by nothing else than a profound misunderstanding rooted in "this habit, ineradicable and becoming ever more inveterate, of the modern mode of thinking for which man is subject" (*Nietzsche IV*, 141 modified). But Heidegger recognizes, on the other hand, that the reason for such a misunderstanding resides also in "the attempt itself," which

> perhaps because it really is something historically organic and not anything "contrived," evolves from what has been heretofore; in struggling loose from it, it necessarily and continually refers back to the course of the past and even calls on it for assistance, in the effort to say something entirely different. Above all, however, the path taken terminates abruptly at a decisive point. The reason for the disruption is that the attempt and the path it chose confront the danger of unwillingly becoming merely another reinforcement of subjectivity. (*Nietzsche IV*, 141 modified)

There is no better way of suggesting that there was in fundamental ontology an element leading to the reinforcement of the Cartesian legacy.

6

The Presence of Nietzsche in *Sein und Zeit*[1]

Nietzsche is quoted only twice in *Sein und Zeit*, in Sections 53 and 76. Each time, the evocation of his name is presented as a self-evident reference and Nietzsche's words quoted by Heidegger seem to bespeak a companion in thinking—or should I say an *alter ego*—without revealing on Heidegger's part the slightest attempt to demarcate Nietzsche's teaching from the analytic of Dasein.

These citations are hardly more than allusive and discreet hints: no more than six words in Section 53 and a page [of commentary] in Section 76. But they are not accompanied by any distanciation from Nietzsche's thought, any reservations, any debate, nor by any attempt at critical probing. Moreover, in both cases, the reference to Nietzsche comes at a decisive point. In both instances, it is inscribed in the context of analyses that play a critical role in securing the approach to the center of fundamental ontology, which is the project aiming at answering in a radical fashion the *Seinsfrage*, that is, the question about what at the deepest level makes our understanding of Being possible. The center of our understanding of Being is authentic temporality, conceived as the finite temporality of the Dasein that resolutely exists for the sake of itself. Temporality forms the transcendental horizon for the understanding of Being.

Sein und Zeit is the book devised to secure the approach to this center, but after proceeding through two stages it stops short of its goal. The first stage is only preparatory: it aims at showing that Dasein exists for the sake of itself (*umwillen seiner*) and that care, as opposed to preoccupation with the useful and solicitude for others, constitutes its Being. In the first stage, corresponding to the first Division of the book, Nietzsche's name is never

---

1. This essay was first published in French in '*Etre et Temps de Martin Heidegger, Questions de méthode et voies de recherche*', under the direction of Jean-Pierre Cometti and Dominique Janicaud, (Marseille: Sud, 1989), pp. 59–75.

mentioned. It appears in the second stage, a Division in which the phenom-enological approach moves from the preliminary stage to what is "origi-nary." Let us sketch how these two stages are linked in order to determine the import of the two references to Nietzsche found in the second Division.

The objective of the treatise is to determine the meaning of Being, that is, to elucidate our understanding of it. Because such an understanding is inherent in the being that we are, it is the mode of being of the being called Dasein that must first be determined. But as long as the determination of the mode of being of Dasein is deficient, that is, as long as it fails to be radical and primordial, no elucidation of the understanding of Being can be reached. The result secured in the first Division is the highlighting of care as the fundamental mode of being of Dasein.

The question which then initiates the second Division is whether the characterization of care developed in the first Division is sufficient to de-termine the Being of Dasein in its totality and to reveal its most primordial character. Because the answer to this question is negative, the second Di-vision attempts to remedy this insufficiency. It shows that Being-towards-death is what determines the totality of the Being of Dasein, that is, the totality of care; and that only in the authentic relation to death does care reveal what is ownmost and authentic in Dasein; lastly, it shows that tem-porality is the ontological meaning of care.

If the analytic conducted in the first division has only a preparatory character, it is because it is—so to speak—burdened by the phenomenal basis upon which it rests: everydayness. For this reason, the first Division cannot determine the Being of Dasein in its totality and primordiality. It is unable to determine Dasein's totality because everydayness has an interme-diary and partial status: it resides between past and future, birth and death, accomplished and future possibilities. It cannot do so primordially because everydayness stands on a ground that is not proper to Dasein, that is not its own—the ground of instrumentality and of the "they." It is not, therefore, in everydayness that we can delineate what in care is ownmost and proper.

The phenomenon of care serves as the guide to a properly existential analysis of death, and conversely this analysis sheds a deeper light on care. If it wants to remain existential, the analysis must guard against confusing the mode of being of Dasein with that of other beings, usable and dispos-able [*manipulables*] beings, extant beings, or even living beings. These confusions can be avoided only by analyzing death in the light of the fun-damental characteristics of care, the Being of Dasein. These characteristics were identified in the preparatory analysis: existing as Being-ahead-of-itself, facticity as Being-already-in-the-world, fallenness as Being-alongside-with usable beings that solicit preoccupation. Let us now consider how death concerns each of these three characteristics intimately and eminently.

First, Being ahead-of-itself is Being in the mode of a potentiality-for-Being. But death is for each of us the always imminent possibility of no longer retaining this potentiality-for-Being. The persistent imminence of the possibility of death therefore throws each and every Dasein upon its own-most potentiality-for-Being. In addition, this imminence is such that in relation to it, Dasein's relationships to others are severed: no one can discharge me of my own death. Finally, the persistent possibility of being there no more cannot be overcome: no one escapes it. Inasmuch as Dasein is characterized by Being-ahead-of-itself in the mode of a potentiality-for-Being, death is not an event-in-the-world, but is Dasein's ownmost, non-relational and not-to-be outstripped potentiality.

Secondly, from the outset, existing is also having been thrown into potentiality-for-Being and death intimately concerns this facticity of existence. The imminence of death is not brought about gradually, by age for example; neither is it something adventitious and surreptitious. As soon as Dasein exists, it is already old enough to die. Thus oriented by the fundamental characteristics of care, the analysis can elucidate the existential concept of death as follows: " 'Dying' is made clear as thrown Being towards its ownmost potentiality-for-Being, which is non-relational and not to be outstripped" (*Being and Time*, 295; 251). To this, we should add that this potentiality-for-Being, as the possibility of impossibility, is certain in its very indetermination. To exist is not to expect the external catastrophe of the end, it is (and from the outset has been) to be on intimate terms with death, it is to be intrinsically mortal, to be Being-towards-death.

This existential elucidation limits itself intentionally to a conceptualization of what can be revealed to each one in the *Grundstimmung* of anxiety, which occurs "without any explanatory or theoretical knowledge":

> Thrownness into death reveals itself to Dasein in a more primordial and impressive manner in that state-of-mind which we have called 'anxiety'. Anxiety in the face of death is anxiety 'in the face of' that potentiality-for-Being which is one's ownmost, non-relational and not to be outstripped. That in the face of which one has anxiety is Being-in-the-world itself. That about which one has this anxiety is simply Dasein's potentiality-for-Being. Anxiety in the face of death must not be confused with fear in the face of one's demise. This anxiety is not an accidental or random mood of 'weakness' in some individual; but, as a basic state of mind of Dasein, it amounts to the disclosedness of the fact that Dasein exists as thrown Being *towards* its end. (295; 251)

Thirdly, it remains for us to characterize the existential connection between death and the third fundamental feature of care: fallenness as Being-alongside-the-intraworldly. This amounts to asking how everydayness conceives of death. It conceives of it as an intraworldly event among others and not as the ownmost potentiality-for-Being of each Dasein. This event is distorted by the tranquilizing idle talk of the "they" by way of an interpretation which obscures the non-relational and not-to-be-outstripped character of death and the indeterminate certainty of its ownmost possibility. Because it hides Being-towards-death from its true character of Being in the ownmost, everydayness holds anxiety at bay inasmuch as anxiety uncovers what the "they" intends to cover up:

> "The "they" concerns itself with transforming this anxiety into fear in the face of an oncoming event. In addition, the anxiety which has been made ambiguous as fear, is passed off as a weakness with which no self-assured Dasein may have any acquaintance" (*Being and Time,* 298; 254).

But if it is true that everyday fallenness covers up Dasein's ownmost potentiality, we still have to consider, ontologically or existentially, what the authentic or ownmost comportment towards death consists in, and to outline the existential conditions of its possibility. This problem is addressed in Section 53, under the title "Existential Projection of an Authentic Being-towards-death." Such a comportment must not be confused with the openness—of understanding and uncovering—by which we attend to a possibility within the world. To open oneself up to a possibility within the world always amounts to seeing to the realization of such a possibility. Far from understanding the possible as possible, intraworldly preoccupation aims at annihilating the possibility of the possible and at transforming it into actuality. Hence no authentic comportment towards death may be found in the realm of preoccupation. Neither does it consist in weighing the odds of one's demise, nor in being on the lookout for its signs, nor in casting a spell against its occurrence, much less in calling for its arrival. Instead it consists in being open to the possibility as such—without any attenuation whatsoever of its character of possibility. Heidegger calls *anticipation (Vorlaufen)*[2] the existential openness to one's ownmost possibility. Anticipation reveals to the existing Dasein that its potentiality-for-Being is radically finite, and frees Dasein for this finitude. Such a finite potentiality-for-Being is unveiled in its entirety by anticipation, which means that anticipation unveils the totality of care. It reveals to Dasein that it is thrown

---

2. The term "*Vorlaufen*" is translated by Macquarrie and Robinson in *Being and Time* as *anticipation.* Hofstadter translates it as *self-precedence* in *The Basic Problems of Phenomenology.* (Trans.)

into the finitude of a potentiality-for-Being that is radically its own. And at the same time, it discloses what everydayness conceals; it discloses the inauthenticity of everydayness by wresting Dasein away from it. Finally, by revealing a singular Dasein to itself, anticipation reveals to it that the potentiality-for-Being of other Daseins belongs to them alone.

Such is in outline the "ontological projection" of the authentic or ownmost Being-towards-death. It goes without saying that the existential possibility of manifesting the totality of care by anticipation can only take place in anxiety, which is radically different from fear. Anxiety is

the state of mind which can hold open the utter and constant threat to itself, arising from Dasein's ownmost individualized Being. . . . For this reason, anxiety as a basic state-of-mind belongs to such a self-understanding of Dasein on the basis of Dasein itself. Being-towards-death is essentially anxiety. (*Being and Time*, 310; 265–66)

Section 53 can therefore be summarized as follows:

Anticipation reveals to Dasein its lostness in the they-self, and brings it face to face with the possibility of being itself, primarily unsupported by concernful solicitude, but of being itself, rather in an impassioned *freedom towards death*—a freedom which has been released from the illusions of the "they," and which is factical, certain of itself, and anxious. (311; 266)

We have now explored the context in which the first reference to Nietzsche is made. It punctuates the analysis of Being-authentic precisely with the possibility *not-to-be-outstripped* of death. Let us consider the terms of this analysis which constitute the particular context in which the quotation appears:

The ownmost, non-relational possibility is *not to be outstripped*. Being towards this possibility enables Dasein to understand that giving itself up impends for it as the uttermost possibility of its existence. Anticipation, however, unlike inauthentic Being-towards-death, does not evade the fact that death is not to be outstripped; instead, anticipation frees itself *for* accepting this. When, by anticipation, one becomes free *for* one's own death, one is liberated from one's lostness in those possibilities which may accidentally thrust themselves upon one; and one is liberated in such a way that for the first time one can authentically understand and choose among the factical possibilities lying ahead of that possibility which is not to be outstripped. Anticipation discloses to existence that its uttermost possibility lies in giving itself up, and thus it shatters all one's tenaciousness to whatever existence one has reached. In anticipation, Dasein guards itself against falling back behind itself, or behind the potentiality-for-Being which it has understood. It guards itself against "becoming too old for its victories" (Nietzsche). Free for its ownmost possibilities, which are determined by the *end* and so are understood as *finite*, Dasein dispels the danger that it may, by its own finite understanding of existence, fail to recognize that it is getting outstripped of the existence possibilities of Others, or rather that it may explain these possibilities wrongly and force them back upon its own, so that it may divest itself of its ownmost factical existence (308–9; 264)

This passage contains only six words of Nietzsche, but they are quoted in such a way as to complement Heidegger's own words perfectly. He introduces them without affectation, and with an approval so spontaneous in the midst of an analysis so decisive that they prompt us now to pause and determine the reason why these six words precisely are singled out from Nietzsche's text. As soon as we look at Nietzsche's text with this goal in mind, we discover many indications of a profound affinity.

The six words Heidegger so completely endorses can be found in the penultimate section of the first part of *Thus Spoke Zarathustra*. Its title is: "*Vom freien Tod*" (On Free Death). In itself, this title reveals a proximity because the very phrasing of the most evocative words of Section 53 is: "freedom for death" (*Freiheit zum Tode*), a formula which we also find in Nietzsche's text. This proximity is confirmed by the examination of the substance of Zarathustra's teaching, which enjoins: "Die at the right time!" This injunction is less in keeping with the end of one's existence than with the way in which existence is related to its end. "Of course, how could those who never live at the right time die at the right time? Would that they had never been born. But even the superfluous make a fuss about their dying" (*Portable Nietzsche*, p. 183).[3] Hence the question is: as opposed to the superfluous, who is it that lives his life at the right time? He is the one who "consumes his life," or, as was said in the previous section ("On Child and Marriage"), the one whose will is "a thirst for the creator, an arrow, and longing for the overman" (*Portable Nietzsche*, 183). In other words, he is the one whose existence measures up to the will-to-power, to an overcoming of oneself which at the same time is transition (*Übergang*)

---

3. *Portable Nietzsche*, trans. and ed. Walter Kaufmann (Princeton: Princeton University Press, 1972).

and loss (*Untergang*), quest for the self (*Selbstsucht*) and offering of self (*Opfer*) (127).

This individual alone has the right to say "I," either in victory or still in the midst of a struggle. He alone is fully individualized, not superfluous. "My death I praise to you, the free death which comes to me because I want it" (184). Free anticipation of death, subscription to one's own demise is at the very core of the *Selbstsucht* inherent in the Nietzschean notion of the will-to-power. The free acceptance of finite existence is therefore the first point of convergence between the Heideggerian analysis and the teaching of Zarathustra. In both cases, such an acceptance entails the contrast between ownmost individuation and a neutralized, anonymous and weak mode of being, i.e., the mode of being of everydayness (in Heidegger's terminology) and of the superfluous (in Nietzsche's). We shall demonstrate later that a certain concept of temporality is implicit in the Nietzschean acceptance of death as "living at the right time" and point out the affinity between the Heideggerian analysis and this teaching of Zarathustra. We shall take up this issue when we consider Section 76 of *Sein und Zeit*. Let us also postpone an inquiry into whether Nietzsche's acceptance of death entails a concept of understanding, and therefore of truth, which would further underscore the affinity. For the time being, it suffices to note that these three points of convergence are—so to speak—bound together in a knot, within the words with which Zarathustra designates the one who wills fully: "Free to die and free in death, able to say a holy No when the time for Yes has passed: thus he knows how to die and live" (*Portable Nietzsche,* 185).[4] Freedom for death, some conception of temporality, and a certain form of understanding, hence of relationship to truth are obviously interconnected in Nietzsche's thought.

Yet if the expression *"Frei zum Tode"* can be transposed without difficulty from Nietzsche's text to Section 53 of *Sein und Zeit,* the same thing cannot be said of the themes of temporality and truth. Indeed, taken in themselves, the six words from Nietzsche hardly exhibit any relationship to time, and say nothing of a connection to truth. And they remain all the more silent in this regard, since Heidegger, as it turns out, deliberately truncated the phrase, short though it was. Zarathustra's teaching was: "Some become too old even for their truths and victories: a toothless mouth no longer has the right to every truth" (184). Although used twice in Nietzsche's text, the word "truth" is now strangely absent from Heidegger's. This is one more reason to suspect that this silence is elo-

---

4. *Frei zum Tode und frei im Tode, ein heiliger Nein-sager, wenn es nicht Zeit mehr ist zum Ja: also versteht er sich auf Tod und Leben.*

quent. But before attempting to confront this silence with the content of Section 76, we should continue our reading of Zarathustra's teaching. To the full acceptance of mortal existence, Nietzsche opposes two types of relationship to death, one consisting in dying too late and the other in dying too soon. It is from the part of the text relative to the first relationship to death that Heidegger selected the passage cited. Those who have become too old for their truths and for their victories are the ones who no longer have a goal or who remain attached to a former goal, and who have been deserted by the movement of willing. They resemble "ropemakers: they drag out their threads and always walk backwards" (184). To the ones, now deserted or never inhabited by a great willing, death always comes too late because "the victor is your grinning death, which creeps up like a thief—and yet comes as the master" (184). In contrast to those who die at the wrong time because they are no longer able to live at the right time, the one who knows how to die and to live stands for lightness against gravity, freshness against decay, and for the passion for struggle against cowardice (*Feigheit*). We need not stress that a similar polarity sustains the movement of Section 53. On the one hand, it is said that the "they" "perverts anxiety into cowardly fear and, in surmounting this fear, . . . makes known its cowardliness in the face of anxiety" (*Being and Time,* 311; 266). On the other hand, it is said that freedom-for-death is "impassioned." To be sure, such a passion is as old as philosophy, dating back to Plato who defined *thaumazein* as *pathos.* But the use—already rare in *Sein und Zeit*—of the epithet "impassioned" is surprising when it is thus linked with a pure ontological "projection." This "impassioned" freedom for death turns out to be less puzzling, however, if we recognize in it the echo of Zarathustra's teaching.

What about the second type of relation to death denounced by Zarathustra, which consists in dying too soon? Most die too old, he says, but a few die too young. Christ is among the latter:

Verily, that Hebrew died too early whom the preachers of slow death honor; and for many it has become a calamity that he died too early. As yet he knew only tears and the melancholy of the Hebrew, and hatred of the good and the just—the Hebrew Jesus: then the longing for death overcame him. Would that he had remained in the wilderness and far from the good and the just! Perhaps he would have learned to live and to love the earth—and laughter too.

Believe me, my brothers! He died too early; he himself would have recanted his teaching, had he reached my age. Noble enough was he to recant. (*Portable Nietzsche,* 185)

The Presence of Nietzche in Sein und Zeit / 183

We can see that denouncing this second type of relationship to death amounts to advocating the joyful science, *gaya scienza,* and its faithfulness to life, against the Christian weariness and longing for another world. Indeed neither Christianity and death, on the one hand, nor joyful science, on the other, can be counted among the explicit themes of *Sein und Zeit.* Yet, they are not completely absent from the Marburg teaching. We find proof of this in the 1925 lecture course on the *Prolegomena to the History of the Concept of Time,* which may be viewed as the first version of *Sein und Zeit.* At the center of the introductory debate, in which Heidegger intends to show the necessity of a radicalization of the Husserlian discoveries, hence the necessity of the analytic of Dasein and of fundamental ontology, we read the following words worthy of attention:

> Philosophical research is and remains atheism, which is why philosophy can allow itself the 'arrogance of thinking.' Not only will it allow itself as much; this arrogance is the inner necessity of philosophy and its true strength. Precisely in this atheism philosophy becomes what a great man called the "joyful science." (80; 110)[5]

The six little words are indeed much more than a display of sophistication in scholarship: they open to a plane that stretches *ad infinitum.* Perhaps Section 76 can help us to outline the characteristics of this dimension and to spell out the affinities between fundamental ontology and its Nietzschean inspiration.

Section 76 is the penultimate in the penultimate chapter of the book. The title of Chapter 5 (II, 5, 424; 372) is: "Temporality and Historicality." If we concede that the next section, devoted to Dilthey and Yorck, has no other value than confirming and illustrating his points for the academic public of the time, we can say that Section 76 is the crowning point of what Heidegger calls "the exposition of the problem of historicality." Its theme is "The Existential Source of Historiology (*Historie*) in Dasein's Historicality (*Geschichtlichtheit*)." It attempts to show that historiology is possible only "in so far as Dasein's Being is historical—that is to say, in so far as by reason of its ecstatico-horizonal temporality it is open in its character of 'having been' " (*Being and Time,* 445; 393). Now as was the case previously in Section 53, the method used is an "ontological projection." The goal is not to derive an induction from a certain number of facts concerning the method of historians, but to allow the *idea* of historiology to spring

---

5. *History of the Concept of Time,* Prolegomena, trans. Theodore Kiesel (Bloomington: Indiana University Press, 1985), G.A. 20

forth from the ontological dimension of Dasein called "historicality." It is in this properly ontological context that the second reference to Nietzsche is found: an entire page on the second *Meditation Out of Season*. Let us examine its essential moments.

> The possibility that historiology in general can either be 'used' 'for one's life' or 'abused' in it, is grounded on the fact that one's life is historical in the roots of its Being, and that therefore, as factically existing, one has in each case made one's decision for authentic or inauthentic historicality. Nietzsche recognized what was essential as to the 'use and abuse of historiology for life' in the second of his studies "out of season" (1874), and said it unequivocally and penetratingly. (448; 396)

To perceive what is "essential" and to say it "unequivocally and penetratingly"—this sort of praise is exceptional in *Sein und Zeit*. Heidegger also wrote at the beginning of Section 77 that the problem of history presented in Section 76 was gained "in the process of appropriating the labors of Dilthey" and had been "strengthened by the theses of Count Yorck." But who could take this claim of allegiance literally after realizing that it is Nietzsche who is credited with seeing and saying the "essential"?

This praise, however, is not without some restrictions. Immediately after explaining what he means by the essential, i.e., the distinction between three kinds of historiology—the monumental, the antiquarian, and the critical—Heidegger adds that Nietzsche failed to "explicitly point out the necessity of this triad or the ground of its unity" (448; 396). Yet this restriction is no sooner issued than retracted, when three sentences later Heidegger adds: "Nietzsche's division is not accidental. The beginning of his 'study' allows us to suppose that he understood more than he has made known to us" (448; 396). We are now presented with a strange sequence. First, Heidegger claims that Nietzsche saw and said the essential. Next, he claims that Nietzsche neither showed nor said "explicitly" that the threefold character he assigns to historiology "is foreshadowed in the historicality of Dasein" (448 modified; 396). Finally, he asserts that the "beginning" of Nietzsche's study shows that he understood more than he made public, and that consequently he somehow did exhibit and say, in a cryptic manner, things which at first sight he seemed neither to show nor say.

Let us take the "beginning" of this study or meditation "out of season." What is to be understood by "beginning"? Does Heidegger mean the foreword to the second *Meditation* or its first sections, those in which Nietzsche distinguishes the three kinds of historiology which he examines in the light of life? In either case, we are invited to think that Nietzsche understood more than he said publicly. But how can one detect such surplus understanding if Nietzsche left it completely shrouded in silence? The answer is obvious: we are invited to find in this teaching the signs of Nietzsche's proximity to what Heidegger says himself. Evidently, the surplus understanding at stake can only consist in what Heidegger expressly says of the "necessity" of the triad detected by Nietzsche and of the "foundation of its unity," which consequently means that the surplus is the ecstatico-horizonal threefold that defines the historicality of Dasein ontologically.

Let us now consider the Foreword of Nietzsche's *Meditation*. The first sentence begins with a quote from Goethe: "Moreover I hate everything which merely instructs me without increasing or directly quickening my activity" (*On the Advantage and Disadvantage of History for Life*, p. 7).[6] Nietzsche reappropriates Goethe's words and turns them against the "spoiled idler[s] in the garden of knowledge" who are the pride of his century. Knowledge for the sake of knowledge, particularly in historical studies, is a symptom of shrinking and decay. In the full bloom of life, knowledge does not detach us from life, but instead stimulates this life even further and fully connects it to action. The second *Meditation* is *out of season* because it is polemical, in strict continuity—as it turns out—with *The Birth of Tragedy* and the struggle against what that book calls "the modern privilege of theoretical man." And now as then, it is as a student of the Greeks that Nietzsche claims to speak. In other words, it is in the name of Greek *theoria*—conceived as a way of life, as *bios theoretikos*, as a comportment aiming at excellence, notwithstanding the distortions imposed by Socrates and Plato on that notion—that Nietzsche denounces the modern theoretical bias [*le théoricisme*]. The fact that on this point Heidegger's path crosses Nietzsche's is hardly doubtful, given the insistence with which the various Marburg lecture courses seek to reactivate the ancient notion of *theoria* as a form of *praxis*, that is, as a way of existing.

But are these points sufficient to justify an anticipation in Nietzsche—in what he says without saying it—of the ontology of Dasein? In order to answer this question, let us consider the broader "beginning," now extended to the first sections of the *Meditation*. What about the first section? Nietzsche mentions here three possibilities for life, or more precisely four that can be reduced to three. First, there is purely animal life, which man has forsaken and for which at times he feels some longing, as in the case of the Cynics. Such life is nonhistorical because the animal immediately forgets what took place and "sees each moment really die, sink back into deep night extinguished for ever." This life "goes into the present like a number

---

6. *On the Advantage and Disadvantage of History for Life*, trans. Peter Preuss (Indianapolis: Hackett Publishing Company, 1988).

without leaving a curious fraction'' (*Advantage and Disadvantage*, 9). Unlike animals, man "resists the great and ever greater weight of the past" (9). If the memory of the past gains predominance, it will indeed give rise to an historical condition, but in a sense detrimental to life, for then the past is "the gravedigger of the present" and memory lacks the "plastic power" (10) required for invention, creation, and regeneration. Then the temptation might present itself to raise oneself in the name of "objectivity" to a suprahistorical point of view, for which past, future, and present are all equal "because one who has adopted it could no longer be tempted at all to continue to live and cooperate in making history" (12). These two possibilities are therefore equally detrimental to life, the former because the weight of the past extinguishes any opening to the future and consequently to any life fully lived in the present, the latter because the equalizing that it brings about treats as meaningless the temptation to live. A fourth possibility remains, which is neither nonhistorical as is the first, nor historical in a destructive sense as is the second, nor suprahistorical in an equally destructive sense as is the third. Of those individuals who take the fourth possibility upon themselves, Nietzsche says:

> Let us call them the historical men. Looking into the past urges them toward the future, incites them to take courage and continue to engage in life, and kindles the hope that things will yet turn out well and that happiness is to be found behind the mountain toward which they are striding. These historical men believe that ever more light is shed on the meaning of existence (*Der Sinn des Daseins*) in the course of its *process,* and they look back to consider that process only to understand the present better and learn to desire the future more vehemently. (*Advantage and Disadvantage*, 13)

They are therefore alive in the proper sense for whom the meaning of existence resides in a process such that their reappropriation of the past aims at the future, and for whom the present is understood as the overlapping [*empiètement*] of reappropriating the past and aiming at the future. Nietzsche said that such men are properly historical because they can strike a balance between the historical sense (i.e., the memory of the past) and a nonhistorical dimension (i.e., the forgetfulness of the past). In other words, inasmuch as they are guided by a project aiming at the future, their memory presents an active selection of a past worthy of being retained. Being capable of such a selectiveness is what Nietzsche calls "drawing a horizon around itself" (10). The meaning of Dasein, as Nietzsche understands it, resides therefore in the unity of a triple movement, a movement which in each case draws a horizon and is related to a retained past, a willed future, and a present understood as the intersection of this withholding and of this willing.

One might object that this interpretation is forced upon Nietzsche, that it projects upon him what Heidegger teaches, that it is ensnared in the hermeneutical circle, and also that the second *Meditation Out of Season,* which focuses on historical studies, is not an ontology of the being that we are. Yet, it remains that Heidegger himself invites us to recognize in Nietzsche the presence of an ontological supplement. Already vigorously outlined in the first section, the ontological supplement becomes more precise at the beginning of the second. Nietzsche here distinguishes three forms of historiology. He states the necessity and the foundation of this triad and therefore does not pass it off as an arbitrary and intellectually seductive classification. Again, let us read Nietzsche's text:

> History belongs to the living man in three respects: it belongs to
> him so far as he is active and striving, so far as he preserves and
> admires, and so far as he suffers and is in need of liberation. To
> this triplicity of relations correspond three kinds of history: so far
> as they can be distinguished: a *monumental,* an *antiquarian* and a
> *critical* kind of history [Nietzsche's emphasis]. (*Advantage and
> Disadvantage,* 14)

The historiological triad is not the final word since it emanates from the living being itself and is connected to, and derives from, the triad of relations that constitute the living being in its Being. To claim that Nietzsche neglected "to explicitly point out the necessity of the triad or the ground of its unity" (*Being and Time,* 448; 396) does not say enough. For, in the Nietzschean text, this triad receives its necessity and its unitary foundation from the triadic ontological structure of the living being that is alive in the proper sense. What does it mean for the living being to act and strive (*Streben*), if not to choose a possibility? What does it mean to preserve and admire, if not to recast selectively a having-been? What does it mean to experience a tension between suffering and liberation, if not to anticipate emancipation from fallenness?

It is therefore not beyond Nietzsche, but in profound agreement with him that Heidegger translates the language of the historiological triad into the language of the ontology of Dasein and of its foundation: ecstatico-horizonal temporality. Moreover, if we consider things closely, the force of the ontological triad is so binding in Nietzsche's own text that each type of historiology is acclaimed as beneficial to life when the triad regulates it, and is denounced as detrimental when the triad ceases to animate it.

Thus we find a remarkable proximity to Nietzsche in these Heideggerian ontological analyses which both have the status of an "ontological projection," and which play a decisive role in articulating its set of ontological problems, because the first concerns the ownmost individuation of Dasein and the second the temporal foundation of its Being. This proximity is all the more deserving of consideration if we contrast it with the treatment generally given by fundamental ontology to those thinkers with whom Heidegger maintained a prolonged dialogue: Aristotle, Kant, and Husserl for example. The difference is striking because it is clear that the attention paid to each of these thinkers involves a twofold approach [*un double geste*]: reappropriation on the one hand, and critical distanciation on the other. It is only the treatment reserved to Nietzsche that gives the impression of a univocal procedure [*geste*] of reappropriation without a distanciation.

But if such is the case, we can surmise that, precisely because it is acknowledged without reservation at two decisive points, this proximity to Nietzsche also inspires many other moments in the project. I shall limit myself to a consideration of the two issues we previously left aside in our analysis of Section 53, the related topics of truth and time. Before considering their link, however, we should note how surprisingly silent *Sein und Zeit* is with regard to Nietzsche's notion of time. In contrast, throughout the notes and the body of the treatise, all of the thinkers who treated time—Plato, Aristotle, Hegel, Kierkegaard, Bergson, Husserl—merit a mention, coupled with a reservation (they were all limited, in one way or another, to the "ordinary" concept of time); all, except Nietzsche, whose eternal return is not even mentioned. Is it because it goes without saying that the eternal return is a variation on the ordinary concept of time? But then, why not say so and comment on it? Is it, on the contrary, because ecstatico-horizonal temporality includes an existential reappropriation of the eternal return? We can surmise that this is the correct hypothesis by developing a certain number of signs.

On the topic of truth, at the time of fundamental ontology Heidegger shares Nietzsche's idea that pure contemplative adequation with a given "objectivity" does not have a primordial status but results from the fall of an active movement of uncovering directed toward the future. For both thinkers, emphasis on this movement amounts to a dismissal of curiosity and avidness for knowledge as fallen modifications of a living understanding. For both thinkers, this fall results from a loss of self. Nietzsche himself writes: "Is it not selflessness (*Selbstlosigkeit*) when historical man permits himself to be flattened to the level of an objective mirror?"[7] For both thinkers, finally, the movement of uncovering is by nature interpretative or hermeneutical. And for both, the nature of this movement is circular because it forces an overlapping of the future and the past, or to speak like Nietzsche, because it transforms a "so it was" into a "thus I willed it." Prior to being thematized by Heidegger, the circle of interpretation forms

---

7. *On the Advantage and Disadvantage*, Section 8, p. 47 modified.

the looming texture of the second *Meditation Out of Season* which says time and again: "*Only from the standpoint of the highest strength of the present may you interpret* (*deuten*) *the past* [Nietzsche's emphasis] (*Advantage and Disadvantage,* 37), and further on: "The past always speaks as an oracle: only as master builders of the future who know the present will you understand it" (38). Nietzsche stresses that in order for life to remain fully alive, such a circular movement needs to be constantly reactivated. By the same token, he suggests that the liberating movement of interpretation entails, at the heart of the living being, a certain circularity of time. This interpretation was soon asserted forcefully by *Thus Spoke Zarathustra* which establishes a link between the will-to-power (the notion which, regarding the concept of life, secretly animates the quest for the highest strength in the second *Meditation*) and the eternal return.

It is therefore not a mere coincidence that Heidegger cites these two works. To be sure, neither the will-to-power, nor (and this point is tantamount to the first) the overcoming of the human by reaching to the overhuman is mentioned anywhere in *Sein und Zeit,* nor, I believe, in the lecture courses which, at that time, sought to implement the project of fundamental ontology. But is it not a sign of an old proximity that the first reading of Hölderlin (1934–35), which was conducted entirely in the language of the analytic of Dasein and of fundamental ontology, contains the following words, precisely about Nietzsche, who, once more, is quoted without any reservation: "Asking oneself about the essence of man, is always thinking the overman" (*Gesamtausgabe* 39, p. 166)? The same proximity is again revealed by the fact that, shortly after the first reading of Hölderlin, the initial part of the lecture course on Nietzsche matches quite exactly the themes of the will-to-power and of the transcendence of Dasein. It is true, however, that Heidegger never expressly assigns any circular character to ecstatic temporality. But how could the "ground structure" of Dasein in *Sein und Zeit,* deeper than understanding of which knowledge is only a fallen derivation, be considered circular (363; 315), if temporality, which is its ontological meaning, were not circular too?

If this assessment is correct, it may help us to understand why, when his relation to Nietzsche ceased to be one of pure proximity and changed to *Auseinandersetzung* (see the 1936–37 lecture course), Heidegger jotted down in a remark to himself that this confrontation [*différend*] is sustained by a "most intimate affinity" (*Gesamtausgabe* 43, p. 277).[8] By the same token it may prompt us to view this *Auseinandersetzung* with Nietzsche as part and parcel of a debate of Heidegger with himself.

---

8. I am very grateful to Michel Haar for drawing my attention to this note.

The First Reading of Hölderlin

In the first draft of his essay on *Hegel et les Grecs*[1] Heidegger reminds us that according to Hegel, "the degree of Greek consciousness is the degree of Beauty" (361). Such a degree, he insists, could only represent for Hegel, the thinker of absolute subjectivity, the preliminary degree of the manifestation of the Spirit: the degree where Being is immediate manifestation, standing and remaining in close proximity to itself, the degree where Being is an objective element, not yet mediated and reflected by its opposition to the subject. Paraphrasing these Hegelian themes, Heidegger condensed their meaning in the following passage:

> Being has not yet found its foundation in subjectivity which knows itself, which is self-conscious or rather "self-knowing." Being is more like pure splendor, pure appearing of what is objective. If it is true that the Greeks lived in the element of pure subjectivity, but failed to understand it as such, how did they correspond to what is objective, that is, to Beauty? From the most ancient times, the Greeks were concerned in displaying and celebrating beings. By making this remark, Hegel shows that he deeply understood the Greek universe. What Hegel saw, we can enunciate in a few words: the fundamental attitude of the Greeks facing Being is one of respectful and reserved emotion in front of the Beautiful. As we ponder about it, we are tempted to hear Hölderlin's voice who in the drafts of his novel *Hyperion, or the Hermit in Greece* thinks Being as Beauty. Hegel was of the same generation as Hölderlin. Together they studied philosophy and theology at Tübingen. But

---

1. "Hegel et les Grecs" trans. Beaufret and Savage, Paris: *Cahiers du Sud* 349 (1959): pp. 355–68. The text given here is the translation of the French text originally translated for Heidegger's presentation (March 1958) by Beaufret and Savage. A later, modified, version of it appeared in German in 1960. See next footnote.

also during the years which decided over their respective paths, the years when their paths were on the verge of growing apart, in Frankfurt, their lives were sustained by the strength of a close friendship. (365)

Such was the assessment that Heidegger made in a lecture given in Aix-en-Provence on March 20, 1958. A second version of this lecture was given with the same title on July 26 of the same year, at a plenary session of the Academy of the Sciences in Heidelberg. However, in that second version, we do not find the passage quoted above. Nor do we read any mention of a kinship of spirits between Hegel and Hölderlin, concerning their approach to the Greek world at a given time of their lives.[2]

What are we to make of such a sudden rescinding? Should we speculate that the recognition of a kinship of spirits between Hegel and Hölderlin was something that could be acknowledged to the French audience of Aix-en-Provence, and not to the German one? This seems unlikely simply because the Heidelberg colloquium was hosted under the aegis of Hans-Georg Gadamer, whose hermeneutics is known to draw both from Hegel's thought and Hölderlin's poetry. Should we hypothesize, then, that the recognition of this harmony of spirits could be overlooked in front of the German audience because, in Germany, it went without saying? I would personally caution against such a premature conclusion, especially because the failure to mention a proximity between Hegel and Hölderlin in the second version of the lecture is coupled with the effort to minimize the theme that originally prompted its mention: the Hegelian understanding of the Greek world as the world of Beauty. Such a theme is not completely absent from the second version, but it appears without any commentary or paraphrase.

Consequently we can say that the second version of the lecture on *Hegel and the Greeks* retracts not only every allusion to an affinity (however temporary and condemned to subsequent disagreement) between Hegel and Hölderlin, but also any form of emphasis on the reason that made the allusion possible in the first place. We can wonder then whether this sudden silence is not a retraction by Heidegger of the point made in the first version of his paper. For the first version does not limit itself to merely stressing that the young Hölderlin and the young Hegel were intellectually close. Such a statement would be unremarkable because their affinity was well-known and mentioning it would not commit the speaker to any philosophical position. The statements of the first version could be taken as such a

---

2. See *Die Gegenwart der Griechen in neueren Denken. Festschrift für Hans-Georg Gadamer zum 60. Geburtstag* (Tübingen: J. C. . Mohr, 1960), pp. 43–57.

commitment, however, if they are intimately connected to the specific kind of attention Heidegger once paid to Hölderlin's poetry. In the first version of the lecture, while saluting the depths of Hegel's insight into the Greek world, Heidegger states that in the words used by Hegel to capture the fundamental attitude of the Greeks facing Being "we are tempted to hear Hölderlin's voice." Is this not to confess that for Heidegger himself, for a moment at least and within certain limits, Hegel and Hölderlin echoed each other? If this admission was made more readily to a French audience than to a German one, could it not be because Heidegger expected his German audience, more than his French one, to remember the insistence with which in his *Erläuterungen* he had stressed the chasm that separates Hölderlin and Hegel? I wish to show that support for this interpretation can be found in Heidegger's first reading of Hölderlin, specifically in the interpretation of the hymns "Germania" and "The Rhine" given during the lecture course of the winter semester 1934–35.[3]

That date is significant. The beginning of the 1934–35 lecture course follows by only a few months Heidegger's resignation from the Rectorate. Anyone concerned with Heidegger's post-war explanations for this episode of his life might expect to find in this lecture course the expression of his disillusionment and the recognition of his blunder. Such an expectation might be reinforced retrospectively if we read this lecture course against the backdrop of the *Erläuterungen* from which any kind of activism seems excluded.

If in addition we strive for a retrospective understanding of the episode not only from the *Erläuterungen* but also from the famous discussion with the Japanese scholar which figures prominently at the center of *A Dialogue on Language* (*Unterwegs zur Sprache*)[4], we might also expect to find in these lectures the first signs of the *turning* (*Kehre*) that toppled the project of fundamental ontology as the science of the meaning of Being and opened the way to the more meditative thinking on the historical withdrawal of Being. Consequently we might expect to detect in the 1934–35 lecture course the first signs of an overcoming of metaphysics and, more particularly, of a dissociation between Hölderlin and the two thinkers, Hegel and Nietzsche, who, according to the meditation on the history of Being, testify to the completion of metaphysics. It seems to me that in both cases (disil-

3. The text is quoted from the *Gesamtausgabe*, Bd. 39, *Hölderlins Hymmen* "Germanien" und "Der Rhein" (Frankfurt am Main: Klostermann, 1980). The translation given here is from the French original. (Trans.)

4. In Martin Heidegger, *On the Way to Language*, trans. Peter D. Hertz (New York: Perennial Library, 1971).

lusionment with National Socialism and the turning) the 1934–35 lectures dash our expectations.

I want to start with the second view (that is, the notion that a turn regarding metaphysics might have occurred as early as 1934–35) because it sheds some light on the first (that is, the hypothetical view that Heidegger was then ready to recognize his blunder of 1933).

At the beginning of the introduction to the first part of the lecture course, the part devoted to the poem "Germania," Heidegger announces: "We do not wish to force Hölderlin into conformity with the present time, but on the contrary: we wish to put ourselves and those who are coming after us under the measure of the poet" (*Gesamtausgabe*, Bd. 39, p. 4).[5] The benevolent reader will take this as a sign of distancing from the regime or at least as indicative of a desire to look above the current unfolding of events. The same reader might even suggest that we witness here the emergence of an opening to the sacred especially because a short preliminary note warns that Hölderlin's poetry is "still without a space and a location" (*Zeit-raum-los*) and that "it has already stepped beyond our historical fuss (*historische Getue*) and has laid the foundation of a new beginning (*Anfang*) for another history (*Geschichte*), the very history starting with the decision concerning the advent or the withdrawal of God" (1). Let me indicate right away that in my opinion such good intentions on the part of the reader are far too generous. However, in order to come to a full assessment of the issues, we must first analyze the categories and the axes which govern the Heideggerian commentary.

It turns out that this articulation originates directly in *Sein und Zeit* and fundamental ontology. It is supported also by a specific recasting of Hegel and Nietzsche. In the very introduction to the lectures, we can find the evidence both of the continuity with fundamental ontology and of the support found in Hegel and Nietzsche. After mentioning a famous passage of a letter sent by Hölderlin to his brother for the New Year 1799, Heidegger concludes:

> Poetry is in no way a game, one's relationship to it is not the playful relaxation in which one forgets oneself. Instead it is the awakening, the shaking-up of the ownmost essence of the individual, by which the latter reaches again into the foundation of its Dasein. If indeed it is from that foundation that each individual originates, then the authentic gathering of individuals in a primordial community has already occurred. The harsh insertion (*Grosse Verschal-*

---

5. The translation is made from the French text. (Trans.)

tung) of the superfluous (*Allzuvielen*) in what is called an organization, is nothing more than a temporary expedient, it is not the essential. (8)

I cannot read these lines without a shudder. But, let us put that grim impression aside for now and consider that there is no need of a long familiarity with *Sein und Zeit* to detect in the call for a return to the foundation of Dasein the echo of the existential problematic of individuation as we have it in fundamental ontology: it is by assuming finite time and in anticipating its death that Dasein reaches individuation and conquers itself from its own forgetfulness. There is no need of a special familiarity with *Sein und Zeit* then to suspect that the first reading of Hölderlin is entirely regulated by the dissociation between fallen everydayness and resolute authenticity. In addition, if it is true that (as suggested by the third sentence of the quote) Being-towards-death individuates both the singular Dasein and the community, there is no need of a long familiarity with Hegel to detect in these lines the echo of the Hegelian concept of the ethical life of a people. The ethical life of a people is described in the *Phenomenology of Spirit* by drawing on an interpretation of Sophocles' *Antigone* that focuses on the foundational link that the relationship to death establishes between the individual and the community. Consequently we will be prone to suspect that there is no distancing from the metaphysics of subjectivity in this first reading of Hölderlin. Finally, there is no need of a long familiarity with the lexicon of Zarathustra to recognize a Nietzschean expression in the term *Allzuvielen* and to be made suspicious that, in Heidegger's reading, the will-to-power and the call to the overhuman will prevail upon ''the respectful and reserved emotion in front of the Beautiful.'' So we might also suspect that the lecture course is not an instance of a distancing from the regime, but rather the futile attempt to distinguish what in it is authentic and what is fallen.

Let us then pay close attention to the terms by virtue of which the first reading of Hölderlin is indebted successively to fundamental ontology, to Hegel and to Nietzsche.

Its debt to fundamental ontology becomes obvious when we consider what it dismisses and what it sanctions positively. The being that we are, in the teaching of *Sein und Zeit*, cannot be circumscribed in its Being so long as we take for granted that the only meaning for Being is *Vorhandenheit*. Likewise, the commentary on ''Germania'' says time and again that precisely because poetry rules over the deepest mode of existing (Dasein) of peoples, it invalidates all empirical attempts to approach poetry in terms of characteristics supposedly present-at-hand in any given text offered to our reading. The phenomenological method of fundamental ontology, in spite of several disagreements with Husserl, was in line with him in rejecting the *Weltanschauungen* as well as the diverse forms of psychologism and naturalism. This is also what the commentary on "Germania" at the outset discards in a clean sweep: Hölderlin was not the author of a *Weltanschauung*, he did not express moods or emotions, his Saying satisfied no biological need. Heidegger's commentary therefore makes no hint at racism and in passing ridicules Rosenberg and Kolbenheyer (26–27). It refuses to turn Hölderlin into the herald of a collective soul à la Spengler and to align itself with the new trend of literary criticism which, after borrowing heavily from the arsenal of psychoanalysis, was at the time obsessed with *Volkstum* and *Blut und Boden* (254).

More deeply, this interpretation of Hölderlin asks us to reject entirely (specifically in light of the insistent preliminary reflections of the first chapter) those various figures of fallen everydayness described in *Sein und Zeit* as obstructing our access to the question: *Who is Dasein?* In line with *Sein und Zeit*, what is at stake in the debate for the sake of thought [*débat pensant*] with Hölderlin's poetry is the question: *Who are we?* (48), not as humans in general, but as this singular people whom the poet addresses and for whom his Saying has the status of a mission: "What is the Being of this very People?" (22). In order to secure a proper access to this question, which ultimately concerns the "Being or non-Being" of that people (58), we must be capable of "withdrawing from everydayness" (22) in which we are endlessly thrown. Everydayness presents itself as an almost unavoidable slope, one against which we must be capable of fighting as if fighting against ourselves (22–23). This tension (authenticity versus everydayness) is also in strict continuity with the *Rectoral Address*, because in both cases, Heidegger maintains a split between the attitude of radical questioning (the only attitude which corresponds to Hölderlin's poetry, or his own radical questioning into the essence of the university) and varieties of everyday fallenness such as: cultural activism, the subordination of thinking and poetry to specific political needs, the administrative decisions of the ministries.

What is decisive in this interpretation therefore is: "remaining within the questioning attitude," or within the essential opening of the question. To this radical attitude, the "they" objects right away: "Questioning, the essential? Why should that be? The answer is what counts as decisive. This is what every petty bourgeois comprehends, and because he comprehends it, it is correct and everything is now termed 'Science for the People' " (41).

Such a tension, or struggle between everydayness and the authentic, is discovered by Heidegger in the very words of the poet:

Full of merit, yet poetically, man
Dwells on this earth.[6]

Heidegger insists that we must understand the conjunction "*doch*" as a "harsh opposition (*herber Entgegensetzung*)" between on the one hand the everyday operations of the productive man and his use of products which contribute to the progress of culture, and on the other hand, what is termed "his authentic Dasein" or his "exposure to Being" which is "as such the fundamental event (*Grundgeschehen*) of the historical existing of man." (36).

Also, according to Heidegger, when Hölderlin writes to his mother that poetry is "the most innocent occupation of all," we must understand that he criticizes the guise that it takes in everydayness (*alltäglich Anschein*). To such a guise, Hölderlin is said to have "heroically" opposed his vocation, accepting the danger of being broken in the process. This vocation meant accepting to stand under the divine lightning, a stance which Heidegger—in line with the central formula of the *Rectoral Address*—construes as "exposure to the excess of Being" (33–35).

The same tension between the poles of the authentic and the inauthentic is present in Heidegger's reading of the fragment "Upon him, akin to the gods, of all goods the most dangerous—upon man, speech was bestowed." One must understand, Heidegger says, that the greatest danger of that "good" is twofold: On the one hand speech is where man "ventures into Being" and on the other hand it is where "the manifestation of beings takes place, not as a secondary expression of something already unveiled, but as the very primary unveiling, but also as (and precisely for that reason) a veiling and its dominant derivation, *appearance*" (61–62). The danger is twofold because on the one hand venturing into Being means being nearer the gods and therefore being exposed to a greater threat of being annihilated by them, and on the other hand, "all essential utterance runs the risk of lapsing into utilitarian idle talk and into the appearance that constitutes it" (63–64).

The same tension again is to be detected in the famous verses:

Many things man has tried
Many heavenly ones he has named

---

6.   *Voll Verdienst, doch dichterisch wohnet*
     Der Mensch auf dieser Erde . . .
See " . . . Poetically Man Dwells . . . " in *Poetry, Language, Thought*, trans. Albert Hofstadter (New York: Harper and Row, 1971), p. 219.

Ever since we were a conversation
And could listen to one another.[7]

Heidegger insists that we must first of all understand the word conversation in its "primordial essence" and not simply as "communication and agreement (Verständigung) with one another" (72). This primordial essence is ontological. Hence what is at issue is not a debate with others, but the debate with destiny concerning the possibility to be or not to be. "It is our Being (Seyn) which comes forth as conversation in an advent such that the gods call us, assign us under their command (Anspruch), bring us to speech regarding the question of knowing whether, and how, we are, how we respond, how we grant them or refuse them our Being (Seyn)" (70). Consequently, Gespräch is first of all exposition to the manifestation of Being and non-Being, permanently threatened by covering-up and fallenness in the ruts and blindness of idle talk. Such an exposure determines the being-together, the "we" that the poet expresses. It is not therefore the capacity to listen to one another that determines and constitutes the community; on the contrary it is the community that determines and constitutes the capacity to communicate. And if the community founds the reciprocal understanding and the communication of the individuals between themselves, the reason is that at the deepest level, exposure not to other beings but to Being (inasmuch as Being is no being, i.e., is no-thingness) individualizes both the individual and the community. In other words, the relationship to death enables us to reach the foundation of dialogue, or conversation. "Death is precisely what each singular man must take upon himself, it is death more than everything else, and the fact of being ready (Bereitschaft) to offer oneself to it, that creates the space of the community" (73).

The exposition of this analysis shows that the first commentary on Hölderlin affirms and continues fundamental ontology also because of the specific assertions it makes and of the way in which it makes them. The Grundstimmung of the poem "Germania" is what the commentary attempts to echo and the "metaphysical locus" of that basic mood is what the commentary seeks to approach. Recall that in the analytic of Dasein the Grundstimmung of anxiety is distinct from fear. Unlike fear (which remains a prisoner of everyday concern and therefore of the "ready-to-hand" [Zuhanden] and of given entities subsisting in the forefront, [Vorhanden]), anx-

---

7.   Viel hat erfahren der Mensch
       Der Himmlischen viele genannt
       Seit ein Gespräch wir sind
       Und hören können voneinander.
The translation is mine. (Trans.)

iety has the ontological function of revealing to Dasein the naked fact (*nackte Dass*) of its temporal existence in the care of itself. The pages on the *Gespräch* just evoked show that anxiety keeps the status of a basic mood (*Grundstimmung*). But anxiety is now included in an even broader *Stimmung*, for, according to the 1934 course, the *Grundstimmung* found in "Germania," and ultimately throughout Hölderlin's entire poetry is sacred mourning.

> No, the Blessed ones who appeared, divine figures,
> On the land of Antiquity, of those
> I cannot invoke the names, rather now
> O live waters of my homeland, when love in my heart raises
> A complaint along with yours, could another desire spring
> In this heart which has accepted sacred mourning.[8]

Heidegger insists that such a *Grundstimmung* concerns the Dasein of a people, but the analysis he makes of it merely transposes and broadens his former analysis of anxiety. *Sein und Zeit* shows that anxiety has a fundamental disclosing function. In *Sein und Zeit*, anxiety is the *Stimmung* that exhibits the ultimate meaning of care, that is, the unitary structure within which all the *existentialia* coalesce. It shows that Dasein is in the care of its own finite potentiality for Being: "it amounts to the disclosedness of the fact that Dasein exists as thrown Being *towards* its end" (*Being and Time,* 295; 251); it shows that Dasein stands in the anticipation of its death, that it "opens itself to a *threat* arising out of its own *there.*" Anxiety is therefore

> anxious *about* the potentiality-for-Being of the entity so destined, and in this way it discloses the uttermost possibility . . . [The anticipation experienced in anxiety] utterly individualizes Dasein, and allows it, in this individualization of itself, to become certain of the totality of its potentiality-for-Being. For this reason anxiety as a basic state-of-mind belongs to such a self-understanding of Dasein on the basis of Dasein itself. (*Being and Time,* 310; 266)

In other words, anxiety reveals individuation as what is ownmost, entirely non-relational and most certain in spite of being radically indeterminate because the outcome (death) is beyond our grasp and is and remains something in the order of a threat.

---

8. The German text is not given in the French original. The translation of this poem in *Hyperion and Selected Poems* (New York: Continuum, 1990; pp. 208–215) does not translate *Heiligtrauernde* as "sacred mourning." This translation is mine. (Trans.)

Furthermore and more deeply, anxiety pervades the internal call (*Gewissen*) thanks to which the singular Dasein can each time take resolutely upon itself who it is in its ownmost, over against what it is not. This call, ultimately, provides the foundation of an existential interpretation of language, in such a way that speech is not primordially interlocution and listening to the other, but a debate within oneself about oneself regarding one's own potentiality-for-Being. Indeed in this call, Dasein and Dasein alone, is at the same time the questioner and the questioned, and even the question and the answer. In both cases, anxiety is involved because "the caller is Dasein, which in its thrownness (in its Being-already-in) is anxious about its potentiality-for-Being" (277; 322) and the resoluteness to which it is called consists in "being ready for anxiety" (Section 60). The interpretation of dialogue, or conversation, (*Gespräch*) in the first reading of Hölderlin affirms and continues this analysis of *Sein und Zeit* by transposing it to the call (the "vocation")[9] of a people.

It is within anxiety finally that *Sein und Zeit* deciphered the primordial structure of time which is neither the indefinite succession of nows (made up of those that are no longer, of those that are not yet and of the one that is presently), nor the intersection of the expectation of future intraworldly events with the retention of previous events—an intersection permitting present events to be encountered. Instead the primordial structure of time is the anticipation of the ownmost potentiality-for-Being, linked to the retrieval or repetition of a thrown condition, at the juncture of which the instantaneous moment of vision reveals resoluteness as the tension between the ownmost and the alien, the authentic and the inauthentic. It is this structure of time, now broadened to the time of a people, that Heidegger detects in the sacred mourning evoked and endured by Hölderlin.

I shall limit myself to highlighting a few points of that structural parallelism. We have seen that the poet does not express his moods. His poetic Saying does not originate in his lived experiences, but in a *Grundstimmung* which is the mourning of the sacred. Mourning however is in no way limited to the suffering and lamentation of an individual who deplores the flight of the gods: the "I" who speaks in the poem, far from lamenting for himself, "laments with the homeland," experiences himself in his link to it, as to "the power of the land on which man in each case according to his historical existence 'poetically dwells' " (*Gesamtausgabe*, Bd. 39, p. 88).

What rules over his own hymn then does not properly belong to him, but to his people. But just as, in *Sein und Zeit*, anxiety individualizes each singular Dasein, this sacred mourning is the test to which the poet calls his

---

9. See *An Introduction to Metaphysics*, p. 38, where the term is also used.

community in order that "the Being of the homeland, that is, the historical Dasein of a people be experienced as the *authentic and unique* Being, from which the fundamental position toward beings in their totality grows and owns its articulation" (121–22, my emphasis).

With regard to the ownmost individuation of a people, the *Grundstimmung* of the poem therefore plays the role formerly played by anxiety pressing for the call of conscience. Just as anxiety, the collective *Grunstimmung* presses for an answer, commands to be ready for hearing a call, which consists, for the Germans, in confronting the question: "Who are we?" (59 ff.) Just as anxiety reveals to Dasein that it exists for the sake of itself (*umwillen seiner*), so the *Grundstimmung* reveals a people to itself, it is "the truth of the people", it is "the disclosure from which the people knows what it wills historically inasmuch as the people wills *itself*, wills being itself" (144).

And just as in *Sein und Zeit* anxiety discloses the primordial time of the individuated Dasein, so the *Grundstimmung* reveals the primordial time of the people called to experience it. This time is ec-static. By renouncing the invocation of the gods of Greece, Hölderlin does not dispute their divinity, but preserves it. Such a renunciation is a loss only for the calculative understanding which is only cognizant of the time of everydayness as the succession of changing days and is blind to primordial time. Very different is the time of which Hölderlin is the poet. In such a time, renunciation is productive and creative (*schöpferisch erzeugend*) (94), the despair over the absence of the gods who once were is metamorphosed into "the awaiting of the imminent new dawn" (107), and the oppression of mourning into the decision of standing ready (*Bereitschaft*) to hail the return of the divine (102). In the time of everydayness, the past is what has vanished and is incapable of reoccurring. But in the primordial time, more precisely in the temporalizing of the time that the people is, "that which has been is what still rules" and remains open to a future or is still to come. Heidegger indeed indicates that it is in the light of *Sein und Zeit* (Section 65, passim) that he deciphers "the essential structure of this primordial temporality and of its essential possibilities" (109). Thus Hölderlin's terms, with their occasional mention of time as what sunders (*die "reissende"*), are absorbed in the terminology of the existential analytic: namely the ec-static displacement (*Entrückung*) that irrupts at the juncture of what has been and what is to come.

Finally, just as the primordial time to which anxiety opens in *Sein und Zeit* turns out to be threatened by fallenness in the inauthentic time of everyday temporality, now the historical time of Germany—revealed in the *Grundstimmung* of the poet—cannot possibly remain without a confrontation of the essence to the nonessence (112). It is the struggle of Being against appearance, of the rise (*Aufgang*) against the fall (*Untergang*), of greatness against pettiness, of the disinterested exposure to the abyss of the earth against the utilitarian (*Nutzen*) exploitation of everydayness.

There is however a major difference between the authentic time of the existential analytic and the ownmost historicality of a people. It resides in the fact that each mortal individual is capable of temporalizing the first one, whereas only some individuals rise and measure up to the second. These individuals are the creators. From the famous pages of *Hyperion* in which Hölderlin considers Athenian harmony in art, in the people's religion, in political life, and in philosophy, Heidegger draws the following assessment at the beginning of his commentary:

> The historical existing of peoples (the rise, the blossoming and the fall), is born out of poetry and thence is carried into authentic knowledge in the form of philosophy, and from these two the Dasein of a people as people is set-into-work (*Erwirkung*) by the State—by politics. The primordial time, which is the historical time of peoples, is therefore the time of the poets, of the thinkers and of the state-creators, or of those who properly found and establish the historical *Dasein* of a people. They are the authentic creators. (51)

These lines can be clarified by reference to the previous analysis of the *Grundstimmung*:

> The *Grundstimmung*, and this means the truth of the Dasein of a people, is primordially instituted (*Gestiftet*) by the poet. But, thus disclosed, the Being (*Seyn*) of beings is understood and articulated, and thus opened up for the first time by the thinker. Thus understood, Being is posited in the ultimate and original seriousness of beings, which means within a *determinate* (*be-stimmte*) historical truth by virtue of this only: that the people is brought to itself as a people. This only occurs thanks to the creation by the state-creator of a state adjusted to the essence of that people. This event taken as a whole has its own timing requirements and consequently its own time sequence. . . . These three creative powers of the historical Dasein are the ones implementing that which solely deserves to be acclaimed as great. (144)

In addition to the fact that this reading of Hölderlin remains indebted to fundamental ontology, it is also obviously indebted to Hegel. First, we can notice that, in these lectures Heidegger is far from dissociating, as he will later on, Hölderlin's poetry and German idealism. Rather he associates them. Thus, concerning Hölderlin's essay "On the Operations of the Poetic

Spirit''[10], he stresses that we cannot understand it "without a real under-standing of the inner core and the fundamental questions of Kant's philos-ophy and above all of German Idealism'' (84). Thus he characterizes as *geistig* the historical existence of the people. Also, after insisting on the intrinsically conflictual character of the *Grundstimmung*, Heidegger stresses that because historical existence founds itself on the "arch-authentic es-sence" of temporality (117), it brings forth in a unitary manner the antag-onism of the most extreme opposites. This polemical cohesion, he claims, is what Hölderlin's most central term, *'Innigkeit,'* designates. At which point, Heidegger evokes Hegel and proceeds to inscribe Hölderlin's understanding of Being within the sphere of Heraclitus's thought.

Let us ponder Heidegger's evocation of Hegel. Since in their exposure to Being, the poet (Hölderlin) and the thinker (Hegel) are of equal rank, an influence of the one upon the other is out of the question. Hence, the sec-tion of the commentary entitled "Hölderlin and Hegel" starts with the fol-lowing words:

> It is in no way a coincidence if the thinker—who in the only philo-sophical system that ever existed in Western philosophy, thought from its foundation and to its end the thoughts of Heraclitus—I mean Hegel, was the friend of Hölderlin. Hölderlin and Hegel grew in the same spiritual world and together they fought for the sake of its new configuration. Hölderlin followed the path of the poet, Hegel that of the thinker. Instead of explaining—as it is cus-tomary—Hölderlin from Hegel's system and also of noticing vari-ous elements of influence of the poet on the thinker, we must attempt the effort of experiencing the great antagonism of the two precisely by taking each one at his most elevated height and on his solitary summit, in order thus to simply understand their true uni-son (*Einklang*). (129)

But the commentary does not study the nature of this true accord: it limits itself to "a few indications necessary to elucidate *from Hegel* the relation-ship that Hölderlin had to Heraclitus and most of all to determine the mean-ing of the notion of *'Innigkeit'* which is the fundamental term used by Hölderlin" (my emphasis). The points which, taken from Hegel, allow us to shed some light on Hölderlin's relationship to Heraclitus, are the concept of philosophy, the unhappy consciousness, and the State.

---

10. See *Friedrich Hölderlin: Essays and Letters on Theory,* trans. and ed. Thomas Pfau (Albany: State University of New York Press, 1988), pp. 62–82.

For Heidegger, the Hegelian concept of philosophy is expressed in this famous passage from the preface to the *Phenomenology of Spirit*[11]:

But the life of Spirit is not the life that shrinks from death and keeps itself untouched by devastation, but rather the life that endures it and maintains itself in it. It wins its truth only when, in utter dismemberment, it finds itself. Spirit is this power, not as something positive, which closes its eyes to the negative, as when we say of something that it is nothing or false, and then having done with it, turn away and pass on to something else: on the contrary, Spirit is this power only by looking the negative in the face, and tarrying with it. This tarrying with the negative is the magical power that converts it into being (*Seyn*). (29)

In the lecture course of 1934–35, these words of Hegel are never held at a distance by Heidegger, who thus does not distinguish them either from his own concept of thinking or from Hölderlin's poetic Saying. When he mentions them, it is instead to point out "the true accord" of the poet and the thinker, each on his own summit. Since no reservation of any kind restricts the preceding quotation, there seems to be no doubt that Heidegger attempted his first interpretation of Hölderlin's *Grundstimmung* in unison with the Hegelian definition of Spirit. Accordingly he maintains, in his interpretation of what the poet calls "destiny," that "the fundamental experience (of destiny) is the experience of death and the knowledge concerning it" and that "therefore no satisfactory concept of Being could be given without the accompanying task of thinking death" (*Gesamtausgabe*, Bd. 39, 173). The fact that this interpretation is conducted along the categories and the axes of fundamental ontology cannot count as an objection, because the 1931 course on *Hegel's Phenomenology of Spirit* had already suggested with sufficient clarity that this ontology conceived of itself as a metamorphosed retrieval of Hegelian phenomenology.[12] And the insistence with which the first lecture course on Hölderlin (1934–35) stresses the ultimately harmonious character of the various tensions under investigation allows us to assert that it is his own way of thinking, as much as Hegel's, that Heidegger has in mind when he characterizes the Hegelian concept of philosophy as infinite thinking: "In-finite is this thinking which thinks alternatively one side and the opposite side, that is to say which thinks the antagonism in unity" (131).

---

11. *Phenomenology of Spirit*, trans. A. V. Miller (Oxford: Oxford University Press, 1977).
12. See supra, Chapter 4.

There is, therefore, unison between the absolute sundering of the Hegelian spirit and the extreme tension which permeates both Hölderlin's *Grundstimmung* and the Heideggerian interpretation of it. This unison is reinforced when Heidegger claims that this infinite thinking, by which "Hegel's insight penetrates into the fundamental positions of the spiritual powers of his time," does not emanate from an "observer," but from someone who, "by bringing the opposites in a universal fluidity, wants to carry their struggle to a decision" (132). This alleged unison is reinforced again by the following assessment of Hegel's infinite thinking:

> In no way is it a well-conceived formula; on the contrary it originates in a fundamental experience from which it is born, the fundamental experience of Western Dasein and of the essence of its Spirit. To this Spirit belongs suffering in the sundering of the most extremely opposed terms. (133)

It is well known that Heidegger links the birth of this "unhappy consciousness" to the flight of the Greek gods. In the unhappy consciousness, Heidegger recognizes the "innermost goad of the Spirit, which along the various figures and stages of the history of the world, pushes History (*Geschehen*), and thus pushes the Spirit toward itself, toward its essence." Such remarks also seem to be in direct alignment with the reading of *Hegel's Phenomenology of Spirit* proposed by Heidegger only three or four years earlier against the backdrop of fundamental ontology. This interpretation highlights the fact that it is precisely because Hegel conceived of unhappy consciousness—the being longing to be a self—as the "Being of self-consciousness," that he achieved (regarding the question of "being a self") "a new concept of Being" and overcame the obstacles imposed by the weight of *Vorhandenheit* upon all the previous modern philosophies of reflection (209 ff.). But of course, between the 1931 course and the 1934–35 course, the categories and the axes of fundamental ontology were broadened to include, as we saw, the Dasein of an historical people. Such a broadening even prepares a third point of convergence with Hegel, specifically on the State.

On this question, Heidegger limits himself to the reminder that for Hegel, the effectiveness of the Spirit in History is the State and (these are Heidegger's words) that

> the State can be what it must be only if it is ruled and carried by the infinite strength of the in-finite Spirit, that is, if it universally implements in a living unity the most extreme opposition of the free self-subsistence (*Selbständigkeit*) of the individual and the free power of the community. (133)

In support of this characterization, he borrows from Section 185 of the *Principles of the Philosophy of Right*, specifically from a remark added by Hegel, a remark from which Heidegger quotes the following lines:

> The principle of ancient cities—which was still too simple— lacked the truly infinite strength, this strength found only in this unity which allows all the contradictions of reason to develop, in order to dominate them, to maintain itself in them and to gather them in itself.

Schematic and general though these indications are, they point toward two precise areas of agreement with the political conceptions of Hegel. When Hegel speaks of a deficient principle for the ancient cities, it is the democratic institution that he has in mind and describes as too simple, because that institution immediately identified the individual and the universal, turning each citizen into a ruler. The criticism of ancient democracies is the first area of agreement between Hegel and Heidegger. As for the living unity of the extremes of individuality and power of the community, it is difficult not to discern here the echo of the Hegelian concept of the ethical life of a people whose power insures that its members really belong to it by exposing them to the danger of death. This defines the second area of agreement between Hegel and Heidegger.

At this point, beyond Hegel, a new thinker is introduced: Nietzsche. Just like Hölderlin and Hegel, he is credited with having stood under "the power of Heraclitus's thinking" (135). This homage is given briefly and presented as obvious, just like the reference to Nietzsche in the interpretation of Hölderlin's "Dionysos" is presented as self-evident. The reference runs: "We know that the last Western interpretation of Being, Nietzsche's, was also preparatory and futural, and names Dionysos too" (191). Nietzsche is therefore no less a herald than Hölderlin. Just like the latter, he awakens the Germans to the greatness of a distress (*Not*), which is at the same time the necessity, urgency, and imminence of an advent, and to the inescapable decision it calls for regarding the flight or the return of the gods. To Hegel's terminology (of the Spirit), Heidegger's commentary now associates Nietzsche's: *Kampf, Macht, Übermacht, Wille, Überwille, Schaffen, Übermensch*. All these words form a constellation in the commentary on the poem "The Rhine" and more precisely in the interpretation of the verses:

> Of the demigods now I think
> And I must know the dear ones

Because often their lives
Have so moved my longing heart.[13]

Recall that the original time of the people (the time of the *Grundstimmung* in which the stark realization of the flight of the gods—inconceivable to everydayness—preserves their divinity and thus opens itself up to the imminence of a return of the divine) is instituted by three creative powers: the poet, the thinker and the State-creator. It is in the language of Zarathustra, as much as, if not more than, in the language of Hyperion, that Heidegger evokes the creators. In the draft of the hymn to Mother Earth, he selects the verses:

And the times of the creator are
Like the mountain which in its surge
From sea to sea
Is waving over the earth.[14]

But Heidegger swiftly dissociates these verses from any reference to the "Holy Father," to "the Pure Law," to "the Almighty" which were nevertheless mentioned in the draft. In other words, he immediately dissociates them from any reference to the Judeo-Christian God and exclusively applies these verses to the only triad of true "creators," in his sense of the term: the poet, the thinker, and the State-creator (51–52).

Because the creators distance themselves from everydayness, because they stand on the peaks of the historical time of the people, because they approach the abyss, they overcome human limits, draw near what is overhuman, and alone are the true measure of destiny, or historical Being. Hölderlin's example of a demigod, Dionysos, is thus described in terms that reveal in him a brother of Nietzsche's Dionysos: he is the figure of the "creative passion" par excellence, of "the awakening to the greatness of a

---

13.   *Halbgötter denk ich jezt*
       Und kennen muss ich die Theuern
       Weil oft ihr Leben so
       Die sehnende Brust mir beweget.
Poems of Hölderlin, trans. Michael Hamburger, Nocholson and Watson, p. 205.

14.   *Und die Zeiten des Schaffenden sind*
       Wie Gebirg, das hoch aufwogend
       Von Meer zu Meer
       Hinziehet über die Erde.
Poems of Hölderlin, trans. Hamburger, p. 205.

necessity," of the exposure to the arch-originary unity of Being and non-Being, of presence and absence, of "the 'Yes' of the wildest life" and the " 'No' of the most awful death and annihilation" (189–90). And just as "the poet has an intimate kinship with the Being of the demigods" (211), so too does the thinker, because "conducting an inquiry into the essence of man always amounts to thinking the overman" (166).

What do we learn about the State-creator? His arrival on the stage is preceded by a commentary on the verses:

Yet the blindest
Are sons of gods.[15]

Heidegger's reappropriation of these two verses has a Nietzschean tone because it construes blindness not as a defect, but as an excess. It has nothing to do with the irresolution and emptiness of a lack of will. On the contrary, it is an "overwill" and "overcapacity for determination." The demigods are not satisfied with "the desire to shape history with the help of inferior men and to expose the small fry as entirely worthless. They are not skilled in the art of the subterfuge or of the meandering path. They are not familiar with what is necessary, and therefore essential, in every attempt to reform the stubborn things of everydayness and to bring them into proper order. Their soul is "unskilled." For the demigods receive their goals, their will and their support from their primordial source, not from the usual course of events. Their doing and their suffering never allow a sanction be imposed on them by the present-at-hand (Vorhanden) as a whole which always speaks against them. The truth of their Being never finds an appropriate sanction because, if something of that nature occurs, their Being has already been torn from its superiority, it has now become fashionable and is diminished" (208–09). After such a delineation of the State-creator, we are not surprised to read, two pages later, the ominous sentence: "The only and true Führer here and now reveals without a doubt in his Being the domain of the demigods" (210).

These words reverberate with a stark and ghastly echo. Their sheer presence is in itself enough to prove that those readers,[16] who see in the lecture course of 1934–35 the evidence of a distancing from a regime which at that time was consolidating itself, are excessively generous. Should we then go the other extreme of contending, despite what the introduction to the lecture course proclaimed, that Heidegger was simply attempting to bring Hölderlin into conformity with the times, that is, with the triumph of National Socialism? To this question we should answer at the same time: absolutely no and absolutely yes. Absolutely no: How can any form of Nazism claim allegiance to the task of endlessly questioning and of discarding into the fallenness of everyday idle talk (and of the "they" of *Vorhandenheit*) the historical realities of racism, national characteristics (*Volkstum*), the slogan *Blut and Boden,* mass organization and normalization (*Gleichschaltung*), which Heidegger feared would soon render thinking impossible? Absolutely yes: How can the call to stand ready to welcome the return of the gods conceivably be opposed to the dictatorship if these gods are exclusively those of the German people and if their return is linked to the unconditional will that this people has to be itself, by willfully confronting its members with the risk of death? What conceivable resistance can emerge from the distinction between authenticity and fallen everydayness if this distinction applied to the Dasein of a people, permits the dictator to rise to the rank of the demigods? What resistance could be derived from an opposition that is turned into a Heraclitean tension, or *polemos* of antagonistic terms, entailing their unavoidable belonging-together? As a matter of fact, after deriding the slogan "Science for the People", Heidegger writes:

> If such a devastation of every authentic thought were not amplified, everything would be in order. For the fact that there exists a misunderstanding and that it is unavoidable can only be puzzling and troubling for someone who does not understand what is authentic (*das Eigentliche*). Astonishment and horror are just as misplaced here, as they would be in front of a beautiful farmstead if someone complained the courtyard contained an imposing heap of manure! Can one imagine a farm without manure? (42)

Should we then say that, because this reading of Hölderlin is articulated along the categories and the axes of fundamental ontology, the latter necessarily contained before the fact this peculiar form of endorsement of the dictatorship? This would be just as reckless as claiming that embryonic Nazism is present in Hegel or Nietzsche, and possibly in Hölderlin. Fundamental ontology aims at determining the meaning of Being with reference to the unique center of intelligibility which is the self-centered temporality of each Dasein existing for the sake of itself. Not in *Sein und Zeit,* nor in the Marburg lecture courses, nor in the Freiburg ones before 1933, are the Being of a people and its State organization taken as objects of reflection. Yet the fact remains that it is in the language of fundamental ontology that the blind trust in the Führer was expressed and justified in 1933. Confronting this evidence, one might still judge that the blindness consisted in transposing to the Dasein of a people what fundamental ontology limits to the singular Dasein and that therefore fundamental ontology is absolved from the mistake of the transposition. Against this suggestion however, I will raise the question: If this transposition is carried out with some blindness, is there no sign of blindness—prior to the transposition—precisely in what it transposes?

It is my overall assessment that, before the transposition, the very articulation of fundamental ontology (and its distinction between what is ownmost and what is fallenness, between authentic resoluteness and everyday preoccupation) contains some sort of prejudice. First, I believe that these distinctions involve a solipsistic concept of individuation, which ultimately precludes any sharing of words and deeds from qualification as authentic. This is something we can witness in the spiraling treatment [le mouvement spiralaire] of language in the existential analytic. At the deepest level, language is extracted from interlocution: it is the call [la parole] which in the solitude of Gewissen, an individual addresses to himself. Second, it is my assessment that the hierarchy established between a resolute way of being and acting (or resolute existence, which alone provides the foundation for the full intelligibility of the meanings of Being) and an everyday way of being riveted to Vorhandenheit, grants a privileged position to the one who is the most resolute or to the one who conceives this intelligibility (the thinker): both (resolute Dasein and the thinker) are ranked above those called "hoi polloi" by Plato. This position involves a lofty disdain for the plurality entailed by human affairs and for the doxa without which this plurality cannot exist. Third, I believe that in spite of the results (and their import is considerable) yielded by the analysis of the fundamentally ec-static character of Dasein, the central formula of the analytic (Das Dasein existiert umwillen seiner) closes the existing being within the impregnable walls of a self-willing. Finally, I believe that there is, in the very project of such an ontology, which conceived the self-understanding of Dasein as the only key to the understanding of Being and to the deconstructed history of ontology, something akin to the culmination of the absolute claims of the modern metaphysics of subjectivity. Such latent paroxysm is what the first reading of Hölderlin brings to the forefront: the three creators described as the most temporalizing beings, the most aware of finitude, are raised to the level of demigods.

It is only fair to add at this point that some years later, in the wake of the famous Kehre which is neither a full spin nor a curve, but rather a profound reassessment and reorientation, Heidegger gave up the attempt to read Hölderlin in the light of fundamental ontology and dissociated the poet from the two thinkers he had first reappropriated in order to read him. At-that time he started seeing Hegel and Nietzsche as the heralds of the modern metaphysics of subjectivity, that is, of an epoch forgetful of Being, and Hölderlin as the first modern whose poetic work takes a first step toward resisting such forgetfulness.

Epilogue

It is in the light of the first reading of Hölderlin that we will suggest now looking at both the lecture course An *Introduction to Metaphysics* (1935) and the essay on *The Origin of the Work of Art.* We shall see that, like the first reading of Hölderlin, the *Introduction to Metaphysics* affirms and continues [*prolonge*] fundamental ontology, while at the same time bringing it to a sort of paroxysm.

It will be easily seen that the *Introduction to Metaphysics* affirms and continues fundamental ontology if we focus on how the course articulates its question and takes it upon itself. Called "the fundamental question of metaphysics," this question is the following: "Why are there beings rather than nothing?". It belongs to this question—the broadest of all because it concerns beings in their totality and the deepest because it searches for their foundation as such—to spring back [*rejaillir*] upon itself and, by virtue of its recoiling [*rebondissement*], to emerge as the most originary. The German word for origin is *Ursprung,* the initial leap. The *Warumfrage* "has its ground in a leap through which man thrusts away all the previous security in which his existence (*Dasein*) resided" (*An Introduction to Metaphysics,* 5–6; 4).[1] The question refers back [*renvoie*] to the questioning activity of the inquiring individual, i.e., to the leap which consists in "forcing the eruption of one's own foundation" (*sich-den-Grund-erspringen*). This reminds us of the articulation of the *Seinsfrage* in *Sein und Zeit* and of the question of the foundation in *Vom Wesen des Grundes* (*The Essence of Reasons*). In the latter as in the former, the central issue is always the onticoontological privilege of Dasein.

That the 1935 lecture course is the continuation of fundamental ontology can also be attested by the insistence displayed by Heidegger, in the wake of Nietzsche's second *Meditation Out of Season,* in bestowing upon

---

1. *An Introduction to Metaphysics,* trans. Ralph Manheim (New Haven: Yale University Press, 1959).

the questioning activity he conducts a historical character, not in the sense of a subordination to the present age, but in the sense of an opening to the future, within the active recasting of "an initial and inaugural having-been" (*Introduction to Metaphysics*, 8 modified; 6).

The continuity with *Sein und Zeit* is equally manifest in the insistence with which inquiring into beings is linked to inquiring into nothingness, in the insistence with which the *Warumfrage* is prevented from degenerating into the search for an explanatory principle—necessarily *vorhanden* because it would apply to a being antecedently conceived in evidence as *vorhanden*—and, finally, in the insistence with which the *Warumfrage* is redirected toward the preliminary question: "What about Being?"

Such a continuity is highlighted with striking vigor when the course lists the "markers" essential for the broadening to which it intends to lead. The list is as follows:

1. The determination of the essence of man is never an answer but essentially a question.

2. The asking of this question is historical in the fundamental sense that this questioning first creates history.

3. This is so because the question as to what man is can only be asked as part of the inquiry about Being.

4. Only where Being discloses itself in questioning does history happen, and with it the being of man, by virtue of which he ventures to set himself apart from beings as such and contend (*auseinandersetzen*) with them.

5. It is this questioning and contention that first brings man back to the entity that he himself is and must be.

6. Only as a questioning and historical being does man come to himself; only as such is he a self. Man's selfhood means this: he must transform Being that discloses itself to him into history and bring himself to stand in it. Selfhood does not mean that he is primarily an "ego" and an individual. He is no more this than he is a "we," a community.

7. Because man as historical being is himself, the question about his own Being must be reformulated. Rather than "What is man?" we should say "Who is man?" (*Introduction to Metaphysics*, 143–44 modified; 109–10).

Except for the theme of "creation" and the connected topic of a "contending with beings," which we shall investigate later, each of these propositions could have been written as such in *Sein und Zeit*.

Even though Heidegger claims that he has given up the term "ontology" for his current inquiry in order to dissociate it from all past metaphysics, we can still claim that the lecture course is the affirmation and continuation of fundamental ontology in light of the insistence with which he distinguishes the primordial questioning activity and its leap from everydayness, more specifically distinguishing what the *Rectoral Address* calls "the resoluteness toward the essence of Being" (*Entschlossenheit zum Wesen des Seins*) from the various forms of decadence (*Verfall*). As in *Sein und Zeit*, such a resoluteness is understood as a knowledge and relies on a primordial *Stimmung*. However, from 1927 to 1935, the location for such a knowledge and for such a *Stimmung* has been broadened: it is no longer the singular existence of an individual, but the existing of a people, of the German people.

The fact that these lectures also bring to culmination or paroxysm the project of completing metaphysics inherent in fundamental ontology is evident from several angles. First consider the totalizing goals of these lectures (they aim at wrenching from "beings in their totality" the secret of their Being); observe next that a "willing to know" regulates the questioning activity; recall thirdly that they emphatically refer to the German people as the "metaphysical people;" and finally consider their praise of German idealism and of the ontological principle of the Spirit.

It is in this context that we witness the emergence of a major correction to the former hierarchy of the forms of action presiding over the articulation of fundamental ontology in *Sein und Zeit*. This correction concerns *techne*. About German idealism, Heidegger writes in the *Introduction*: "It was not German idealism that collapsed; rather, the age was no longer strong enough to stand up to the greatness, breadth, and originality (*Ursprünglichkeit*) of that spiritual world, i.e. truly to realize it, for to realize (*verwirklichen*) a philosophy means something very different from applying theorems and insights" (45–46; 35). *Verwirklichen* means to implement, to set-into-work, and in Greek corresponded to *energein*; according to Aristotle, it is connected to the activity of *poiesis* which receives its light from a specific knowledge, *techne*—the very activity which *Sein und Zeit* and the lecture courses from the 1920s relegate into the inauthentic sphere of everydayness. Thus, concerning the epoch (the first part of 19th century) and its failure to measure up to German idealism the *Introduction* continues: "Dasein began to slide into a world which lacked the depth out of which the essential always comes to man and comes back to man, thus compelling Dasein to become superior and making it act in conformity to a rank" (46 modified; 35).

When he is writing these lines, Heidegger apparently feels quite confident that the 1933 Nazi revolution has brought this sliding to a halt. Since the aspiration could never be merely to repeat German idealism as such— spiritual energies are each time *jeweilig*, developing at a different pace—

but instead must be to summon a new world of the Spirit to a new age of strength and vibrancy (and so to implement it), there is now room for a setting-into-work which is preeminent instead of being a mode of fallenness. In other words, there is now room for a *techne* which, instead of being limited to everyday circumspection, is of the same rank as the resoluteness (*Entschlossenheit*) by which Dasein accepts its most authentic possibility for being, and which is of equal rank to *theoria*, the thinking of Being in which authentic action (*Handlung*) culminates. The thinking of Being is not merely the highest form of *praxis*, but also essentially the highest form of *poiesis*. Directly aligned with the topic of creation previously elaborated in the first lecture course on Hölderlin, the *Introduction to Metaphysics* characterizes philosophy as "one of the few autonomous creative possibilities and, at times, necessities of man's historical being-there" (9; 7). The few who get involved in it "initiate creative transformations" (*schaffend verwandelnd*, 10;7) and achieve a transmutation (*umsetzend*).

The *Rectoral Address,* which points out that the Greeks conceived of *theoria* as "the implementation of the highest form of *praxis,*" at the same time insists on the old Greek legend that had Prometheus as the first philosopher. The *Address* also maintains that it was concerning this first philosopher that Aeschylus wrote: "*techne d' anagkes asthenestera makro,*" which Heidegger translates and comments as follows:

"Knowing however is much weaker than necessity." This means: all knowledge concerning things is first of all delivered to the overpower of destiny and falters in front of such overpower. That is precisely why, if it is to truly falter, knowledge must display its highest challenge, in front of which only the power of concealment of beings is erected. (p. 10)[2]

At the same time as it is *theoria-praxis,* philosophy is also therefore *techne,* which obviously means a knowledge adjusted to a *poiesis,* to some implementation over which it rules.

We find similar proclamations in the first reading of Hölderlin, and we see them thematized now in the light of the Pre-Socratics by the *Introduction to Metaphysics.* We shall not attempt to follow Heidegger's first reading of the Pre-Socratics which he conducted under the heading "The Limitation of Being," but only to highlight further the major correction mentioned above.

---

2. *Rectoral Address* (Frankfurt am Main: Klostermann, 1983). The translation given here is from the French text. (Trans.)

The convergences that Heidegger detects between Parmenides' poem, Heraclitus' fragments, Pindar's poems, and Sophocles' tragedies can be summarized in the following manner:

Being-human defines itself from out of a relation to beings as a whole. The human essence shows itself here to be the relation which first opens up Being to man. Being-human, as the need of apprehension and collection, is a being-driven into the freedom consisting in undertaking *techne,* the sapient setting-into-work of Being. This is the character of history. (*Introduction to Metaphysics,* 170; 130)

Why are we now assigned to *techne* and to setting-into-work? Because Being whose initial names are *phusis* (upsurge and maturation remaining within themselves), *logos* (gathering of antagonistic forces), and *dike* (the ordering which provides adjustment and assignment), is by nature fundamentally polemical. It is an uncovering which on the one hand stands within itself, and on the other hand is threatened with lapsing into pure appearance (*aletheia*). Thus understood, Being threatens with unfamiliarity, wrenches from the ordinary and is disquieting. It is an overpower (*Übergewalt*) to which man must be responsive. And responsive he can be only by seeking to be the disrupting and violent one. The issue for him is to operate "a taming and ordering of powers by virtue of which beings open up as such when man moves into them. This disclosure (*Erschlossenheit*) of beings is the power that man must master (*bewältigen*) in order to become himself amid beings, i.e., in order to be historical" (157 modified; 120). This violent activity is that of *techne.* "It is therefore *techne* that provides the basic trait of *deinon,* the violent; for violence is the use of power against the overpowering: through knowledge it wrests Being from concealment and makes it manifest within beings" (160 modified; 122). Thus understood, *techne* is at the same time a knowledge and a power. It is a knowledge inasmuch as it comports itself as "the initial and persistent seeing looking out beyond what is directly given before the hand (*vorhandene*)" (159 modified; 122). It is a power (*Können*) inasmuch as it is the "capacity to set-into-work Being as a being which each time is this or that," and inasmuch as it is "a manifest setting-into-work of Being in beings" and "brings them to display as beings" (159 modified; 122).

As knowledge and power leading to a work, this *techne* has three fundamental modalities: artistic, philosophic, and political. Heidegger writes: "Unconcealment occurs only when it is achieved by work: the work of the word in poetry, the work of stone in temple and statue, the work of the word in thought, the work of the *polis* as the historical place in which all this is grounded and preserved" (191; 146). These works refer to the "cre-

ators'' celebrated in the first course on Hölderlin: the poet, the thinker, and
the state-creator. It is at this point—in our opinion—that a metaphysical
paroxysm engulfs fundamental ontology.

To be sure, Heidegger stresses, in connection with Sophocles, and with
Heraclitus, that

> the *violent one*, the creative man, who sets forth into the un-said,
> who breaks into the un-thought, compels the unhappened to hap-
> pen and makes the unseen appear—this violent one stands at all
> times in venture (*tolma*, line 371 of the Antigone chorus).

And he adds that:

> in venturing to master Being, [the creator] must risk the assault of
> the non-being, *me kalon*, he must risk dispersion, in-stability, dis-
> order, mischief. The higher the summit of historical Dasein, the
> deeper will be the abyss, the more abrupt the fall into the unhis-
> torical, which merely thrashes around in issuelessness and place-
> less confusion. (161 modified; 123)

If conceivably such words allow the figures of Creon and Oedipus Rex on
the one hand and the image of the Führer on the other to overlap, perhaps a
reader might detect in them, and in Heidegger the fear that the outcome of
the 1933 revolution will be a race to the abyss. On the other hand, is not
this interpretation made untenable by the following words which, in contradistinction, seem to give massive support to the necessary ambiguity of the
attitude of those creators who are state-builders?

> Pre-eminent in the historical place, they become at the same time
> *apolis*, without city and place, lonely, strange, and alien, without
> issue amid beings as a whole, at the same time without statute and
> limit, without structure and order, because they themselves as cre-
> ators must first create all this. (152–53 modified; 117)

In any case, there is evidence of the metaphysical paroxysm of fundamental ontology in the unquestioned recasting of two major philosophical
notions of Platonism, which are closely bound together: the philosopher-
king and the city as a work. In spite of his strong insistence on the contrast
between the polemical ambiguity of *aletheia* in the early Greeks and the
univocal clarity of the Idea in Plato, Heidegger in fact aligns himself
with Plato. In one stroke he turns the city into the work of a creator, and
assigns it to the activity of *poiesis* from which precisely—as we indicated
earlier—action in the Greek *polis* intended to distinguish itself. As for philosophy, it is no longer conceived in 1935 as a way of life, or *praxis* only,
but also as preeminent *poiesis*. ''To be a man,'' Heidegger says now, ''means

to take upon oneself . . . the sapient setting-into-work of appearing, and so to administer unconcealment, to preserve it against cloaking and concealment." And further:

An inquiry into Being that is concerned not only with the Being of beings but with Being itself in its essence calls explicitly for a grounding of Dasein in the question of Being. For this reason and *only* for this reason we have given this grounding the name of 'fundamental ontology' (See *Sein und Zeit*, Introduction). (*An Introduction to Metaphysics*, 174–75; 133)

Philosophy remains, consequently, fundamental ontology, and acquires now a foundational status as setting-into-work, in the sense that it founds the existence of a people. The importance assigned in the *Introduction to Metaphysics* to the essence of philosophy, resides in this:

a thinking that breaks the paths and opens the perspectives of the knowledge that sets the norms and hierarchies, of the knowledge in which and by which a people fulfills itself historically and culturally, the knowledge that kindles and necessitates all inquiries and thereby threatens all values. (10; 8)

And further: "We can speak of historical destiny only where an authentic knowledge of things dominates man's being-there. And it is philosophy that opens up the paths and perspectives of such knowledge" (11; 9). To philosophize is therefore to rule, to govern (*beherrschen*). But because Being should not be leveled off to *Vorhandenheit* within which "the many" remain, "it must itself have, and maintain, a rank," from which one can see that "the true is not for every man, but only for the strong" (133; 102).

The themes of philosophy as ruling and of the city as the setting-into-work under a master-workman, reactivate not only two themes central to Plato's *Republic*, but also two comparable ones, central in Hegel. Concerning philosophy, let me simply recall the sentence found at the beginning of Hegel's 1812 *Logic*, which Heidegger at the time liked to quote: "A people without a metaphysics is like a temple without a holy of holies." Concerning the city, it should be sufficient to mention, first, that the notion of the "founding tyrant" allows the *Realphilosophie* of Jena to dispense with a social contract,[3] and, secondly, that it is only in the register of setting-

---

3. See our work *Naissance de la philosophie hégélienne de l'Etat* (Paris: Payot, 1984), pp. 60–62. Also see "Hegel and Hobbes" in *Dialectic and Difference*, ed. and trans. Robert Crease and James T. Decker (Atlantic Highlands, N.J.: Humanities Press, 1985), pp. 25–26.

into-work (the production of itself by the Spirit), i.e., in the register of *poiesis* to the exclusion of *praxis*, that Hegel thinks the status of the political realm. This is particularly obvious concerning the *Phenomenology of Spirit*, which views the Greek ethical life (*Sittlichkeit*), that of the *polis*, as the *production* by the citizens of a work—the city-state—in which they recognize and contemplate their own activity.[4] There still remains the third form of setting-into-work, the third modality of *techne* as knowing and power, namely the implementation of *aletheia* in art. In a commentary on Heraclitus, Heidegger writes:

> The Being of beings is the supreme radiance, i.e. the greatest beauty, that which is most permanent in itself. What the Greeks meant by "beauty" was taming. The gathering of the supreme antagonism is *polemos*, struggle (as we have seen before) in the sense of setting-apart . . . For the Greeks *on* and *kalon* meant the same thing (presence was pure radiance). The aesthetic view is very different; it is as old as logic. For aesthetics, art is representation of the beautiful in the sense of the pleasing, the pleasant. But art is disclosure of the Being of beings (131–32 modified; 100–101). [And further:] The Greeks called art in the true sense and the work of art *techne*, because art is what most immediately brings Being (i.e., the appearing that stands there in itself) to stand, stabilizes it in something present (the work). The work of art is a work not primarily because it is wrought, made, but because it brings about Being in a being; it brings about the phenomenon in which the emerging power, *phusis*, comes to shine. It is through the work of art as being that everything else that appears and is to be found is first confirmed and made accessible, explicable, and understandable as being or not-being. (159 modified; 122)

These themes are precisely the same which the essay on *The Origin of the Work of Art* was to analyze—an essay for which there are two versions: one dating from the same year as the lectures on the *Introduction to Metaphysics* (1935), the other from 1936. In an investigation of the second version conducted some time ago,[5] we attempted to show that in some ways it confirms the Hegelian completion of the metaphysical concept of art, while the essay moves away from this concept at the same time. The weight of the Hegelian legacy is even more noticeable in the first version, inasmuch

---

4. See *Phenomenology of Spirit*, trans. A. V. Miller (Oxford: Oxford University Press, 1977), pp. 424–425.

5. "Le dépassement heideggérien de l'esthétique et l'héritage de Hegel" in *Recoupements* (Brussels: Editions Ousia, 1982), pp. 175–208.

as precisely this version is more closely akin to the *Introduction to Metaphysics*. To prevent any misunderstanding, let us emphatically rule out the notion that the first version operates a transposition of Hegel's *Aesthetics*. Let us also dismiss any suggestion made from the preceding analysis that the *Introduction to Metaphysics* gets engulfed in a metaphysical paroxysm because it reactivates Hegel. Such claims could never be made for the simple reason that Hegel never adopts a Promethean stance. The Hegelian philosopher does not struggle for the sake of Being, he contemplates it. And if, according to him, the identity of Being and thinking is conquered through a struggle, he is not himself the one conducting it; rather, he limits himself to a commemorating survey of its stages. But, in the *Introduction to Metaphysics*, Heidegger finds this limitation reproachable: "Hegel and his friend Hölderlin were both under the great and fruitful spell of Heraclitus, but with the difference that Hegel looked backward and drew a line under the past while Hölderlin looked forward and opened up the way to the future" (126 modified; 96). Because we were not previously[6] attempting to inscribe these lines in their context, or to pay attention to all the tribulations, shifts, new turns and reversals that occurred throughout Heidegger's itinerary, we saw looming in them the contrast between absolute knowledge and the reserved thought of finitude which is also a meditation on the enigma of Being. But this interpretation cannot be sustained in light of the Promethean connotation of the first Heideggerian reading of Hölderlin, also present in the *Introduction to Metaphysics*. The paroxysm of metaphysics is triggered in this Promethean stance.[7] The *Introduction* seeks a will-to-found instead of a Hegelian commemoration (*Erinnerung*). Such a will concerns the Greek beginning, perceived only confusedly by Hegel who remained prisoner of the Platonic Idea. This Greek beginning, which Hegel assigned to a recollection, should now be assigned to decision. The "superior knowledge" of the Greeks of the great period implied a risk which con-

---

6. In our 1982 essay "Le dépassement heideggérien et l'héritage de Hegel." See note 5.

7. Given the central place of this Promethean attitude, it is hard to see how the *Introduction to Metaphysics* could have initiated a confrontation with the essence of technology. Consequently, we view the famous parenthesis—added in 1953 to the 1935 text and opposing "the inner truth and greatness of the Nazi movement" (199) to the official ideology of the regime—as a retrospective projection (see Hartmut Buchner, "Fragmentarisches", in Günter Neske, ed., *Erinnerung an Martin Heidegger*, 1977, p. 49). It is true that the "unleashing of technology," allegedly characteristic of Russia and America, is mentioned in the lectures, along with "the rise of mediocrity" and "the flight of the gods," among the symptoms of "spiritual decadence." Still how could a Prometheus stand up against the alleged unleashing?

sisted in "struggling to measure up to Being, non-Being and appearance, which means in taking existing (*Dasein*) upon oneself by bringing it to the decision between Being, non-Being and appearance" (115 modified; 86).

It is not this kind of beginning, conceived in the resolute confrontation of risk, that prevailed over the Western world. It is only in its decline, by means of Platonism, that Greece prevailed: "The philosophy of the Greeks conquered the Western world not in its original beginning but in the incipient end, which in Hegel assumed great and definitive form" (189; 144). But in 1935, Heidegger seems to be confident that it will indeed be possible for the German people, the center of the future history of the Western world, to repeat the initial Greek beginning. He writes:

> To ask "How does it stand with Being?" means nothing less than to recapture, to repeat the beginning of our historical-spiritual existence, in order to transform it into a new beginning. This is possible. Indeed, because it begins in the fundamental event, it is the crucial form of history. But we do not repeat a beginning by reducing it to something past and now known, which need merely be imitated; no, the beginning must be begun again, more radically, with all the strangeness, darkness, insecurity that attend a true beginning. (39 modified; 29–30)

The aspiration to a second beginning was embraced by Schiller, the young Hegel, the young Hölderlin and the young Nietzsche, and it is this aspiration which we find now in the first version of the *The Origin of the Work of Art*. What this text shares with the young Hegel and the mature one, is the idea that so far there has been only one kind of great art: Greek art. Such an art gathered the entire people around its gods and permanently shaped the destiny of this people. The temple, the statue of the god, and the tragedy: these are the topics around which this text gravitates.

What the first version of *The Origin of the Work of Art* also shares with both the young and the mature Hegel is the idea that art is only properly art when it manifests beings in their totality and their foundation, in short—to borrow from Hegel's terminology which, incidentally, is used by Heidegger—when it corresponds to an "absolute need." We see without ambiguity that such a need is metaphysical in the ontological sense of the term, when we pay attention to the terms used to define it in the first lecture course on Nietzsche, given soon after the first version of the essay:

> Great art and its works are great in their historical emergence and Being because in man's historical existence they accomplish a decisive task: they make manifest, in the way appropriate to works, what beings as a whole are, preserving such manifestation in the

work. Art and its works are necessary only as an itinerary and
sojourn for man in which the truth of beings as a whole, i.e., the
unconditioned, the absolute, opens itself up to him. What makes
art great is not only and not in the first place the high quality of
what is created. Rather, art is great because it is an "absolute
need." (*Nietzsche I*, 83–84)[8]

But what differentiates Heidegger from the young Hegel is the fact that
his language is in no way one of nostalgia, and what differentiates him
from the mature Hegel is that he does not speak the language of *Erinnerung*, commemoration, but rather the language of decision (*Ent-
scheidung*). At this juncture the theme of the creator reappears, borrowed
from Nietzsche much more than Hölderlin.

Art is the implementation, the setting-into-work of truth as a striving
between the world and the earth. "The world is the jointure that tightly
presses upon our Dasein, and it is in conformity with the requirements of
this jointure that everything that bears upon us is connected to us and consequently must be decided by us."[9] The work opens (*aufstellt*) the space of
a decision, and at the same time produces (*herstellt*) the earth as a
"ground, which because it essentially closes upon itself, remains an abyss
and makes itself present as such in the work." The work is strife and struggle, staged out in the open. In this *polemos*, "an 'open' is opened, a
'there', a 'clear space of dis-play' " which is truth itself as *aletheia*. Concerning the question of "how is this there?" Heidegger says in the first
version of *The Origin of the Work of Art* that it exists in the mode of an
extension toward a future and of a retrieval of the past, at the intersection
of which one can attend to a present. Here we recognize the language of
Nietzsche's second *Meditation Out of Season*, such as it was reappropriated
in *Sein und Zeit*. The 'there,' that is to say truth, exists in the mode of
historicalization of history. To the question of knowing "who takes upon its
Self the keeping of this 'there,' " the answer is: "the people." "It is only a
people who can be historical, i.e., futural, having-been and present in the
sense previously indicated."

Because this implementation of truth is essentially historical in the
sense just mentioned, art is not attached to current affairs, to what is

---

8. *Nietzsche*, I, "The Will to Power as Art," trans. David Krell (New York:
Harper and Row, 1979).
9. The text was quoted in the French original from the first version of the essay
on *The Origin of the Work of Art*, translated by Martineau, available only in a
privately circulated edition. The English translation was made from the French original, and the page numbers correspond to Martineau's French translation.

present now before the hand (*vorhanden*). Instead, it is *poiesis* characterized by the terms formerly reserved to the project of *praxis* in *Sein und Zeit*. Every art is *Dichtung*, poesy, or poietic project, extending beyond what is usual, common, current, *vorhanden*. Such a project presses a call to the Dasein of an entire people, it casts itself forth (*zu-geworfen*). But because this very Dasein has already been thrown into existence, "its truly poietic project is the openness of *that* into which historical Dasein has already been thrown." Thus the "earth is here exclusively understood as the earth of a people" and, ultimately, what is opened by the poietic project is "nothing foreign, but only the ownmost characteristic—so far hidden—of historical Dasein" (First version of *The Origin of the Work of Art*, 41–43). Art confronts us with the unfamiliar and the disquieting, only so as to bring Dasein back to itself. What it reveals as being "different from anything ordinary" is that which the Dasein of the people already was, something, therefore, that this Dasein must take upon itself in a project. Thus in the end, the poietic project does nothing but reveal this Dasein to itself. We witness here a strange intertwining of a Hegelian legacy and of a Nietzschean one, involving the themes of the mirror and the will. This intertwining is noticeable too when the essay analyzes what is specific to creation. For the striving that the work is, is wrought by a solitary creator and him alone. By creating, he merely brings into the open "this 'there' that a people chooses to be" (48–49). This intertwining concludes the first version of the essay. Heidegger writes:

> In the context of the broadest and most nearly definitive meditation on the essence of art which the Western World has ever had, Hegel's *Lectures on Aesthetics*, one can read the following sentence: 'We no longer have an absolute need to bring a content to representation in the form of art. Art, with respect to its highest destination, is for us a thing of the past.' (S.W. T.X., 1, p. 16).

Such a sentence, which registers a stage of the spirit in the Hegelian commemoration, is transformed by Heidegger into a question, and submitted to a "decision," the one concerning precisely the reiteration of the beginning. Hegel's sentence remains true for us, i.e., for us the German people, inasmuch as we have not decided that art can and must be an "essential guise within which the truth decisive for our historical existing occurs" (First version of the essay on *The Origin of the Work of Art*, 54–55), that is, inasmuch as we have not decided whether art is a simple "presentation" connected to a present time or, in opposition, a project into the future by means of a primordial leap (*Ur-sprung*) which is always a leap forward (*Vor-sprung*). In *Sein und Zeit*, an answer to the question "Who is it?" was central for Dasein. The point now, since Dasein is the Dasein of a people, is to give a decisive answer to the question "Who are we?" Now, what can this decision possibly entail if not the will to be a Self? This confirms fundamental ontology.

Nevertheless, it is in the midst of Heidegger's meditation on the origin of the work of art that we can detect the collapse of the Promethean stance which allowed fundamental ontology to be engulfed in a metaphysical paroxysm.

A detailed confrontation of the two versions of the essay goes beyond our objective here. On first inspection, the 1936 version seems to broaden the 1935 version. Yet, from the outset, the difference of tone between the two is striking. The demand for a decision, the appeal to the will, the call to the German people, in short the previous tone of proclamation and Promethean style have all but faded away in the 1936 text. And the very manner in which themes found in the 1935 version are now treated anew and broadened, is indicative of a distancing from the Promethean stance. We shall indicate only a few signs of this distancing.

Nowhere in the 1935 text is the question "What is a thing?" raised. But this question now animates the first third of the 1936 essay. In it, two points clearly break from the former Promethean stance.

First, we read the following remarks by way of concluding the criticism of the traditional definitions of the thing and the highlighting of their deficiencies as well as the thing's resistance to their ensnaring:

> The unpretentious thing evades thought most stubbornly. Or can it be that this self-refusal of the mere thing, this self-contained independence, belongs precisely to the nature of the thing? Must not this strange and uncommunicative feature of the nature of the thing become intimately familiar to thought that tries to think the thing? If so, then we should not force (*erzwingen*) our way to its thingly character. (*The Origin of the Work of Art*, 31–32)[10]

In this theme at least, everyone will agree that no Promethean trace can be detected. The *Erzwingen*, formerly the prerogative of the thinker-creator, is no longer deemed acceptable.

Secondly, it is to a painting by Van Gogh that is assigned the mission of displaying both the essence of equipment (the reliability which entrusts the earth to the world and vice versa) and the essence of the work of art (the setting-into-work of truth). Now, it is difficult to see what kind of unanimous people could be called forth by such a painting, and what kind of a

---

10. *The Origin of the Work of Art*, in *Poetry, Language, Thought*, trans. Albert Hofstadter (New York: Harper and Row, 1971).

leap forward (*Vorsprung*) to the resolute assumption of their destiny such a painting could enjoin. This is all the more difficult to see because Van Gogh was deemed a degenerate painter by the Nazis.

Moreover, the second third of the essay deals with "The work and truth." Obviously understood as *aletheia,* truth was connected in the 1935 text to the 'there' (*Da*) which the historical existing of a people, and it alone, is entrusted to take upon its Self. Such a perspective has faded away in the 1936 text. The locus for truth is no longer Dasein. Unconcealment is now a "clearing" in the midst of beings in their totality, a clearing to which humans belong and are exposed more than one they institute (*The Origin of the Work of Art,* 53). Consequently, resoluteness (*Entschlossenheit*) undergoes a deep change of meaning: it forsakes its initial call to the will, its project of being a Self. Now it means "un-closedness" (*Entschlossenheit*), i.e., an exposure to the reserve and the enigma present at the core of the *Lichtung* (67).

Finally, the last section of the 1936 text deals with creation. Concerning this topic too, the Promethean inspiration has all but disappeared. In 1935, the creator was the one who affixed measure and rank in the register of greatness. No such assignation is present in the 1936 text. What is viewed as most essential in the work, as a created thing, what in it is valued as most extraordinary, is no longer its capacity for anticipating in a leap what a people wills to be and for affixing what its measure (*Mass*) should become.[11] Much more modestly what is most essential in it is "that it is at all, rather than is not" and that it offers as a gift its very emergence into Being (*The Origin of the Work of Art,* 65). As for the creator, it is still a striving that he sets into work, the struggle of world and earth, but he himself is no longer a contestant. Witness the words concerning the attitude thanks to which the artist ushers in his work: "Creation is such a bringing forth. As such a bringing, it is rather a receiving and an incorporating of a relation to unconcealedness" (62). "Receiving," "incorporating," these words, decidedly, contain nothing Promethean.

---

11. See the 1935 text, first version of the essay on *The Origin of the Work of Art,* pp. 48–49.

Index

9401